New Readings vs. Old Plays

Richard Levin

New Readings vs. Old Plays

Recent Trends in the Reinterpretation of English Renaissance Drama

The University of Chicago Press • *Chicago and London*

The University of Chicago Press, Chicago 60637
The University of Chicago Press, Ltd., London

© 1979 by The University of Chicago
All rights reserved. Published 1979
Phoenix edition 1982
Printed in the United States of America
89 88 87 86 85 84 83 82   2 3 4 5 6

Library of Congress Cataloging in Publication Data

Levin, Richard Louis, 1922–
  New readings vs. old plays.

  Bibliography: p. 247.
  Includes index.
  1. English drama—Early modern and Elizabethan,
1500–1600—History and criticism.   2. English
drama—17th century—History and criticism.
3. Criticism—History—20th century.   I. Title.
PR651.L48   822'.3'09   78–10695
ISBN 0–226–47520–4 (cloth)
       0–226–47521–2 (paper)

To Muriel

Contents

Three

Four

Five

Preface

Surely one of the most striking features of current criticism of the drama of the English Renaissance has been its remarkable proliferation of reinterpretations or "new readings" which, if they were accepted, would radically alter our traditional views of a great many of these plays— views held, so far as we can tell, by virtually all spectators and readers down to the present time. Most of the new readings, I believe, can be attributed directly to certain recent trends or approaches in interpretation, and since these trends have now become so widespread and well established, and have come to dominate so much of the criticism of this drama, there would seem to be a need for an extended investigation that could examine, in some sort of rigorous and systematic way, their basic assumptions, their techniques, and their consequences. This book attempts to present such an investigation, which I think should also be of more general significance. For while it is limited to the operation of these trends in studies of English Renaissance plays (primarily those of Shakespeare and Jonson), the trends themselves certainly are not; their influence now pervades the interpretation of works in just about every genre and period, so that most of what I have to say about them should apply, with only minor modifications, to most other fields of literary criticism today.

Almost all of the studies that I will be dealing with have appeared since 1950, and the great majority since 1960. I settled upon the former year as a kind of cutoff point because it was at about this time that these trends achieved their present dominant position in the critical arena; but they did not, of course, begin then, and I have drawn on a few examples from the thirties and forties which are indicated in the text. Unless there is such an indication, therefore, the reader can assume that all the unidentified quotations come from books or articles which were published no earlier than 1950, and that most of them are much later.

These unidentified quotations call for an explanation. The reader will soon see that my presentation requires a large number of quotations—most of them quite brief—from studies of the plays, which must be used to illustrate the various aspects of the trends that are being examined. But there are several reasons why I did not wish to single them out with the usual documentation. For one thing, it would have been inappropriate to the aim of this investigation, which is concerned with these particular studies not in themselves but only insofar as they represent the general trends. I wanted to keep attention focused upon the trends as such, and the problems and issues they raise, without the distraction of what were really extraneous considerations. Moreover, it would have been unfair to the authors of these studies, since they were selected quite arbitrarily to exemplify a point and were no more "guilty" than many others who could have been quoted for the same purpose. And I feel that it would have been gratuitously personal and so could only have rendered even more uncomfortable the role I have taken on in criticizing the work of my colleagues. I bear no ill will toward any of them (in fact I am grateful to them, for without their work this book could not have been written), and I hope that they will take my arguments in the spirit in which they are offered here.

For the same reasons, whenever one of these quotations refers to another critic, I have substituted "Critic X" for his name, which seemed appropriate because his product, like Brand X in a commercial, always turns out to be inferior to the sponsor's. Otherwise I have tried to reproduce these passages exactly as they appear in the original studies (with the one exception noted below), indicating any alterations with the usual ellipses and square brackets. And I have tried to present them in a way that did not distort the author's meaning, although I realize that I cannot always have conveyed the nuances provided by his context. The studies from which they were taken are all listed in the back matter in order to give the reader some general sense of their provenance (and to comply with copyright law), without the need to make particular iden- tifications. On the other hand, whenever I have drawn upon the work of another in my own arguments, this debt is of course acknowledged with the customary footnotes.

To facilitate reference I have also listed at the end each English play mentioned in the text, with the edition used for quotations and citations. If it is an old-spelling edition, I have modernized the spelling and punctuation. Where the critical passages that I quote contain quotations or citations based upon a different edition, I have for the sake of consistency altered these to conform to the one named here. This list also serves as an index.

I would like to thank the National Endowment for the Humanities and the Research Foundation of the State University of New York for generous fellowships which enabled me to complete this investigation, and the staffs of the British Library and the London Library for the many kindnesses extended to me during my work there. Portions of the book have appeared in different form in various journals, noted in the Acknowledgments, and I am grateful to their editors and publishers for permission to make use of this material.

Acknowledgments

Material from the following articles has been incorporated into this book, with the kind permission of the original editors and publishers: "Some Second Thoughts on Central Themes," *Modern Language Review*, 67 (1972), and "Third Thoughts on Thematics," *Modern Language Review*, 70 (1975), by permission of the Modern Humanities Research Association and of the Editors; "The New *New Inn* and the Proliferation of Good Bad Drama," *Essays in Criticism*, 22 (1972), and "The Proof of the Parody," *Essays in Criticism*, 24 (1974); "Thematic Unity and the Homogenization of Character," *Modern Language Quarterly*, 33 (1972); "'No Laughing Matter': Some New Readings of *The Alchemist*," *Studies in the Literary Imagination*, 6 (1973); "The King James Version of *Measure for Measure*," *Clio*, 3 (1974); "On Fluellen's Figures, Christ Figures, and James Figures," *PMLA*, 89 (1974), and "The 'Fluellenian' Method," *PMLA*, 90 (1975), by permission of the Modern Language Association of America; "Refuting Shakespeare's Endings," *Modern Philology*, 72 (1975), and "Refuting Shakespeare's Endings, Part II," *Modern Philology*, 75 (1977); "My Theme Can Lick Your Theme," *College English*, 37 (1975), © 1975 by the National Council of Teachers of English; "Shakespeare or the Ideas of His Time," *Mosaic: A Journal for the Comparative Study of Literature and Ideas*, 10 (1977): 129–37, published by the University of Manitoba Press; "The Delapsing of Shakespeare," *Shakespeare: Pattern of Excelling Nature*, ed. David Bevington and Jay Halio (Newark, Del.: University of Delaware Press, 1978); and "Working Hypotheses in Shakespearean Interpretation," *Hebrew University Studies in Literature*, 6 (1978).

One

Readings and Approaches

If ours is an Age of Criticism, as we have frequently been told, then it can also be called the Age of the Reading, since that is the dominant form in which most of our criticism is taught and practiced. The term itself regularly appears in the titles or subtitles of numerous books and dissertations and articles, and even where it does not it is tacitly understood by both the author and his audience, for we have come to expect that an extended commentary upon a literary work will be a "reading" of it. The general acceptance of this concept would suggest that it is not limited to any particular approach, and this is borne out by the fact that almost all of the schools of criticism flourishing today make use of it as a matter of course; however much they may differ in the kind of reading that they give us, they seem to agree that the critic's task is to give us a reading of some kind (thus we now hear of Marxist readings, symbolic readings, and so on). Indeed the identification of literary criticism—or more precisely, literary interpretation—with the reading has become so well established that it is usually assumed without question, and as a result we can easily forget that this is a relatively recent phenomenon. The great critics of the past may have occasionally used the word, but they have not left us anything that we would recognize as a reading in the modern sense.

This modern sense of "reading" may require some explanation, since its meaning, like its identification with criticism, is also usually assumed without question. We all think we know what it signifies, because we all deal with readings every day, as producers or consumers, in the library or classroom or study. Yet, like many similar conceptions that are frequently employed and seldom discussed, it has over the years accumulated a number of implications, closely related but analytically separable, of which we may not always be fully conscious. It should be helpful then to attempt to spell out these implications, so long as we realize that not all of them hold true for all readings, since what we will be describing is a general attitude (or collection of attitudes) rather than some explicit doctrine, a kind of composite or ideal reading to which most individual readings conform for the most part.

First of all, then, we assume that *a reading is an interpretation of a single literary work*. The unit of criticism here is the work itself—nothing more and nothing less. Larger entities such as the author's canon, his life, the age, or the genre may be invoked to shed light upon the work, but they are not themselves the subject of a reading. Nor, usually, are the smaller entities which make up the work. Although we sometimes encounter readings of a single character or scene or even a speech, these are almost always presented as components of the real reading, which is of the work in its entirety.

Second, *a reading is a complete interpretation of the work*. It claims that it will provide an explanation of all the parts and aspects of the work, by demonstrating that each of them has an essential function in the work as a whole. This claim, one must admit, is not always fulfilled, but it is the assumed goal of the reading.

Third, *a reading is an interpretation of the meaning of the work*. This now seems so obvious that we tend to forget that there are other modes of interpretation which do not concentrate in the same way upon meaning—modes which attempt to analyze the work, for instance, primarily in terms of how the author addressed the problems involved in producing the response he desired, or of how that response is evoked in the audience. Such considerations can enter into the reading, of course, but here they serve its elucidation of the work's meaning, which most often turns out to be, as we shall discover, some sort of idea. This emphasis upon meaning is a very important characteristic of the reading, since it leads directly to the next point.

Fourth, *a reading is an interpretation of the real as distinguished from the apparent meaning of the work*. The opposition between these two kinds or levels of meaning may be stated in various forms—deep vs. surface, subtle vs. obvious or simplistic, symbolic vs. literal, covert vs. overt, oblique vs. direct, ironic vs. naive—and sometimes is not stated at all, but it usually seems to be assumed. For the reading does not aim at an interpretation of the ordinary sense of the work (which is routinely dismissed as mere paraphrase or summary), but at a *translation* of that sense into something else which the author really meant, as M. H. Abrams has observed:

> This modern polysemism, which splits all poems—or at least the most noteworthy poems—into two or more levels of meaning, one overt and nominal (which other readers have detected) and the other covert but essential (whose discovery has usually been reserved for the critic making the distinction), is extraordinarily widespread. . . . And at the risk of giving away a trade secret, it must be confessed that most of the time, when we critics come out with a startling new interpretation of a well-known work, it is through the application of this very useful interpretative stratagem.[1]

Fifth, *a reading is the one true interpretation of the work*. This follows from the preceding point, since each reading claims to be presenting the "real" meaning intended by the author of the work, and so usually asserts or implies that it is the only correct (or at least the best) interpretation, and that all others are deficient in some way. Many readings in fact begin by lamenting the failings of their predecessors.

Sixth, *a reading is a justification of the work*. This may be seen as a consequence of the second point, because the demonstration that each of its components has an essential function is in effect a vindication of the work itself. The older criticism could condemn some parts of a work and even some entire works, for various reasons, but that is not the purpose of the modern reading. "The critic's business in general," a recent book tells us, "is to make the best of the text that, broadly, has come down to him, not to complain of its (and his) inadequacies." The assertion that any aspects of the work are defective, in other words, is now regarded as a confession of one's inability to justify them.[2] And the way to justify them was indicated in the fourth point: the reading will show that what seemed to be defects to earlier commentators, who judged them in terms of the work's apparent meaning, turn out to be virtues once we have grasped its real meaning. We shall find that a number of readings base their claim to superiority upon just such a revaluation of the work, and that two of the approaches—the thematic and the ironic—which have been responsible for so many of them are ideally suited to this task. As a result of such readings the works of our major authors have now attained perfection, and those of even minor writers have suddenly become very much better than anyone had ever guessed before.

Seventh, *a reading is a justification of a thesis about the work*. The critic will frequently claim or imply that the reading is to serve the function of testing his conception of the work's real meaning, which is presented initially as a kind of hypothesis. And his hypothesis always passes this test, because the reading, for reasons we shall examine later, is a self-confirming demonstration—the thesis used by the critic to construct his interpretation of the work will necessarily be validated by that interpretation, since this thesis provides the principle in terms of which all the parts of the work are explained (point two) and the work itself is justified (point six). Thus while this aspect of the reading would make it analogous to a scientific experiment, which is also set up to test a hypothesis, there is a crucial difference between them: the experiment can produce negative results, but no reading on record has ever failed to prove the critic's thesis.

Eighth, *a reading is close*. Many would probably regard this as a tautology, for the terms "reading" and "close reading" have become interchangeable. Almost all interpretations, no matter how far off or far out they may seem, now claim to be based upon "a close reading of the text," because few critics would care to admit that they were engaged in any other kind of enterprise. Consequently one cannot tell just what it is, although it is obviously a good thing. Yet its purpose is clear enough. A close reading is designed to set up the crucial distinction noted in point four, by discovering that the real meaning of the work is very different from the apparent meaning yielded by the presumably unclose readings of previous critics. Curiously, we often find that the closer the reading professes to be, the farther is the distance between these real and apparent meanings. In one of the most extraordinary performances that I have seen, a recent article which undertakes to prove that Falstaff is actually "a covert St. John" with "a heavenly vocation," the author is concerned that we may feel his reading is *too* close—that we may, in his own words, "object that my interpretations require an unbelievably close reading."

Ninth, *a reading is new*. This too has become a tautology, but many of the pioneer readings made a point of advertising their newness. The earliest example of this that I could find is the title of an article published in 1919, "A New Reading of *Henry V*" (the article announces, in italics, that *the play is ironic*," and goes on to show that it is "a satire on monarchical government, on imperialism, on the baser kinds of 'patriotism,' and on war"). Today most critics would not bother to insert the word "new" in their titles since it has come to be assumed;[3] if the reading were not new there would be no reason for proposing it (and little hope of publishing it). And we have just learned why it will be a new reading—because it will emerge from a close reading which reveals that the work does not really mean what everybody thought it did (thus the article of 1919 begins by stating that "None of Shakespeare's plays is so persistently and thoroughly misunderstood as *Henry V*").[4] Of course, this places the critic in something of a dilemma, since he must claim that the real meaning of the work was never conveyed to anyone before, so that his reading will be new, and at the same time claim that it is conveyed by the work with flawless artistry, we found in point six, so that his reading will be a vindication. As Alfred Harbage has observed, the meaning is somehow supposed to be "unmistakable and yet hitherto mistaken, perfectly expressed, yet in need of 'interpretation'."[5]

Tenth and last, *a reading is a tour de force*. It is regarded as an exhibition of the critic's skill, of his ability to discover and to demonstrate an interpretation of the work which no one else ever thought of. The reading is therefore peculiarly his own property, since in composing it he is not so much the explicator of a work already in existence as he is the creator of a new work, and so deserves the same kind of credit given to the original author, or at least to a translator. This aspect of the reading has been noted by E. D. Hirsch: "It became fashionable to talk about a critic's 'reading' of a text, and this word began to appear in the titles of scholarly works. The word seemed to imply that if the author had been banished, the critic still remained, and his new, original, urbane, ingenious, or relevant 'reading' carried its own interest."[6] And this would apply as well to those modern theatrical or film directors whose productions of the older drama embody new and personal interpretations which can also be considered "readings" in the same sense (and which often reflect the same approaches responsible for many of the critics' new readings, as we shall see). We could therefore speak with some justice of Critic X's *Hamlet*, just as we do of Barton's *King John* or Polanski's *Macbeth*, for they are not really Shakespeare's.

The following chapters will not attempt to pursue this examination of the reading in general, which would not get us very far, but will instead investigate the specific forms that it takes in the three recent trends or approaches which have generated most of the new readings in the field of English Renaissance drama, and in most other fields of criticism today— the thematic, the ironic, and the historical. I believe they can be grouped together in this way as approaches to interpretation because they all seek to determine the intended meaning of the work (as opposed to the many other things one might do with it), but they are not all approaches in the same sense. Perhaps only thematism, which has been the most influential of the three and therefore will be taken up first, would qualify as a full-fledged critical approach, since behind it there lies a complete philosophic system which, even though rarely invoked by the critics themselves, gives it a coherent rationale, in its conception of the literary work and of the interpretative process, and a universal applicability lacking in the other two. (A fourth trend, Fluellenism, is relegated to an appendix because it is not actually an approach at all but only a technique that may be used in many different approaches.) One clear proof that these approaches are not really coordinate is the frequency and ease with which they are combined; the same reading can derive from two and even all three of them, as we shall discover. Moreover, there are still other approaches, such as the Freudian, the Marxist, the archetypal, and so on, which cut across them and also may combine with them, for they are defined on different levels and thus are not mutually exclusive. So long as we bear this in mind, then, it should do no harm to treat these three trends as distinct critical approaches, since this investigation is not concerned with the ultimate theoretical basis of such distinctions, which belongs to the realm of aesthetics.

It is concerned, rather, with an intermediate range of problems lying somewhere below the cloudy abstractions of aesthetic theory and above the mundane particulars of practical criticism found in the readings of individual works. This is the area which, I believe, is now most in need of investigation. For we have had no shortage of studies in aesthetics (thanks largely to the philosophers), and certainly more than enough new readings, but very little discussion of the grey region in between, which does not even seem to have a name. It might be called the area of critical methodology, where one would examine the actual procedure employed in each approach to discover and demonstrate the meaning of the work, as well as the assumptions (seldom stated or even recognized) that this procedure implies, and the results that it achieves. Few aestheticians descend to this area, and still fewer practical critics ascend to it, since most of them are not at all self-conscious about the approaches they are using, which apparently just grew over the years by a process of imitation and repetition, until they attained the status of new critical orthodoxies, with no need to be explained, much less justified, by their practitioners. As we shall learn in the following chapters, the typical thematic and ironic and historical readings simply take for granted the validity of their method of interpretation and its applicability to the work being interpreted. Many of them in fact do not even betray any awareness that they have adopted a particular methodology, or that there are other possible alternatives.

It is just as difficult to find any systematic discussion on this level by those who question the value of these approaches. For I am certainly not the only one to do so—indeed my position would be quite untenable if I were. A number of critics, including some of the most respected in the field, have raised objections to them, which I have tried to record, but these have for the most part been limited to brief and incidental remarks made in the course of presenting their own studies. (A notable exception is the controversy which has developed over aspects of the historical approach, and which will be touched on in chapter 4.) One can understand why these critics would prefer to devote their time and energies to pursuing their own work, rather than to challenging the work of others. Even on the level of practical criticism, we are confronted with what John Peter has called "the melancholy rule that it is easier to propound a misreading than correct one."[7] The effective refutation of a wrong interpretation can be a very troublesome undertaking, often more troublesome than the development of the right interpretation, and the result is certainly much less satisfying. Anyone who doubts this has only to ask himself just how easy and enjoyable he would find the task of proving that some play was not about a central theme, or that it was not ironic, or that it was not written to please King James. And the attempt to challenge or correct an entire approach must necessarily appear much more onerous and, for most people, even less rewarding. Indeed many would say that it is not the critic's proper job, since he should be engaging the literary work, positively and directly, instead of criticizing criticism of it.

Many people undoubtedly also feel that such an undertaking would be a breach of professional etiquette. Although it is quite acceptable to controvert the work of our colleagues in private conversation and, as was just noted, even in print, briefly (and usually decorously) in our introductions and footnotes, we are not accustomed to seeing a full-scale, systematic investigation directed against them. The prevailing attitude in much of the critical arena today seems to be "live and let live"—a kind of intellectual laissez-faire in which each entrepreneur minds his own business of turning out new readings and expects his competitors to do the same, so that any disputes among them are kept within narrow bounds and do not raise the sort of basic issues that might hold up production. (Thus we shall find in the next chapter that the thematists very frequently disagree on what central theme any given play is about, yet never question the assumption that it must be about a central theme.) But this attitude is a perversion of true academic freedom, which guarantees us the right to present our readings to the public, but surely does not guarantee these readings the right to escape scrutiny, even impolite scrutiny. If the interpretation of literature really matters—and this is the fundamental faith of all criticism—then it must be important to challenge a dubious interpretation, and still more important to challenge a dubious approach to interpretation. For these approaches are far from harmless, since they have been responsible for generating most of the serious misreadings we encounter, and have now reached the stage where they can multiply such readings in the manner of a self-sustaining chain reaction. The thematists have imposed their conception of "thematic unity" upon so many Elizabethan plays that it has come to be regarded as a principle of the playwrights themselves, rather than of this school of critics; now one of them can begin an article by announcing that among the "modes of dramatic unification conventionally resorted to in the Elizabethan period . . . the most potent, though not always the most obvious, was the thematic," and then proceed, on the basis of this supposed convention, to the discovery of yet another central theme in yet another play. The new revelations of pervasive ironies also tend to reinforce each other, because the demonstration that one drama after another was "not meant to be taken at face value" builds up the impression that it was the normal practice of dramatists of this period to conceal their real meaning (this is actually asserted in that "unbelievably close reading" of *Henry IV* mentioned earlier, where the author, who is one of the foremost ironizers of Shakespeare, assures us that "Renaissance artists valued obscurity"). A similar effect has been produced by the recent proliferation of occasionalist readings: as Alfred Harbage pointed out, claims that certain plays were composed for a special occasion are now "functioning as ghostly precedents" to support further claims of this sort, since they seem to prove that playwriting on commission was also a standard practice of the period.[8] And the use of the Fluellenist technique has advanced to the point where its practitioners can apotheosize new dramatic "figures" of Christ or King James by showing their similarity, not to the original personages, but to other alleged Christ or James figures produced by other Fluellenists. Within each of these approaches, then, the new readings beget still more new readings, with no end in sight. I believe that the situation calls for an investigation, for a long and hard look at the methods of interpretation which have brought us to this pass, even if that be considered bad manners.

This investigation is the subject of the following chapters, but since some portions of it have already been presented in articles and in papers read at various professional meetings, I have had the benefit of what is now called feedback, both from those who were sympathetic and those who were not, and so am able to anticipate and attempt to answer two possible objections to my procedure. One is that I am not really dealing with these three approaches in themselves, but only with their abuses, through my selection of illustrative examples, and that this is unfair because every approach can be misused by incompetent critics. A problem of definition is involved here: if any of these approaches is given its broadest and vaguest meaning, then the particular methodology that I am discussing can be thought of as just one manifestation of the approach, and therefore as an "abuse" of it. But at the beginning of each chapter I have tried to separate out from this more general meaning and to define (in terms of that particular methodology) the specific approach I will be considering; and within this definition, I would argue, my investigation is directed at the entire approach and not merely its abuses. The assumptions, the interpretative techniques, and the consequences which I go on to examine are inherent in the nature of the approach itself, as it has been defined, and so do not depend upon the idiosyncrasies of the individual studies chosen to exemplify it.

Now it is certainly true that any approach to interpretation, no matter how good or bad it may be, will yield better results when employed by a critic who is informed, sensitive, and responsible than when it is employed by one who is not, and this also holds for the three approaches in question. But that platitude does not allow us to dismiss the approach as unimportant—a view which is frequently heard and which has the attraction of providing an easy way out that avoids confronting the issues involved (it is in fact another aspect of the attitude of laissez-faire, applied not to readings but to approaches). For the converse is equally true: any critic, no matter how competent or incompetent he may be, will produce better results with a good approach than with a bad one. In all interpretations of a literary work, the approach used is a significant and analytically separable factor, and it should therefore be possible to characterize and to judge the three approaches which are my concern in their own terms. Just as their nature does not depend upon the individual peculiarities of the studies I have selected as my examples, so their value does not depend upon the individual abilities of the authors of those studies.

I would not deny that a few of these examples are pretty silly and have been included largely for their entertainment value (although I could have chosen far worse, especially if I had gone to the writings of the lunatic fringe that hovers around Shakespeare). With this very minor exception, however, all of the studies were selected because they are truly representative of the kind of readings which the three approaches have been producing, and some are among the most widely known and admired examples of each approach. A glance at the list at the end of this book will show that they come from the mainstream of academic criticism of English Renaissance drama, which is about the only stream (except for the aforementioned lunatic fringe) now watering that field. Almost all of them were written by teachers of literature in our colleges and universities, including some of the most prestigious, and were published either in the standard scholarly journals or in books issued by a university press or reputable commercial house. This is the proof that they have been taken seriously by the profession, and my reliance on them here means that I am taking them seriously as well, which I hope their authors will accept as a kind of compliment. If they are all to be considered abuses of these approaches, then I would like to know where the nonabuses can be found.

The other major objection which has been made to my procedure is that it is entirely negative and so puts me at an unfair advantage, since I can fire at my colleagues without offering them a target in return by presenting my own approach to interpretation. I do have one, of course, which those who are interested can find in my earlier criticism; but it is not my purpose here to advocate it or any other approach. I am not arguing that there is a single valid method of interpreting literary texts, but that these three methods are invalid. And in my final chapter I do suggest some positive things that can be done about them, and about the general state of criticism today. Even aside from that, however, I would not agree that the results of this investigation will be wholly negative, since it attempts not only to challenge the three approaches but also to bring out and clarify some of the basic problems of interpretation which they have raised. And I hope that this will lead to a further and fuller discussion of those problems, which would even include the practitioners of the approaches in question. I certainly do not expect that they will suddenly see the light and abjure their interpretative sins, but I would like to believe that at least a few of them will now pause in their production of new readings in order to consider what they are doing, and then try to explain and defend it in some sort of rational conversation with the rest of us. If this book helps in any way to promote such a conversation, then I think it will have served a very positive and very useful purpose.

Two

Thematic Readings

Since the term "thematic" is applied to literary criticism in two different senses which are sometimes confused, it is important to make the distinction clear at the outset. In its more general meaning it refers to studies that trace the recurrences within a work (or among works)[1] of various motifs or conceptions, embodied in the direct statements of the characters, the action and situation, the diction and imagery, and other components. Such an undertaking is often very useful, but it does not constitute an approach to interpretation because the tracing of these recurrences cannot in itself determine what any critic will do with them, and in fact studies of this sort have been employed in many very different approaches. It becomes an approach, however, when the critic attempts to find in one of those recurrent conceptions the real subject of the work he is examining. This is the more specific definition of "thematic criticism" and the one I am concerned with: it is the approach that interprets a literary work as the representation or expression of some abstract concept, which will therefore give the work its unity and its meaning. (This concept is usually called "the central theme," or simply "the theme," of the work, but may be referred to as its "informing motif," "governing idea," etc.—obviously the determination of whether any reading is thematic, according to this definition, does not depend upon the presence of the word "theme" in it.) The term is most commonly used in this sense today, and it designates what has certainly become the most

11

common approach to English Renaissance drama and to virtually all other fields of literature. Indeed one would be hard put to overstate its influence upon contemporary criticism, which is now so pervasive, as we shall soon see, that many people cannot even imagine any other method of interpretation.

The Thematic Scene

Probably the easiest and quickest way to impart some sense of the nature of thematism and its influence is through a collection of representative quotations from recent readings of the plays of Shakespeare and his fellow dramatists which illustrate the kinds of conclusions reached by this approach, and which therefore should provide a useful introduction to the current thematic scene. Each statement is by a different critic, and all have been published within the past fifteen years.

> Love's Labour's Lost might be considered as a prelude to the more extensive commentary on imagination in A Midsummer Night's Dream.

> A Midsummer Night's Dream can . . . be reasonably regarded as a sustained meditation on reality and illusion.

> [A Midsummer Night's Dream is] Shakespeare's first attempt to explore and to justify the distinctive qualities of his art as a way to knowledge.

> Much Ado about Nothing . . . must take its place in Shakespeare's incessant debate about the conflict between appearance and reality.

> [Julius Caesar] may be regarded as a dramatic essay on the nature of [political] power.

> Hamlet continues on a more sophisticated level the discussion of appearance and reality that begins in Richard II.

> Troilus and Cressida . . . emerges as perhaps Shakespeare's finest philosophical contribution to the Renaissance debate on honor.

> [In Measure for Measure] Shakespeare is above all concerned with an analysis, in dramatic terms, of "authority."

> Othello [is] a tragic statement about love in general, . . . [an] exploration of romantic love and marriage.

King Lear clearly offers an inquiry into nature—into the nature of man and his relation to the natural order.

The great tragic exploration of the theme of man in society is in *King Lear*.

[*Antony and Cleopatra*] continues the discussion—and critique—of "romantic love" of *Romeo and Juliet* and *Troilus and Cressida*.

Timon of Athens, Coriolanus, Measure for Measure and *All's Well That Ends Well* investigate more specifically the distinction, often a fine one, between negative and positive pride.

It is almost as though Isaiah xxix were the lesson, and *The Tempest* a dramatic sermon embodying its theme.

Marston's *Dutch Courtezan* [is] a play that explores the issue of "the normality of concupiscence."

[In *A Mad World, My Masters*] Middleton is examining the age-old problem of liberty versus restraint.

[In] *The Revenger's Tragedy* . . . the playwright [is] concerned with the theoretical function of the play itself. . . . [He] is, in the final analysis, writing about his art.

[*Volpone*] is one of the greatest essays we possess on the ontology of selfhood.

The Alchemist is a religious, not a social, tract.

The Broken Heart is a deontological argument.

These quotations share four characteristics which I believe are closely related. Firstly, we should note the class or genus into which they place the play, for it has become an analysis or exploration or examination of some idea or issue, an argument or debate, a commentary, a critique, a discussion, an essay, an inquiry, an investigation, a meditation, a sermon, a statement, a tract—all terms that, in their literal sense, refer to modes of logical discourse. Of course the thematists use this terminology as a kind of metaphor, but it is a metaphor that indicates very clearly how they define the play and hence how they will proceed to interpret it. Secondly, we find that none of these statements mentions or even points toward any particular characters or actions, and it is difficult to see what significance they could have within this definition of the play, except as exemplars of the thematic idea. Thirdly, there is no suggestion in the statements that these plays produce any emotional effect in us, other than the sort of contemplative mood with which we might peruse a philosophical treatise, so in this respect the plays cannot be differentiated—the tragedies do not seem to evoke anything recognizable as tragic feelings, and the comedies have apparently been decomicalized. And fourthly, the thematic ideas seem more or less interchangeable, since many of the formulations could fit many of the plays, and vice versa. We are led to suspect that the connection between theme and play must be rather tenuous, and this is confirmed by the fact that, even in our small sampling, we find the same central theme attributed to very different plays, and very different central themes attributed to the same play.

This last point is certainly one of the most striking and disturbing features of the thematic scene today. The great success of this approach has been accompanied by a great deal of controversy among its practitioners, for while they are all agreed on the essential role of the central theme, they very rarely agree on the identity of that theme in any given play. Indeed, the standard procedure is for the critic to begin his reading by announcing that the central themes proposed by his predecessors are all inadequate, before advancing his own candidate, which in turn is found to be inadequate by his successors. A typical result may be seen in a survey of fourteen readings of Jonson's *Volpone* published since 1937, which yielded the following central themes:

1. avarice
2. money and the power it confers
3. lust and greed
4. immoderate desire
5. disorder
6. disinheritance
7. disease and cure
8. the unnaturalness of sin
9. the folly of worldliness
10. the false estimation of reality
11. the idea of "playing"
12. corrupted creativity
13. the comic spirit itself
14. the centrifugal personality

Similar lists could be compiled for many other plays of the period, and much longer ones for some, such as Shakespeare's tragedies, which have attracted much more thematic criticism. Thus the triumph of thematics has presented us with an embarrassment of riches, which grows more embarrassing every year when the bibliographies reveal that the number of different central themes discovered in each drama has again increased in direct proportion to the number of thematic readings of that drama rolling off the academic presses.

At the same time we are confronted with the converse but equally embarrassing enrichment in the number of apparently dissimilar plays, of all types and genres, which turn out to have the same central theme.

This situation has usually been brought about quite unintentionally through the accumulation of individual readings made over the years by different critics, each laboring independently in his own thematic vineyard; but it can also be the intended result of a single critic's pursuit of his favorite theme over a larger tract of drama. In the studies of *Volpone* just cited, for instance, critic five claims the "theme of disorder" is central not only to that play, but also to "Shakespeare's plays of the same period," while critic six says, "The main theme of *Volpone* is a comic distortion of a theme that is tragic in *Hamlet* and tragicomic in *The Malcontent*, the pervasive Jacobean theme of disinheritance." According to critic thirteen, many of Jonson's other plays are also about "the comic spirit," but critic fourteen believes the theme of the centrifugal personality embodies the basic "issue at stake" in "most of the works in Jonson's large canon— including the tragedies and comedies, verse and prose," and a recent book on this dramatist asserts that "Jonson's plots are concerned with three principal themes: the discovery of real relationships, the curing of wrongheadedness, and the exposure of chicanery. . . . Every play Jonson ever wrote revolves around some combination of these three central issues. The plots play variations on his principal theme, endless inversions of the same leitmotiv. . . ." We are told in another study that each of Shakespeare's plays is also "an individual variation on one grand theme," since they "make a series of statements about order," and in another that "the theme of appearance and reality is almost infinitely extendable in Shakespeare's work," and another deals with "Shakespeare's near obsession with the antithesis between appearance and reality."

This theme of appearance vs. reality has proved to be the most ubiquitous of them all. Some of us may not be so certain that Shakespeare was obsessed with it, but there can be no doubt that the critics were, since by now they have demonstrated that it is indeed extendable not only to all of Shakespeare's work, but to almost every other significant play of the period. Its popularity is waning, however, because there are fashions in themes as in most things; when a theme has been applied too widely, it is no longer useful for creating new readings and so will be turned in for some later model.[2] Another favorite theme-for-all-plays has been the conflict between two hypostatized mental faculties: in one common version we have a virtuous "reason" attempting to control unruly "passion," while in another "reason" is demoted to a calculating prudence which opposes the superior truths of "intuition" or "imagination." The present popularity of this second version is related to the rise of what appears to be the new leading candidate for all-purpose thematism—the theme of aesthetics, which we have already encountered in *A Midsummer Night's Dream, The Revenger's Tragedy*, and *Volpone* (entries 12 and 13). Critics pursuing this line are now revealing that play after play is actually about itself, since its real subject is the nature of poetry or drama or art in general; and, thanks to their efforts, this growing field of reflexive thematics has recently been dignified with a name of its own: "metadramatic criticism." It has obvious connections with yet another current vogue (to which I once succumbed) that is promoting the theme of communication and language—as one study explains it, "the nature, condition, and role of the spoken language ... is what the plays are *about*." And there are of course older hardy perennials, such as good vs. evil, order vs. chaos, freedom vs. restraint, etc., which continue to crop up in a wide variety of plays. Thus this embarrassment, like the first, increases in direct proportion to the proliferation of thematic readings; each year we learn that the same central theme has been found in more different plays, and that more different central themes have been found in the same play. Perhaps, as in the Marxist dialectic, the success of this critical system necessarily carries within it the seeds of its own destruction. At the very least, we can conclude that all is not well in the current thematic scene, and that an investigation of this approach is long overdue.

The Thematic Assumption and the Thematic Leap

We will return later to these four characteristics of the thematic conclusions exemplified in our sampling, but it seems more appropriate to begin our investigation at the beginning, by trying to learn how the readings that led to those conclusions were generated. It is a commonplace that the sort of interpretation one derives from a literary work will depend upon the questions one asks of it, for these determine what one will seek and find there. The initial question which the thematic reading appears to be addressing (and which turns out to be resolved, of course, by the central theme it has discovered) is, quite simply, What is the play about? (Many of these readings actually begin by asking how the play is unified, but this is just another form of the same question, since what unifies the play will be what it is about.) Now to ask what a play is about may seem like a perfectly innocent and neutral starting point, but to the thematist it is not, because for him it already implies a certain kind of answer which is very different from that sought by the rest of us (and by the thematist himself, I suspect, when he is not practicing his vocation). Let us try to picture, for instance, the following conversation between Ben Jonson and William Shakespeare in a tavern on the Bankside:

B. J.:   What have you been doing lately, Will?
W. S.:   I've been working on a new play.
B. J.:   Oh, what will it be about?
W. S.:   It will be a sustained meditation on reality and illusion.

I think we can imagine Ben's response, once he had calmed down. It probably would be much the same as our own if we asked a friend what a play or movie he had seen was about and received such an answer. We would still want to know what it was *about*, by which we would mean, I take it, some specific information concerning its characters and action.

In the strange world of thematics, however, this works the other way around. When a critic of this school asks what the play that he is interpreting is about, he really means what *idea* it is about. We must therefore go on to consider just what is supposed to be the relationship between the play and that thematic idea which is its alleged subject. The thematists themselves will not be of much help on this problem, since they very rarely discuss it, even though it is fundamental to their entire approach. They continually speak of the play as being "about" its theme; but here it is essential to make a logical distinction which will require some belaboring of what I trust is obvious. In the assertion, "*Hamlet* is about the discrepancy between appearance and reality," the term "about" cannot possibly have the same meaning as in the assertion, "*Hamlet* is about Hamlet's attempt to avenge his father," or in the assertion, "Descartes's *First Meditation* is about the discrepancy between appearance and reality." A philosophic treatise is literally about abstract conceptions; but a Shakespearean play is literally about particular characters and their actions, and so can only be said to be about an abstract concept through a form of metaphorical shorthand which replaces this literal subject with one of a totally different order. For the thematic subject, unlike the characters and actions, is not actually "in" the play at all, but must be sought outside it by generalizing from these particulars to some genus to which they belong. The relationship of theme to play, therefore, is the same as that of "woodenness" or "brown-ness" or "rest" to a bed, or of any other abstraction to any other concrete object. And that relationship creates serious difficulties for the thematic approach, as we shall soon discover.

These critics are aware, of course, that the play is not literally about their thematic idea, but they get around this by means of a distinction (explicit or often implicit) between real and apparent meaning, which we have seen is characteristic of readings in general. The particular actions represented in the play are only its apparent subject, and so can be dismissed very quickly as pertaining to the lowest level of interpretation, or to some level below interpretation ("preliminaries," one critic calls them). They assume that the play cannot really be about what it seems to be about, because it must be about an idea if it is about anything, or anything important. This assumption is spelled out at some length in the introduction to an essay on *The Merchant of Venice*:

> What, then, is it about, if indeed it is "about" anything at all. There are, of course, those who think that it is not about anything at all, that it is only a fairy tale, a delightful fantasy . . . and not to be taken seriously. . . . Let us assume, however, that the play *is* about something, and that it is not about the doings of Jews in England or in Venice. We can say, of course, that it is about a Jew who almost takes a pound of flesh from a Christian merchant, and it is about a young man who wins a young lady by passing a strange test. . . . But this is to summarize the plot, to say what happens rather than to say what the happenings add up to. When we turn from *what* happens to what the happenings are *about*—from plot to theme—we tend to allegorize. . . . To say that the play adds up to something, that we make something out of it, and that it lends itself to a sort of allegorical interpretation is really not to say anything very daring about a work of literature. Surely literature is about something, and is not merely pretty sounds.

At the beginning of a widely anthologized reading of *Much Ado about Nothing*, another critic presents us with the same kind of choice: "*Either* this is all trivial . . . and we are foolish to look for anything in any way deep, ourselves solemnly making ado about nothing; *or* it is a . . . love-fantasia on the theme of deception by appearances." Here the italics (in the original) bring out the thematic assumption very clearly: the theme is the thing, and presumably the only thing, that can make a play "deep"; or, putting it negatively, a play that is not about a theme—i.e., a play that is merely about its literal subject—is really "about nothing" and therefore "trivial." Another critic, in his study of *A Midsummer Night's Dream*, complains of the "historical failure to take the comedies seriously,"[3] and undertakes to refute "the view that the play means nothing much at all." As he puts it, "Unless we see that these mature comedies are thematically serious we shall never get them right. . . . The point is that all the comedies are 'problem' comedies; that *The Two Gentlemen of Verona* is a legend of Friendship, . . . *A Midsummer Night's Dream* of love, *As You Like It* of courtesy, and *The Merchant of Venice* of justice." Yet another insists that in *Volpone* "we are dealing with ideas, not simply with the interplay of characters in a one-dimensional action." Some of us might find the prospect of one-dimensional action rather intriguing, but the "simply" tells us that we are supposed to regard it as a grossly inferior alternative to "ideas." And another explicitly states this assumption as a universal law:

> All commentary is allegorical interpretation, an attaching of ideas to the structure of poetic imagery. The instant that any critic permits himself to make a genuine comment about a poem (e.g., "In *Hamlet* Shakespeare appears to be portraying the tragedy of irresolution") he has begun to allegorize.

According to this law, it would seem, to "make a genuine comment" about a work is to abstract (or "allegorize") from its literal subject to a thematic idea ("irresolution").

Since the thematic approach, we noted, can begin by asking how the play is unified rather than what it is about, we often find this assumption stated in terms of artistic unity or form rather than subject. A very influential reading of *King Lear* (published in 1948) starts off by asserting that the unity of the play "lies very little on the surface . . . indeed, as in all high art, it is a question of theme"; the parenthetical insertion is not explained or defended, presumably because it is thought to be axiomatic. The dust-jacket blurb of a recent book on Shakespeare's comedies announces that the book's "purpose is to identify the form of each comedy; that is, to relate the governing idea of each play to the action that expresses it." The author of a more general study entitled *Construction in Shakespeare* tells us that those who concentrate on the plots and emotional effects of the plays "are far too narrow," because "they quite ignore design, the organization of parts with relation to an idea." And another critic, quoting him, adds that "psychological analysis is inadequate to the consideration of general design, that 'organization of parts with relation to an idea' which seems accessible only to thematic criticism." Numerous examples could also be cited to show how this equation of unity or form with central theme is assumed without question in readings of individual plays. Note, for instance, the use of "obliged" in this comment on *Much Ado about Nothing*: "Those who claim a structural relevance for the Dogberry scenes . . . are obliged to recognize a theme which is articulated in all three of the actions"; or of "must" in another critic's remarks on *The Merchant of Venice*: "If then the play will work neither as a Jew-baiter, nor as its opposite, there is nothing to conclude except that either Shakespeare did not know his business, or we have misunderstood it. The latter is more likely. . . . We must try again, and seek a unifying theme that will include these opposites of race and religion."

This is perhaps enough to make the point about the thematic assumption. Anyone who doubts its power or its prevalence has only to observe the automatically thematic responses of students in a college English class (any class, from freshman composition to a doctoral seminar) when they are asked about the subject or structure of some work—or, better yet, observe their consternation when this kind of response is challenged. Most of them have apparently never encountered, and cannot even conceive of, any other way of discussing literature. Throughout their school careers, they have learned from their teachers and textbooks and "cribs" and other study aids that they must always "look for the theme" in every work they will be questioned on (which all too often means guessing what theme the teacher has in mind), just as their parents were trained to look for those Freytagian pyramids of "rising" and "falling" action. Indeed we find one of the earlier thematists justifying his approach because of its superiority to this mode of geometric analysis, as if that were the only alternative:

> The most obvious approach to the structure of drama is to equate structure with plot and then to describe plot in terms of those familiar and yet somewhat elusive elements sometimes called rising action, climax, dénouement, etc. . . . But at best such descriptions of the action yield only superficial information. A likelier route into the heart of the play is to define the structure in terms of theme.

Today our thematists feel no need to provide any such justification, because of the general acceptance of the thematic assumption. For this assumption does not, of course, only affect the critics who state it, but operates even more potently upon those—now apparently the great majority—who are not aware of it. Implicitly or explicitly, they all now seem to assume that the thematic definition of subject matter and of form is a universal law, since I have not seen any of them attempt to demonstrate that the play under discussion possessed some special qualities which called for a thematic interpretation, rather than some other kind. (The passage on *The Merchant of Venice* quoted above is the most elaborate defense of a thematic reading that I could find in recent criticism, and it is completely general and completely circular, being, as was said, nothing more than a spelling out of the assumption.) They apparently take it for granted that all plays require such an interpretation, and that there are no other valid approaches to be reckoned with. That is why, at the beginning of the typical thematic reading, the critic does not pause to ask *whether* this play is about a central theme, but proceeds immediately to the question of *which* central theme it is about, and so to the refutation of the themes proposed by others. Thus the new orthodoxy has produced a curious paradox, for it expects us to begin with the assumption that a play cannot be about what it obviously seems to be about—namely, particular characters engaged in particular actions—because it must be about something entirely different—a general idea—which is not at all obvious, since the thematists themselves rarely agree on it.

Perhaps I had better make it clear at this point that my argument against the thematic assumption is not an argument against the existence of thematic plays. Nor am I suggesting that we should begin our interpretation of any play by assuming that it cannot have a general idea as its subject, for this would be just as arbitrary as the thematists' assumption, and could be just as misleading. Some plays really are organized around a central theme and therefore require a thematic mode of analysis. We will never be able to identify them, however, or to distinguish them from other kinds of plays, if we adopt the thematic assumption, since it simply begs the question. We must come to the play with another sort of working hypothesis, which will be discussed in the final section of this chapter.

We are not quite through with the thematic assumption, however, because there is another kind of argument which has been used to justify the application of this approach, and which therefore should be examined here. Sometimes a critic will claim that the play itself is asking us a general question that can only be answered with a thematic reading. I have collected a few examples of these questions—each one, again, by a different author, and all published within the past twenty years.

> The question the play [*Hamlet*] asks is, "How can man do anything successfully?"
>
> The two basic questions which underlie the whole significance of *Hamlet* [are]: Who or what is Hamlet? and, Who or what is Man?
>
> The whole play [*King Lear*] is a dramatic answer to the one question in which all Lear's questions are subsumed: the question, What is Man?
>
> Shakespeare's question [in *Macbeth*] remains open for the

audience if not for Macbeth's killers: What is a man, and of what is he capable as part of his sex and of his race?

Throughout *Caesar*, Shakespeare forces us to consider the nature of man. Of what is he made? What parts go together to form . . . the "whole man"?

[In *Troilus and Cressida* and *Othello*] the dramatist is posing the question of how men come to deliver themselves to illusion.

The material of the play [*Coriolanus*] is ordered about a central question: what is the proper relation between an individual and his state?

The questions raised in *The Alchemist* are related to metaphysical and theological problems: what are the limits of man's knowledge?

[In *Bartholomew Fair*] the epistemological question will become also an ethical one and very nearly a religious one: "Do you have Adam's warrant?"

[In *Bartholomew Fair*] Jonson is asking a . . . most devastating question . . . Who is responsible for the folly and evil we see around us?

Unfortunately, it is impossible to learn from these readings just how the play can ask this kind of general question, or—even if it could—just how one can determine what that question is. And a moment's reflection should tell us that, in any literal sense, these plays do not present us with questions at all; they present us with particular actions, from which we can abstract all sorts of general questions if we have a mind to. We may conclude, therefore, that these questions cannot justify the application of the thematic approach to a play since they are themselves the consequence of that approach: it is only because the critic is asking the thematic question of the play—what idea is it about?—that he finds the play asking a thematic question back at him. Moreover, the connection between any such question and the play which is said to be asking it seems no less tenuous than that between any central theme and the play which is said to be expressing it, for the results have proved just as embarrassing (although on a smaller scale)—very different questions have been derived from the same play, and the same question has been derived from very different plays. (There are even critics who discover their favorite questions in a whole body of drama, just like those all-purpose themes: in one study we are told, for instance, that throughout his canon there is one "crucial question Shakespeare asks . . . Has man authority to know what is authoritative in his nature and in his position?" and in another that during Middleton's early period "two burning questions ... turn up in one comedy after another," namely, "Why do people fall into sin?" and "What is the effect of individual sin upon society?") In fact, the dependence of these questions upon the critic's own predisposition is acknowledged in a reading of *Hamlet*: "The Christian may find the fundamental question the play raises to be 'How can man be saved?' The existentialist, 'What is man's essence?' Are not both right?" At least we can agree that one is no more "right" than the other, or than dozens of additional questions of this type which could be abstracted from the play by the same arbitrary technique.

This technique is the direct result of the thematic assumption and is basic to all thematic interpretation. It is actually quite simple; it consists of seizing upon some particular components of the drama and making them the representatives or exemplars of a general class, which then becomes the subject of the play and of the critic's analysis. The technique, in other words, "thematizes" these concrete particulars by transforming them into abstract ideas, and therefore can be employed both to discover the central theme (or central question) that the play is supposed to be about, according to the assumption just examined, and to work up the thematic reading of the play that is supposed to confirm this discovery. I call it the "thematic leap," since it is the means by which the critic rises from the level of particulars to the level of abstractions, from the apparent, literal subject of the play to its real thematic subject.

This technique is most often applied to the characters themselves, who usually come to represent entire groups of people (Cleopatra "is all womankind, rather than a single woman," Prince Hal stands for "youth," Sir Epicure Mammon for "knighthood"), or else those hypostatized mental or moral states, already mentioned, which these critics are so fond of (thus Iago and Desdemona exemplify the opposition of reason vs. intuition, or hate vs. love, or wit vs. witchcraft, or good vs. evil, and Middleton's Deflores "is, in a sense, the personification of the irascible appetite"). But it can be used to thematize the character's situation (in Othello's marriage we see the "implications of any love relationship"), or an action of his (Prospero's "rejection of the masque becomes part of a larger rejection of passive life in general"), or a speech (Dogberry's directions to the Watch turn out to be "disquisitions on the methods of securing knowledge, of confirming likely hypotheses"). The same technique can also be applied to the imagery, by detaching it from the particular context and making it part of an autonomous "pattern" that comments directly upon the theme, and even to the setting, as in a reading of *Antony and Cleopatra* which finds a thematic conflict embodied in "the vast containing opposites of Rome and Egypt, the World and the Flesh." And it can function as well in interrogative thematics, by discovering that some event in the play is asking, or forcing us to ask, a general question: according to a study of *A Woman Killed with Kindness*, when Mountford kills two of Acton's men in I.iii, "our question now is, What must he do to pay for his error?, or abstracted, What is the proper penance for a sin of passion?" But further illustration would be superfluous, since the technique has now become part of the critic's standard operating procedure, as may be seen, for instance, in the account of it given in one of those study aids referred to earlier which train students in theme-hunting:

> The supercharging of the action leads the audience to levels of greater generalization. As the play proceeds, it becomes more than just a story about straw men created by the dramatist. . . . We talk, therefore, not of individual characters and their faults, but instead begin to use abstract nouns. The play is about *avarice*, *lechery*, *self-delusion*, *over-ambition*, and *hypocrisy*. It has become symbol.

We must bear in mind that this thematic leap is performed by the critic and not the characters, for it depends upon the crucial distinction between real and apparent meaning. The characters, tied down to the apparent level of particulars, are not aware of the thematic significance of their words or actions, which is supplied by the critic through his insight into the real level of abstractions; thus, while Dogberry is giving us those disquisitions on epistemology, he thinks that he is only instructing the Watch, but the critic knows better. It is true that occasionally a critic will make the characters themselves behave as if they were self-conscious thematists: another study of *Much Ado about Nothing*, which locates its theme in the opposition of "faith" and "fashion," tells us that "to distinguish between faith and fashion is the task which Beatrice has imposed upon herself," and that "she undertakes this dialectical search" with "deep commitment";[4] and the reading of *Antony and Cleopatra* quoted above explains that Cleopatra kills herself because of the irreconcilability of the two abstractions represented by those "vast containing opposites of Rome and Egypt," which must be the most unlikely and the most obligingly thematic motive for suicide on record. But these are atypical aberrations of overenthusiastic thematic leapers, and should not be allowed to complicate what is really a very simple and straightforward technique.

There is, however, one kind of complication which is not atypical but seems to be inherent in the nature of this technique. Once it is asserted that some particular dramatic component stands for a general class, there is then no way to determine how general that class should be. And since, as we are about to learn, the critics of this school often seek a central theme for a play that is more "inclusive" than those proposed by their predecessors, the leap by which this theme is discovered will have to carry them ever higher up the ladder of abstraction to ever more general classes. Thus one thematic leap tends to beget another, and the result is a kind of thematic leapfrog. A reading of *The Alchemist* claims, for instance, that "in mocking Mammon and his dreams, Jonson ... mocks not only Mammon's sensualism but all escapism," while another insists that Mammon must be viewed as a representative, "not merely" of "avarice," but of "sin," and many similar examples could be cited. But there is no reason for the process of abstraction to stop even at this level, since it can just as easily go all the way. In fact, we have already seen this occur in some of the thematic questions in that collection, which leapfrog over all the intermediate classes to arrive at what would seem to be the most general class of all, mankind itself. As the critic who asked us to jump from "Who or what is Hamlet?" to "Who or what is Man?" explains it, "Through Hamlet's search for identity, Shakespeare makes his audience aware of the larger significance of 'everyman.'" The reference, of course, is to the Everyman or Mankind figure of the early Morality plays, who clearly was meant to represent all humanity, and who for that reason has become a popular goal in thematic leapfrog.[5] Another critic states that "Shakespeare framed the role of Hamlet to represent the life-journey of everyman"; and another that "Macbeth is an Everyman"; and another that "*Othello* is not a treatise on mixed marriages, but a drama about Everyman"; and a recent book on Middleton finds "an Everyman figure" in Richard Easy of *Michaelmas Term* and Penitent Brothel of *A Mad World, My Masters*. At least one critic has even managed to leap over this ultimate abstraction by asserting that "Lear's story, as the story of Man's life, is much more universal than the theme of *Everyman*." We are not given the name of the more universal class that Lear stands for, but the claim should not surprise us, since the entire thrust of this technique points toward it. Once the critic has taken the decisive step (or leap) by declaring that a character is not to be regarded as an individual but as a class representative, he finds himself in a competition to make that class as general as possible. And in this competition there are no controls or limits provided either by the interpretative approach or by the data of the play.

I would argue that the thematic leap is arbitrary in two distinct senses. For one thing, the choice of the general class is wholly arbitrary, since any character or event belongs to many different classes and subclasses. There is no reason, for instance, why Sir Epicure Mammon should be taken as a representative of all escapism, rather than of all pride, or unnaturalness, or self-transmutation (as he has been in other thematic readings of *The Alchemist*). And for a much more complex character such as King Lear, the number of possible classes would be very much larger, even if they were restricted to the same level of abstraction. But of course there is no such restriction, since we have just seen that any of these classes can be subsumed, by the leapfrog technique, under more general classes, and those under classes still more general. It seems clear, therefore, that in both the horizontal and vertical dimensions, the critic is free to leap from any character (or event) to just about any class he wishes. And this is confirmed when we try to proceed in the opposite direction, from the general class to the character. For if someone in the *Henry IV* plays is to represent "youth," why should it be Prince Hal rather than Hotspur, who is presumably of about the same age, or Prince John, who must be younger? If "all womankind" is embodied in Cleopatra, then what is poor Octavia? And why should Iago stand for "reason" in *Othello* when the Duke seems much more rational? There are no answers to such questions, since the choice of the character who is supposed to exemplify any class is just as arbitrary as the choice of the class that any character is supposed to exemplify.

The thematic leap is also arbitrary in a second and more basic sense. Not only is there no reason why these characters should be regarded as the representatives of any given class, but there is no reason why they should be regarded as the representatives of any class at all. No one would deny that some characters in these plays actually are defined in this generic way—Messenger, a Servant, 1 Soldier, 2 Plebian, etc.—but the thematic leapers do not meddle with them. They operate upon the major figures, which include some of the most highly individuated characters in our literature. But this individuation must inevitably be diminished to the extent that we view them as class-representatives, for they will then possess only those traits shared by all members of the class—thus when the thematists make some character stand for "reason," the other aspects of his personality will either be ignored by them or else distorted to fit their formulation. And the more universal the class which these characters are supposed to represent, the less individuality they will retain, because as the scope of the class increases, the number of traits shared by its members must decrease (in the language of the logicians, the

larger the "extension," the smaller the "intension"). Therefore the assertion that "Lear's story . . . is much more universal than the theme of
Everyman," though intended as high praise, would really mean that he
was even less individualized than Everyman, if it were true. But of course
it is not true. Everyman is explicitly presented as the representative of all
men; his experiences in the play are those which (according to the
dramatic postulates) everyone must face, and he is not given any past
history, any human relationships, or any traits of personality that do
not belong to the general run of mankind. But that could never be said of
King Lear. How many men have been in his situation, or undergo what
he does, or possess his tremendous capacity for rage or suffering? Now
Lear certainly is a man (among many other things) and shares our
common humanity, or else we could not understand or sympathize with
him; but is he any more representative of mankind than Oswald or Kent
or the Gentleman who carries Kent's message to Dover? Indeed, of the
four, the nameless Gentleman would seem to be the most representative
because he is the least individualized, and so comes closest to Everyman,
while Lear is the most individualized and therefore least representative.
Nor is this simply a question of logic, for it goes to the heart of our
dramatic experience. What makes Lear's story so important to us—so
interesting, so memorable, so moving—is surely not his representativeness but his uniqueness, his complex and extraordinary personality
that differentiates him from every other character in the play and from
Everyman. And that is just what is lost when we treat him as the
exemplar of *any* class, even one much less universal than mankind. But
the same is true of every major character in these plays, although they do
not all, of course, have as much individuality to lose. Even Sir Epicure
Mammon will suffer a terrible diminution if he is flattened out into a kind
of personified Sensuality or Escapism, and so will all the others, in
varying degrees, when they are elevated, or reduced, by means of the
thematic leap to the status of Morality figures. If we look back, then, at
the passage quoted from that study aid, which asserted that this process
of "generalization" (i.e., the leap) is what makes the characters something more than "straw men," we must conclude that exactly the opposite
is true. It is when they are generalized into symbols of a class (or, in the
words of the study aid, into "abstract nouns") that they become straw
men, for then they can no longer be regarded as individual characters
who are significant in their own right.

Since the thematic leap exacts such a heavy price, the critics who ask
us to make it might be expected to show us that the characters in question
have been presented by the dramatist in a special way which indicates

that they are to be interpreted as class representatives rather than as individuals. But one searches in vain for any such demonstration in these readings (and it is not easy to imagine what evidence they could produce in the case of characters whom the dramatist has taken such pains to individualize), just as one does for any demonstration that the play in question possesses some special qualities which call for a thematic interpretation. The justification for both of these operations seems to be assumed automatically; indeed, one assumption demands the other, for if the critic begins by asking what idea the play is about, he must then work out a reading of the play that transforms its characters and events, through the thematic leap, into representations of an idea.

My Theme Can Lick Your Theme

We have seen why the thematists seek the subject of the play in the realm of ideas, because of their basic assumption, and how they are able to find it there, by means of their basic technique; but we have yet to consider another crucial problem of this approach which has been the source of most of the controversy among its practitioners. That is the problem of determining *which* idea is the subject of the play and hence the goal of each thematic leap—of determining, in their own language, the play's "central theme." In our earlier discussion of the relationship between the play and the thematic idea which it is supposed to be "about," we saw that this idea must be abstracted from the particular action presented in the play, and so is related to that action in the same way that "woodenness" and "brownness" and "rest" are to a bed. The trouble, of course, is that very many different abstractions can be derived from any particular object, even from such a relatively simple object as a bed. And the greater the complexity of the object (in the quantity or variety of its parts and of their interconnections), the greater will be the number of abstractions derivable from it, so that when we are dealing with a play, this number must be very large indeed. Yet every one of these abstractions would appear to have the same legitimate claim to be considered a "theme," so long as it was generated by something in the play. It need not be universally applicable to all the play's components, since this is not possible and is not demanded of other forms of abstraction (even in the bed, none of the suggested "themes" applies to every part). Nor need it be universally acceptable to all readers or viewers of the play, which is equally impossible and equally irrelevant, because the process of abstraction in this situation will be determined by each abstractor's temperament and interests. Therefore it does not seem unfair to conclude that a dramatic theme is any general idea that occurs to anyone experiencing a drama— or, more accurately, after experiencing it, for I suspect that very little of this abstracting takes place while one is in direct and active contact with the work.

We cannot stop here, however, because the thematic critic insists that the idea he has abstracted from the play is not merely one of its many possible themes, but "the central theme," and thus its real subject. We must therefore try to discover just what is the nature of this claim that one theme in a play is "central," or "more central" than the others. In theory, this would seem to be as illogical as the claim that the bed was really wooden rather than brown, or more brown than restful. And we have already noted that, in practice, the thematists themselves have not been able to convince each other by the arguments they have advanced to demonstrate the centrality of the theme they favor. It will be useful to examine these arguments to see whether they can shed any further light upon this problem.

Virtually all of them turn upon an appeal to the conception of "thematic unity," in which the critic asserts that his candidate for central theme is the architectonic principle (and the only such principle) that "includes" or "comprehends" or "informs" or "organizes" all the disparate components of the play and so unifies them into a coherent whole. Sometimes this appeal is couched in the language of discovery, as if the theme constituted a special insight, a kind of gestalt, finally making sense out of a work which had hitherto remained for the critic (and presumably for the rest of us) a mere aggregation of unrelated parts:

> Grasp this, and instantly a dozen things in the play fall into
> place, and nearly every character in it is seen to be one thing on
> the outside and another underneath—so inherent, so little mere
> adornment, is the casket theme. It ramifies into a hundred details
> and into every corner of the play.

This sales pitch—which, we might notice in passing, relies on the usual separation of a real ("underneath") from an apparent ("outside") meaning—may sound very persuasive, until we learn how many other central themes have been discovered in the same play (it is *The Merchant of Venice*) since these words were printed, each of which, according to its discoverer, ramifies into every corner and makes everything fall into place. Unfortunately, one thematist's gestalt is not another's, which would suggest that these unifying insights, like those first investigated in gestalt psychology, are really a form of optical illusion residing in the eye of the beholder rather than in the object beheld. And this suspicion is confirmed by those critics mentioned earlier, who manage to see their favorite theme in one play after another, although for them it might be more appropriate to adopt the terminology of a rival psychology and say they are "projecting" their own thematic obsessions onto the innocent plays or playwrights.

Our interest here, however, is not in the psychological mechanisms that may underlie the discovery of a central theme, or the rhetorical flourishes that may herald it, but rather in the actual arguments employed to assert and defend its centrality against the claims of other candidates. Such arguments are not difficult to find, since they have become the standard opening of most thematic interpretations—one which I call the my-theme-can-lick-your-theme gambit, wherein the critic tries to justify his "new reading" by proving that the central theme he has found in the play is superior to those proposed in earlier readings. Because the case for any central theme depends upon its alleged ability to encompass and thereby unify the entire play, he usually contends that the previous candidates are not as "large" or "wide" or "inclusive" as his own. It is on these grounds, for instance, that several of the critics represented in that survey of readings of *Volpone* assert the superiority of their central themes over "avarice," the theme of critic one. Critic four says that this play portrays

> the horrors which any immoderate desire . . . will engender. Venice, with its oriental trappings, happens to permit what else-where might seem an unlikely course of avarice; this minute localization suggests all the more strongly reasons for not sup-posing the vice to be just hunger for money.

And critic eight:

> *Volpone* is about nature. Our central objection to Volpone is that his activities are unnatural, not simply selfish. . . . *Volpone* is not simply a satire of avarice in Jacobean England. It is not a play of topical interest; it is a play for everybody concerned with the eternal verities.

And critic nine:

> The unifying theme of the play is the folly of worldliness. Cer-tainly folly seems a more inclusive concern of the play than the commonly suggested avarice.

But critic ten feels he is being even more inclusive than critic nine:

> If . . . we take Folly to be the central theme of the play, it must
> be in an older and wider sense of the word. . . . Folly, in its
> widest Renaissance sense of a false estimation of reality or the
> Nature of Things, is the object of the moral satire.

And critic fourteen begins by acknowledging that critic eleven has

> rightly stressed the theatrical bent of the two principal villains.
> I am inclined to see these propensities as part of the larger por-
> trayal of the centrifugal personality.

The thematic criticism of Shakespeare provides a great many similar examples, but we can content ourselves here with a triad of studies of *Troilus and Cressida*. The first begins by asserting that its candidate for central theme is the worthiest because it includes what had previously been regarded as two separate themes. According to this critic, we must conceive of

> the theme of the play as somewhat different from the conven-
> tional view. The play, as I read it, is not "about" love and war,
> or love and honor, or policy and emotion, or about any pair of
> conceptions or qualities. Rather it deals with the single problem
> of corruption and its causes; and the war story and the love story
> simply manifest different aspects of the same essential decay.

The cause of this corruption is the "false equation" of "prideful will and appetite" with "honor and glory," which therefore qualifies as the one true central theme; but its qualifications were soon challenged by another critic who objects that it is still not quite inclusive enough:

> [The] argument that the unifying theme of the play is a corrup-
> tion which consists in mistaking "prideful will and appetite" for
> honor and glory will be seen to have its parallels to my own
> reading, though it stops short of seeing the uses to which this
> idea is put in the play, and the larger theme which it serves.

That larger theme, espoused by his reading, is the "effect of time"; but yet another critic objects that time itself serves a larger theme which brings us back full circle:

> Critics have made it abundantly clear that Time has a special
> significance in the play; [but] this is superficial. . . . The the-
> matic function of Time here is simply to define the sensibility of
> Troilus and, consequently, that of the play: Time is appetitive,
> sensual and limiting. . . . And Troilus, with his mercenary-
> mindedness and appetitiveness, is but an abstract of the corrup-
> tive spirit which the play as a whole is "about."[6]

This kind of argument can involve two different claims, although they are often combined (as in some of these quotations): theme A may be larger than theme B because it includes more of the play, or because it includes theme B. The second claim implies the first, since if theme A includes B it must also include those components of the play encompassed by B and presumably others as well; but the first claim need not imply the second, and so can be examined separately. It is of course a quantitative claim, which is equivalent to the assertion that the bed is more brown than restful, and even more difficult to argue. Although it purports to measure the "amounts" of two (or more) themes in a play, there is no way to determine what dramatic components should be counted as the units in this measurement, since a theme may be found in any part or aspect of the play. Often these units are scenes or episodes which, according to the critic, are subsumed under his theme but not his predecessor's:

> Love's Labour's Lost is organized around a central theme, but this
> fact is obscured by the usual approach to the play as a satire of
> overelaborate language. This interpretation accounts for the
> witty talk and suggests that the outcome of the action is due to
> the lords' excessive verbal play. It is difficult, however, to see the
> relevance of the academy plan, the commoners' role, or the
> startling final act of the play in terms of "wit." . . . Wit is only
> one aspect of a larger concern. . . . Love's Labour's Lost presents
> a conflict between fancy and achievement, a conflict which is
> ultimately one between artifice and nature.

But the measurement can also be made in terms of the forces motivating the action:

> The theme of a play, if dramatically significant, is worked out
> in action, and conversely a particular action can be translated
> into theme. If you say, as does [Critic X], that the theme of Much
> Ado is love's truth, the governing action (the activity guiding the
> characters) could be formulated as the search in love for the truth
> about love—though where this would leave Dogberry is a bit
> hard to say. In a keen study of the comedy, [Critic Y] found
> pride or comic hybris the binding agent in [the] action. . . . The
> analysis is illuminating, but I believe it . . . understates the role
> of wit, which in both its main senses drives the play.

Or in terms of emotional power:

> What is the object of Shakespeare's rage in King Lear? The play
> has several important themes, including the dangers of political
> disorder, the infirmities of old age, conflicting conceptions of

nature, and others [proposed in earlier readings]. But the theme with the highest emotional temperature is the theme of charity in human relations.

Or interest:

> The Broken Heart furnishes an answer to a question every reader of Ford must ask himself: what is laudable and meaningful in a villainous world? . . . The claims of romantic love, the violated contract of betrothal, and the conflict of reason and passion [the central themes found by previous critics] may be arranged behind this concern as questions and problems of lesser ultimate interest.

Nor does that exhaust the possibilities, for other arguments of this sort have used as their unit of measurement the characters, the imagery, word counts, the locales, the atmosphere, and so on. But since these are all incommensurable entities, they do not admit of quantitative comparisons: when Critic A asserts that most of the episodes in a play fall under his theme, and Critic B that most of the motivation falls under his, how does one decide which theme encompasses more of that play? And even when the dispute is limited to a single unit of measurement—say, the characters—we still have the problem of judging the relative weight of these components, since they cannot be of equal importance: if Othello, Iago, and Desdemona are claimed for Critic A's theme, and Othello, Desdemona, Emilia, Cassio, and Roderigo for Critic B's, which is more inclusive?

A still more basic problem, however, is involved in all of these quantitative arguments. For even in the unlikely event that two critics with rival themes could agree on the identity and the weight of the components to be counted, there would be no way to determine which of these components should be placed under one theme rather than the other. It is true that a critic will often name specific parts of the play which he contends are irrelevant to his opponent's theme but relevant to his own (as in the quotation above on Love's Labor's Lost), but the situation is rarely if ever that clear-cut. I have yet to find the critic who would admit that even one significant dramatic component was not encompassed by his central theme,[7] and there is no reason why he should, since we saw that he can "leap" from each part of the play to just about any theme he wants to. And he is no less free when he proceeds in the opposite direction, for each theme can be expanded to include just about any part of the play (certainly in Love's Labor's Lost it would take very little ingenuity to extend the theme of "wit" to the academy plan and commoners and final act). The extreme flexibility of this relationship between the dramatic component and the thematic idea is the most serious difficulty faced by these quantitative arguments, and it would appear to be insurmountable.[8] Because of it, we have no way of testing the claim that one central theme includes more of the play than another candidate.

The second claim, that one central theme includes another candidate, may seem more promising, because it involves a purely logical relationship between two ideas which should be relatively easy to ascertain (much easier, as Hume taught us, than the relation of the ideas to the particular facts of the play). And indeed we often find these critics asserting confidently that some theme proposed in an earlier reading is subsumed under, or subordinated by, or enveloped within, or a part of, or a means to their own larger and higher thematic abstraction, so that anyone who has mistaken it for the play's central theme is left feeling very small-minded indeed. We are told by one of them, for instance, that the "chief unifying theme [of *The Spanish Tragedy*] is not revenge but the problem of justice," since "the element of revenge is part of . . . the larger theme of justice"; and by another that "outwardly [*Hamlet*] is a study of the need for revenge, but for Shakespeare, revenge is the catalyst by which he will activate truth about humanity" through the real "central theme," which is "Hamlet's search for his identity, and . . . the search of all humanity for itself"; and by another that "for Shakespeare the theme of identity is the controlling force in the story [of *The Two Gentlemen of Verona*]—even the concepts of love and friendship are subordinate to it." And another rejects the "common view [that] the main theme of *Henry IV, Part I* is . . . the idea of honor": "Honor is surely a theme of this play; but it is not the main theme. . . . Our formulation of the main theme therefore includes but subordinates the idea of honor. The main theme of *Henry IV, Part I* is the politic concealment and exhibition of seminally transmitted virtue."

Another critic disposes in the same way of a number of rival themes found in *The Merchant of Venice*:

> The play is concerned to explore and define Christian love and its various antitheses. Many critics have suggested that the play is essentially concerned with the contrast and evaluation of certain moral values—such as money, love, and friendship; appearance and reality; true love and fancy; mercy and justice; generosity and possessiveness; the usury of commerce and the usury of love. . . . All these, however, may be subsumed under the central concern, Christian Love.

Love is not enough, however, for a critic dealing with *A Midsummer Night's Dream*—

> We must look upon the play as something more than a slight *divertissement*, interesting mainly for its charm and innocent humour on the foibles of lovers. The immediate subject may be love but the larger concern, enveloping that of love itself as one theme, is the nature of illusion.

or for another in his reading of *Romeo and Juliet*:

> The tragedy is not primarily concerned with love. . . . The play exploits a love-centered situation to explore problems of larger import, the abiding concerns of time, death, and immortal aspiration.

And several readings of *Othello* have warned us not to settle for mere jealousy as the play's central theme, since it really subserves a much grander thematic idea, although they have very different ideas about what that idea is:

> Errors almost inevitably result when the critic fails to see, however dimly, what the play is about. *Othello* is the story of an idolatrous love. . . . The reduction of the presentation of so large a theme as this to a tale of mere jealousy has led to endless error and an understanding of the play usually little better than that of Thomas Rymer.

> The main theme . . . is *not* the passion of jealousy, but the problem of which jealousy is the symptom. . . . The constant preoccupation of the play is the problem: how, given the external data of behavior, can one relate it to the minds of the actors? This problem, applied to Othello and Desdemona, is in the forefront of the play, and therefore creates the misleading impression that the play is about jealousy. But it is not: jealousy is simply a consequence . . . of a failure to resolve this general human problem.

> The problem here is to see that *theme* is not understood too haphazardly and coarsely. Thus it is possible to conceive of *Othello* as a study in jealousy. . . . [But] the "coarse" theme of jealousy . . . would still be, I think, peripheral; a more central thematic approach would be to consider *Othello* . . . a play about love. . . . The central tension is between the love of Othello and the hate of Iago, the specific forms taken in this play by good and evil.

The most elaborate argument of this kind that I have come upon introduces a reading of *Measure for Measure*:

> The dramatic conflicts of the play are built around several op-
> posing forces, mainly in the form of ideals or intellectual
> concepts. Mercy and justice, appearance and reality, chastity
> and sexual license, and the basic opposition of life and death,
> all are part of the general pattern of the play. . . . However . . .
> on the thematic level the basic conflict is between freedom and
> restraint; and certainly the other oppositions of the play may be
> subsumed under this one. Justice is a restraint imposed from
> without. . . . Its opposite, mercy, like grace, is a free gift. . . .
> Appearance may be seen as a restraint on truth, while reality
> is a freedom from falsehood. Chastity implies restraining one's
> sexual drives. . . . On the other hand, complete freedom of sexu-
> ality quickly degenerates into mere sexual license. And, of
> course, life suggests freedom of movement, and death may be
> equated with final constraint.

And the most poetic concludes a summary treatment of the entire Shakespearean canon:

> The two superintending themes of identity and authority flicker
> and fade in the primary ambiguity of appearance and reality.
> Other thematic developments, so numerous that they can hardly
> be exhausted, are reducible only and ultimately to this, from
> the early plays of the wry comic disguises where all the world's
> a stage, through the middle ones haunted by ubiquitous, ghostly
> delusions, to the late ones whose glassy essences claim kinship
> with the audience in the stuff of dreams.

It should immediately be obvious that in most of these examples,
despite the critic's claim, his own theme does not include the rival
candidate (or candidates) in the same sense that, say, "animal" includes
"man." There is nothing in the intrinsic relationship of the ideas themselves which requires us to subsume "love" under "illusion" or "identity,"
or "identity" under "appearance vs. reality," or "appearance vs. reality"
under "freedom vs. restraint"; indeed in each case it would seem just as
logical, or illogical, to reverse the subordination. Perhaps some of the
critics may simply be contending that their theme subsumes the other one
within the structure of the particular play, rather than in the abstract; but
this can only mean that it encompasses more of the play, which brings us
right back to the quantitative argument with all of its uncertainties. For
in these readings the movement up from one thematic idea to another

that is supposed to include it may be as arbitrary as the leap from the dramatic components to the thematic idea that supposedly includes them: from any given theme the critic can abstract (or leapfrog) to almost any "larger" theme that he fancies. And the movement down is no less arbitrary because the nature of these thematic ideas—or at least of the thematists' reasoning about them—is such that they can be expanded indefinitely, through analogical extensions and equations, to subsume almost any other idea (just as they can encompass almost any part of the play). This is especially true of those cosmic dichotomies so much beloved by the thematists, which, like similar two-term dialectics in other fields (classical vs. romantic, bourgeois vs. proletarian, life force vs. death force, Dionysian vs. Apollonian, Yin vs. Yang, etc.), will necessarily divide between them and thus conquer everything that they encounter, as we have seen in the treatment of "freedom and restraint" in *Measure for Measure*. Of course, according to the rules of my-theme-can-lick-your-theme, only the critic's central theme may be expanded in this way to engulf his opponents', because if their themes were permitted the same sort of expansion they would just as easily engulf his own. Thematic imperialism, like its political counterpart, always works for the subsumer and against the subsumed.

Putting aside these objections, however, let us assume for the moment that the critic's claim is valid—that we can logically demonstrate, from the relationship of the two ideas themselves, that his theme does include the rival candidate—and go on to ask how this bears upon its relationship to the play. It must mean that his theme is a more universal term than the other by virtue of its higher position on the ladder of abstraction; but if this is the route to better themes, it is not at all clear where or why we should stop. If "folly" is more central to *Volpone* than "avarice" because it includes "avarice," as critic nine asserted,[9] then the theme of "mankind" should be even more central because it includes "folly," and so on up the ladder, or the Platonic divided line, to something like "Being," which includes every other possible theme and so would qualify as the most central of all. The problem is no longer merely hypothetical, for we have already observed that the internecine warfare of the thematists is now caught up in just such an escalation of "inclusiveness."[10] This is a major cause of the second embarrassment of thematic riches noted at the outset: as the themes grow more and more universal they will of necessity be applicable to more and more plays. But unfortunately this enrichment is accompanied by a corresponding impoverishment, since the more plays that a central theme can apply to, the less it can tell us about any particular play (the larger the "extension," the smaller the "intension"). The route toward ever more inclusive themes, therefore, really draws us further away from the unique center of each play, so it would seem that the critic should be asserting that his theme is more central than those of his predecessors because it is *less* inclusive than theirs.

This line of argument has actually been attempted, although it is very rare, since the whole thrust of the thematic leap and leapfrog (and of the quest for thematic profundity, soon to be discussed) is toward greater abstraction and generality. The clearest example that I have been able to find introduces a recent reading of *Much Ado about Nothing*:

> [Critic X has suggested] that the play is about "man's irresistible propensity to be taken in by appearances." . . . [He] attributes all the confusion to man's innate "giddiness" . . . but the term is perhaps too imprecise to clarify the particular limitations of the protagonists. Perhaps a more helpful suggestion is made by [Critic Y], who considers almost all the characters to be "self-willed, self-centered, and self-admiring creatures . . . [who] fool themselves." . . . But self-centeredness and self-deception are such generally pervasive flaws in Shakespearean comedy that without being further discriminated they are not very useful. . . . In this essay I want to try to sharpen the meaning of the various mistakings and discoveries of *Much Ado* . . . by relating them to an opposition which the play develops between two ways of perceiving the world. One mode of perception, . . . which may be called "wit," relies on prudential reasons; . . . the other, the opposite of wit, rejects practical reason for intuitive modes of understanding.

The obvious objection is that this claim of greater particularity seems no more justified than were the claims of greater inclusiveness in most of the earlier examples, since the theme of wit vs. intuition is at least as general as the two rival themes it is supposed to supplant, and is not subsumed under either of them. But even if this claim is granted, we are still faced with the same basic problem posed by the escalation of inclusiveness— the problem of determining where to stop. For if one theme is to be judged superior to another because it is more specific, then there does not seem to be any reason why we should not proceed still further down the ladder of abstraction to themes much more specific than the one proposed here—or even descend all the way to the specific facts of the play itself, which would mean the end of thematic criticism.

There remains, finally, one more tactic of my-theme-can-lick-your-theme which is sometimes encountered, and which must be the most unkindest cut of all, since here the critic asserts that the rival candidate for central theme is not merely uncentral but is not even a theme!

> Time, then, is not a philosophic theme above the play, con-
> taining and unifying the dramatic action [as contended by Critic
> X]. . . . The characters of *Troilus and Cressida* share a special
> and heightened awareness of time, which is appropriate to the
> world they live in . . . . Their appeal to ultimate Time . . . is a
> means of escape from the present. . . . The dramatic function of
> time is to serve as a means of evading the present.

> Virtuous action [is] the play's dominant theme. . . . I do not
> accept [Critic X's] contention that "the theme of *The Tempest* is
> not regeneration through suffering, but the eternal conflict
> between order and chaos." The subject of form and disorder
> is not a theme in *The Tempest* so much as it is a recognition
> underlying Prospero's virtuous action.

> To the Elizabethans it was a commonplace that the world is a
> battle ground between good and evil; and a commonplace is not
> a suitable theme for the profound interpretation, or rather rein-
> terpretation, of human experience, which makes literature great.
> It is the ground, the datum, on which the drama is built, not
> the building. The storm within Lear's mind goes beyond good
> and evil. . . . The meaning of the tragedy goes deeper than the
> conflict of good and evil, into the more fundamental problem of
> wisdom and folly.

The trouble with this argument is that we have no thematic qualifying test—no way to determine what ideas may or may not become themes. (The law, promulgated in the third passage, that a "commonplace" is unsuitable for a theme would disqualify, on a conservative estimate, at least 90 percent of the central themes which have been discovered so far, including the one endorsed by this critic.) It seems clear, however, that in each of these examples the critic is actually contending that his oppo-nent's candidate is not *the* theme of the play, because it is subsumed under his own. Thus the first passage treats time as a "means" to the real central theme (which turns out to be the mechanism of escape or eva-sion); and the author of the second goes on to explain, in one of those exercises of thematic imperialism discussed above, that his central theme involves "the contrast of nature and nurture (other variations of which are revenge and virtuous action, disorder and order, black magic and white magic)." This tactic, then, is really just another version of the claim of greater inclusiveness, and is certainly no less arbitrary. There is no logical reason, for instance, why the "conflict between order and chaos" should be subordinated to "virtuous action," rather than the other way around, or why the "problem of wisdom and folly" should be considered deeper or more fundamental than the "conflict of good and evil." But we have been through all this before.

In our survey of the kinds of arguments employed in the my-theme-can-lick-your-theme gambit, we have not found one capable of proving that any candidate for central themehood is superior to (or more central than) any other candidate. But the cumulative effect of these arguments is even more devastating, for it reveals a serious problem at the heart of the thematic enterprise—one that is bound to get worse with the publication of each thematic new reading which sets out to refute all of the central themes proposed by all of the older new readings of the same play. The problem is not merely that the strategies used in these refutations are so unconvincing, as we have seen, but that they are ultimately self-defeating, because no central theme ever has been found or ever could be found which cannot be refuted by their means. Since there is no way to measure the "amount" of a theme in a play, one can always outnumber any given theme by claiming that some other encompasses more dramatic components and so is quantitatively more important. And since each theme must be located somewhere on the ladder of abstraction, one can always outflank it vertically by discovering another which is either more general or more specific. And since it is impossible to define the kinds of ideas that qualify as themes, one can always outlaw any earlier candidate by the simple assertion that it is not really a theme at all, but an underlying recognition or ground or datum or whatever else one chooses to call it.

It is difficult to avoid the suspicion, therefore, that these arguments are not concerned with anything substantive—certainly not with anything susceptible of proof or disproof. I once suggested that the critics' strategies in my-theme-can-lick-your-theme could be compared to the quarrelers' "degrees of the lie" described by Touchstone in the last scene of *As You Like It*, since they are both designed for wholly verbal games which are kept going by the tacit agreement of the participants to a set of procedures without any meaning outside the game itself. A major difference, of course, is that in the thematic game all of the participants are winners, at least in their own publications, but for that very reason it must seem to the rest of us that they are playing a losing game. For they have succeeded in demonstrating, far more effectively than could any opponent of this approach, that there is no rational basis for choosing one possible theme of a play over another. Therefore, if we return to the

various themes discovered in *Volpone*, or in these other plays, we will
have to conclude that any or all or none of them could be considered
"central," which is equivalent to admitting that the concept of central
theme has no real meaning here.

Theme and Structure

These critics, however, do not rest their case upon the refutation of their
predecessors, but upon the reading of the play which follows it, and
which shows how the dramatic components are organized in a structure
that embodies the central theme being proposed (hence it has come to be
known as a "theme and structure" study, and these two terms, or
synonyms like "idea and form," appear in many titles). This reading
constitutes the thematist's real argument, since it is supposed to justify
his thesis about the play—that being, as we noted, another characteristic
of readings in general. And some of them can be very persuasive,
although this should not surprise us because they are of necessity self-
confirming. The problem is not so much that the critic selects those
facts of the play which support his thesis and passes over any which do
not, but that the significance of the facts he does select has been defined in
advance by the thesis they are intended to prove, for they present
themselves to him, and so are presented to us, as representations of the
central theme—as data already "thematized." Or, reverting to our earlier
physiological analogy, out of all the manifold aspects of each dramatic
component, the "eye" of the analysis can only see those which its theme
has brought into focus. Anyone who doubts this circularity has only to
compare two thematic readings of a single play to be shown how readily
the same facts are accommodated to wholly different themes (which need
not require any actual distortion of the facts, although some of that is
scarcely avoidable). Thus, to take a simple example, the legacy-hunters
in *Volpone* will be avaricious if that is the central theme, or centrifugal if
that is central, or the audience for Volpone's and Mosca's theatrics if that
is what the comedy is about. We found earlier that each dramatic fact is
almost infinitely malleable in this approach because it does not exist as a
literal *donnée* but only as a stimulus (and jumping-off place) for the
critic's thematic leap to whatever abstraction he chooses; and that abstraction, we saw, can be expanded during the analysis to encompass
whatever facts he selects, so that it would be an unimaginative thematist
indeed who could not produce a plausible fit. And this circularity affects

not only the separate components of the play but even the overall structure which organizes them, since it will not present itself to the critic as a literal sequence of particular actions but as a "thematic structure" of abstractions designed to explore or express the central theme—that is, as another prethematized datum.

These thematic structures come in two basic varieties, which might be called homogeneous and dialectical. In the homogeneous structure the central theme is reflected directly and independently in each of the dramatic components being considered, so that they all turn out to exemplify the same idea: they are homogenized. Almost any kind of part or aspect of the play can be used for this purpose, although most readings concentrate on just one or two. Sometimes it is the separate episodes or plots. A study of *The Jew of Malta*, for instance, begins by announcing that this play possesses "a remarkable unity of theme, for not only is the main theme of the play Barabas' desire for wealth, but each of the subsidiary plots has its basis in the same motive," and then proceeds to demonstrate "this consistency of idea" in each of those subsidiary plots (the two friars, to take just one example, "not only represent the covetousness of the religious orders, but, by so doing, ineluctably connect this sub-plot . . . with the general theme of the play"), and concludes that "it is this universality of idea which makes the *Jew of Malta* a highly integrated drama."

The same thing can also be done with the play's imagery, as in a study which traces images related to the theme of "seeming and being" throughout *The White Devil* and finds that "the unrelenting repetition of this kind of figure binds all the scenes of the play into a whole of the highest possible unity." Similar claims are made for this sort of "thematic imagery" in many other readings (in fact the combination "theme and image" appears almost as often as "theme and structure" in their titles), and it is easy to see why: since most of these plays contain a great many images to choose from, and since most of these images can be connected to a great many themes, the imagery in almost any play will turn out to be unified by, and therefore prove the centrality of, almost any theme the critic has in mind, and if some images are left over they can always be assigned to "subordinate themes" contributing to the main one. This mode of analysis has even been extended to inanimate objects; one reading of *The Spanish Tragedy*, which views it as a play about the problem of "communication," explains that at the end Hieronimo "finds himself, ironically, unable to make those around him understand what has actually happened. In frustration he bites out his tongue and stabs himself and his last tormentor, the Duke, with an instrument designed to facilitate communication, a penknife." I think most of us will be willing to suppress any doubts we may have about this account of Hieronimo's motivation in our delight at the triumphant homogenization of that penknife.

The characters themselves, however, have proved to be the favorite quarry of these homogenizing critics. They have produced a large and growing number of readings which set out to demonstrate the essential similarity of all, or almost all, of the major characters in play after play by herding them into a single thematic corral. The earliest example of this trend that I could find is in a very influential book of the thirties, which states that *The Changeling*

> may be described as a study in the conflict of passion and judg-
> ment, and of the transforming power of love. All the characters
> (save Alsemero) are entirely at the mercy of their feelings. . . .
> Alsemero is the only character whose "will" does not overpower
> his judgment.

By now this homogenization of character has become so common that it is difficult to know which studies to cite, so I have limited myself to just a few representative examples, each by a different hand. The critic quoted earlier, who said *Love's Labor's Lost* "is organized around a central theme" defined as "a conflict between fancy and achievement," goes on to tell us that "ultimately everyone in the play spends most of his time and effort" in "fancies" which "all fall short of achievement." Another finds a thematic unity in the characters of *Henry IV, Part I*: "They all live, to some extent, in self-made worlds of illusion; each of them, in his own way, twists reality in order to make it conform to his own desires." Another asserts that most of the characters in *All's Well That Ends Well* partake of "the theme of sin (or vice) as self-treason"; and another that everyone in *Measure for Measure* is "in bondage," which is what "the play is literally and in many shadings of figure about." Almost all the characters of *Much Ado about Nothing* enact the theme of "deception by appearances in love" resulting from "hearsay," according to one critic; or "the theme of giddiness," according to a second; and a third, who unifies the play around "the theme of appearance and reality," claims "they [are] all asses because they deemed themselves wise."

One might suppose that these homogenizers would have some diffi-culty with plays in which the literal structure clearly differentiates and sets in opposition two distinct groups of characters, but they have proved more than equal to this challenge. Something like a minor in-dustry has grown up around their attempts to construct a single thematic formula (a different one for each critic, of course) that would encompass, and therefore equate, the Greeks and Trojans in *Troilus and Cressida*. Each of the three readings of the play quoted on page 31 places both groups under its central theme, as does the reading quoted on page 39, which urges us to pass over (or under) the "subtle variations among Greek and Trojan leaders," since "beneath an apparent diversity" all of them— "the Troiluses, the Hectors, the Achilles and Ulysses of this world"— exemplify the same idea of "evasion." Another critic finds that major figures on both sides are "remarkably alike," since each is an "exemplum" of "the overpowering of Right Judgment by Passion," the "central theme which binds together the seemingly unrelated parts"; and another that his theme, which is "the universal flaw in all human exchange," is equally present in Greeks and Trojans (since, among other things, they are all guilty of "linguistic mismanagement"); and yet another locates the central theme in "the mistaken conception of honor," which homogenizes the two warring camps: "in respect of their attitude to honor there is very little difference between the Greeks and the Trojans."

Similar attempts have been made to obliterate the distinctions between different groups or kinds of characters in Jonson's comedies. Most of the readings represented in the survey of criticism of *Volpone* insist that their central theme includes Volpone and Mosca as well as the legacy-hunters (and sometimes even Bonario and Celia). A reading of *Epicene* joins the wits and their victims through a thematic extension of the title; the play "explores the question of . . . the decorum of the sexes" and "nearly everyone in the play is epicene in some way." Another critic uses the title of *The Alchemist* for the same purpose: "The rogues and gulls of *The Alchemist* share a common desire to be 'sublimed.' . . . They all want to be raised—socially, sexually, religiously, metaphysically; they all hunger for the transmuting miracle of their respective alchemies"; and other critics, showing the usual disagreement, have equated these two groups under their own central themes of "avarice" or "pride" or "self-delusion" or "impiety." And in *Bartholomew Fair*, according to one reading, "both the individuals who go to the Fair and those who are part of it are in one degree or another representations of aspects of Vanity," while another has all members of both of these groups embody the "theme of vapors" which is the "basis of the play's unity" and symbolizes a single "universal comic truth" about "the limiting physical basis of human nature."

A stodgy literalist might raise the objection that in every one of these plays there are important characters to whom these generalizations do not apply, but that would only betray his failure to appreciate the absorptive power of the thematic abstractions and the adaptability of the dramatic facts, as well as the ingenuity of the critics who are determined to connect them. Thus the theme of "deception by appearances in love" resulting from "hearsay" in *Much Ado about Nothing* can be extended to include Dogberry by a series of rhetorical questions:

> Is it exaggeration to bring even Dogberry into this pattern? to
> point to his manifest self-admiration . . . and to hint that the
> little arrow that wounds *him* "by hearsay" is magnificent
> language and "wit"? Are not words and wisdom his Cupids?
> No doubt that stretches "love" too far. But self-love is a common
> term to all three of the splendid comedians of the piece.

Celia and Bonario can be brought under the "central theme" of "folly" in *Volpone* because in them "we see perhaps a distant reminiscence of the 'folly' of Lear's Fool, which is the unworldly wisdom of the simple and innocent."[11] Even though Dauphine and Truewit are "apparently normal men," they can still be called "somewhat ambiguous, sexually," and so be accommodated to the "epicene" theme of Jonson's comedy, since they are friends of Clerimont, whose relationship to his Boy is suspect. And while Surly is "the one apparent exception" to the universal hunger for sublimation in *The Alchemist*, we soon find that this exception, too, is not real: "once in the house, his righteous anger modulates into cupidity for Dame Pliant's fortune, and he demonstrates that he is in fact no more impervious to the stone than are the objects of his contempt."

There is no point, however, in lingering over the question of accuracy here, for even if a particular theme cannot be stretched to fit every character, or vice versa, it is quite simple, if one wants to homogenize them, to formulate a "more inclusive" theme that can, as we have already seen. The real question is why anyone should want to homogenize the characters in the first place, or should present this homogenization to us as a great artistic (and critical) achievement. It is certainly a curious reversal of the attitude of the Restoration and eighteenth-century critics of Elizabethan drama, who thought they were bestowing high praise upon a play when they could say that it contained "many persons of various characters and humours," who were "perfectly distinguished" or "diversified with the utmost nicety" or "with great variety," or that it was "remarkable for the variety and number of the personages, who exhibit more characters appropriated and discriminated than perhaps can be found in any other play."[12] One is almost tempted to posit the operation of a kind of compensatory zeitgeist to explain why the Age of Reason and of the neoclassical unities should delight in the variety and differentiation of dramatic characters (which of course led to its own critical excesses and blind alleys), while our nominalistic and relativistic age should try so hard to homogenize them. There does seem to be some connection between our moral relativism, with its distrust of the heroic or romantic values of the Elizabethan playwrights, and these efforts to equate their characters, for it is no coincidence that in each of the preceding examples the central theme employed for this purpose is something very undesirable. The ascent up to a homogenizing theme must necessarily bring us down to the lowest common denominator encompassing all the characters, and so will assimilate the more admirable character to the less admirable, rather than the other way around. If everyone in *Troilus and Cressida* exemplifies "the mistaken conception of honor," then Hector is really in the same class as Achilles and even Thersites. And similarly Dauphine is reduced to the level of the Collegiate Ladies, Grace Wellborn to that of Cokes, and so on, because they must turn out to be only "apparent exceptions" to the basic—and base—uniformity. Thus the modern shift of interest from "variety" to "thematic unity" of character can be explained in the same terms as the parallel shift in interpreting the relationship of the Elizabethan clown to the protagonist, from a contrasting "foil" to an assimilating "parody," which also requires us to emphasize the similarities and minimize the differences between them, and also answers to our need to deflate the protagonist and his values.[13] But this brings us into the area of ironic readings, which will be discussed in the following chapter.

More to our purpose here, however, is the explanation given by these critics themselves for their activity, because they usually present it as an aesthetic rather than an ethical demonstration, aimed primarily not at negating the characters' values but at affirming the play's unity. And since the kind of unity they are offering us in these homogeneous structures will be the same whether the components involved are the characters or episodes or images or any other aspect of the play, we can consider it separately, apart from the problem of irony. It is like the unity of a heap of pennies, which may be called "one" only in the sense that every object in the heap partakes of "penniness"; and it is a minimal unity, because the number or arrangement of the pennies can be changed without affecting the "oneness" of the heap or its "penniness." (Even if an object is found there which does not seem to be a penny, we could still claim unity for the heap merely by formulating a more inclusive class, such as "metallicity," or else by arguing that the apparent exception is really some sort of penny after all.) I do not see how this conclusion can be avoided, for if the unity of a play depends solely upon the fact that all its parts (however they are defined) reflect the same theme, then it would be no less unified if we reordered those parts, or removed some, or added others that reflected this theme.

Consequently, one cannot accept the claims made by these critics, in the quotations above, that the homogeneous structure gives us "a highly integrated drama" or "the highest possible unity," or the statement in another recent study (of *Julius Caesar*) that it produces "what most of us know as organic unity—the characteristic present when the essential aesthetic principle of a work informs all constituent elements of that work." On the contrary, such a structure would result in a very loosely integrated drama and in the lowest possible unity. Nor would it be at all like organic unity, for the parts of a living organism are certainly not homogeneous and are unified, not through their simple and separate participation in some "informing" idea, but through a complex system of functional interactions, which will be damaged or destroyed by any significant addition or subtraction or transposition of those parts. This kind of unity, which is what we actually find in an effective drama (or any other work of art),[14] is obviously much more difficult to create. And it is much more difficult to analyze, since it cannot be discovered or demonstrated by the sort of verbal manipulation of part and whole that we have just witnessed.

We may have some trouble understanding, therefore, why the homogenizers should feel that what they are showing us represents a remarkable achievement on the part of the dramatist—or, for that matter, on the part of the critic. It would take no great artistic ability to put together a collection of characters or episodes related only, or primarily, as exempla of a single idea (in fact, the plays of the period that come closest to this kind of structure—Jonson's *Every Man* comedies and *Cynthia's Revels*, for instance, or Middleton's *The Phoenix* and *Your Five Gallants*—are usually among their authors' earliest and weakest productions). Nor does it take great critical ability to find an abstraction that encompasses any collection of dramatic components, no matter how diverse they may be. That is why we said that the question of truth is irrelevant to these homogeneous readings. They are all true, even those which contradict each other, for we have seen that almost every part of almost every play can be shown to embody almost every theme now in fashion. The real question, still unanswered, is why these critics should want to produce such readings, since the feeble kind of unity which they give as their explanation would surely not justify this reduction of the rich variety of characterization and incident in these plays to a flat and dreary uniformity. To find the answer, I think we must go back again to the thematic assumption that each of the plays is about an idea, because this search for homogeneity makes sense if, and only if, one is more interested in an abstract theme than in the differentiated individuality of the characters and events which the play presents to us. This does not mean, of course, that these critics deny the differentiation; they simply regard it as "apparent" and not "real," since it must be less important than, and therefore subordinate to, the one universal idea which they seek behind or above all of those many particulars. And the easiest way to proceed from the Many to the One is by means of this homogeneous structure.

The dialectical thematic structure is more complex than this because in it the parts are heterogeneous and interact with each other, rather than simply exemplifying the central theme. Here the theme is usually one of those pairs of mighty opposites, which are supposed to be locked in some sort of conflict—enacted between groups (rational Romans vs. passionate Egyptians) or individuals (Desdemona's love vs. Iago's hate) or within an individual (appearance vs. reality in Lear's soul)—that the play finally resolves through the victory of one abstract entity over the other, or a compromise between them, or their transcendence in a higher abstraction. But there is no necessary connection between these two-term themes and the dialectical structure. We encountered them in some homogeneous readings (for example, the one that had everybody in *Troilus and Cressida* suffering from "the overpowering of Right Judgment by Passion"), and one-term themes are utilized in some dialectical readings, such as those which have the play exploring a single general problem (communication, identity, etc.), although here the problem is typically defined as an opposition between two abstract alternatives which is resolved in one of the ways just indicated.

Since these dialectical structures are much more complicated and varied than the homogeneous form, they cannot easily be illustrated or surveyed by a collection of brief quotations. They all seem to fall, however, into two basic categories, which I call the schematic and the sequential, and so I thought it might be helpful to examine in greater detail one representative example of each. The schematic structure can be seen very clearly in a recent reading of *Othello*, where the critic begins with the explanation that he will "isolate the theme of *Othello* by studying the series of relationships through which the play unfolds." He then discusses the relationships between Iago and Roderigo, Brabantio and Roderigo, Othello and Brabantio, Iago and Othello, Iago and Cassio, Cassio and Bianca, Iago and Emilia, and Othello and Desdemona,

showing how each bears upon what he finds to be the central theme of
the play, the "general human problem" of judging people from "the
external data of behavior," which turns out to be another manifestation
of the ubiquitous "appearance-reality dualism."[15] Among these relationships, that of Iago and Emilia is "the most important" and "provides the
core of the play," because "it is paradigmatic to the play's main theme"
and "best embodies" it ("since I see the unresolvable appearance-reality
dualism as the center of the *Othello* design, I regard Emilia-Iago as the
play's central relationship"). According to him, "the problem is debated
by Roderigo, Brabantio, Iago, Cassio, Bianca, Emilia, and the Venetian
leaders," in those relationships, as a question of "belief" or "trust," and is
finally brought to this conclusion: "The answer to the problem, in human
terms, can only be made thus: that trust, arrived at after a full intuitive
and intellectual grasp of the data, should be an absolute value."

I call this structure schematic because it treats *Othello* as an essentially
static presentation of "a range of behavioral data," as the author puts it,
designed to demonstrate a proposition. This, for him, constitutes "the
pattern of the play." Although the various relationships between characters are taken up, for the most part, in the order in which they first
appear in the play, there is no sense of a sequence of action here;
presumably their debates could be rearranged without significantly affecting the "pattern" or its "answer to the problem." And any actions
which fail to qualify for the pattern or to illuminate the problem do not
form part of this structure: Othello's suicide, for instance, is completely
ignored, and his killing of Desdemona is mentioned just once, only to be
dismissed as "the mere dramatic and emotional consequence" of his
"failure to resolve this general human problem." Nor is there any suggestion that this "behavioral data" is meant to evoke any feelings in us.
We are much too busy, apparently, following what the author terms "the
intellectual argument" of the play and being edified by its conclusion.

A sequential structure, on the other hand, has a distinct temporal
movement which is supposed to correspond to the play's line of action.
In the example I have chosen, a recent reading of *Measure for Measure*,
the critic announces that the central theme is "the basic conflict . . .
between freedom and restraint," and then proceeds to trace its progress
in the events of the drama, many of which are found, by means of the
thematic leap, to be making general statements or raising general questions about the conflict of these "intellectual concepts." Thus Claudio's
arrest in I.ii shows that "excessive liberty leads inevitably to imprisonment, an excessive form of restraint, and further that this proposition is
true in every case. . . . Beneath this general proposition of moral law,

however, lurks the question of whether the reverse is also true: does excessive restraint lead to excessive freedom?" The answer of course is yes, for in the next scene the Duke reveals that the laws have not been enforced because of his own "lack of social involvement," which turns out to be another kind of excessive "restraint," so "it would appear that too much restraint in the ruling power leads invariably to too much liberty in the people." And when Angelo, who is also guilty of "inordinate restraint" (not only in denying his sexuality but also in rejecting Mariana before the play began), attempts to seduce Isabella in II.iv, "Our earlier question, 'does excessive restraint lead to excessive freedom?' seems to be answered, by his actions, in the affirmative." The movement of the play is described as an "educational process" involving "certain lessons which the dramatis personae finally learn" about the relationship of these two concepts to each other and to Original Sin. In that process the bed-trick "is symbolically important" because it "is the turning point in resolving the initial tension between freedom and restraint" (for here "both the duke and Isabel symbolically share the sin of Angelo and Mariana" and so abandon some of their "restraint"). And this tension is finally re-solved in the marriages at the end, which also "are symbolic" since they represent "a stasis in which freedom and restraint are equally balanced." (Marriage, happily, "lies between . . . unnatural restraint . . . [and] un-restrained sexuality.") But we are warned that "the balance is precarious":

> We cannot assert that there is any great likelihood that the married couples will live happily ever after. In a sense, mar-riage is only one solution, at best temporary, for a recurring human problem. As the play ends, we have a feeling that continuing adjustments will be necessary for the characters— if we may project them into an imaginary future—in maintain-ing that delicate balance between freedom and restraint.

Although this sequential structure differs from the static "pattern" of the reading of *Othello* because of its dependence upon the temporal unfolding of the play, it is, like the *Othello* pattern, a structure of abstractions rather than of particular actions. For these actions are not significant in their own right, but are "symbolically important," as we saw, in enacting the dialectic of "intellectual concepts" which is the real temporal sequence here. In fact the characters themselves become dialec-ticians: they are found "discussing sexual liberty" in I.ii, for instance, and in I.iv engage in "a discussion of liberty and restraint" (just as the characters of *Othello* "debated" its thematic problem). And again there is no suggestion that their activity should elicit any emotional response in us, other than the sense of enlightenment in the "lessons" which we presumably learn along with them, and which include (in addition to the insights into marriage just quoted) the following revelations: "Freedom cannot always have a plus value, nor can restraint always be regarded as a human evil." "Just as in restraint, there are different types of freedom." "Neither restraint nor freedom is good in and of itself."

These two examples are not, I believe, an unfair sample of the dialectical readings which are now inundating us; indeed there are many far worse. I have been examining a large number of them, and have yet to find one that really worked—that produced even a reasonably close "fit," which would stand up under scrutiny, between the thematic structure created by the critic and the literal structure created by the playwright. In all of them, to a greater or less extent, the thematic abstractions have been manipulated in order to subdue the dramatic facts, and the dramatic facts themselves— the components of the play and their interconnections and propor- tions—have been distorted or slighted to accommodate the thematic abstractions. There is, for instance, an obvious manipulation of theme in the reading of *Measure for Measure*, where Claudio's imprisonment and the Duke's aloofness and his leniency and Angelo's strictness and even his desertion of Mariana are all equated under the term "excessive restraint." And there is an equally obvious distortion of dramatic proportions in the assertion, by the critic of *Othello*, that Iago and Emilia constitute "the most important" and "central relationship" of the play. Many similar distortions could be cited from other thematic readings. Although any literal interpretation of *Henry IV, Part I* would recognize Prince Hal as the protagonist, we find one critic arguing that Falstaff is "the focal point . . . at the centre of the play" because he is "the embodiment" of its theme of "illusion," being himself "the supreme illusionist," while another makes Hotspur central since he is "embodying" the "play's major theme of disorder in that he is himself a figure of disorder." Another critic claims that King Lear's counterpart in the subplot is not Gloucester but Edgar, because his efforts to "discover his personal identity" parallel Lear's. And even though the literal structure of *Bartholomew Fair* clearly groups Overdo, Busy, and Wasp together and separates them from the other visitors, one critic has placed Cokes in the same thematic category with Overdo and Busy since all three operate on the assumption "that any qualities divide the essences from the elements composing the object."

It can be seen from these quotations, however, that when a thematist speaks of the importance or centrality of dramatic characters or events, or of their relationship to each other, he is not really referring to the literal structure at all, but to a kind of Platonic scheme in which the many particular facts of the play take on significance only as they "symbolize" or "embody" the one governing Idea floating above them that gives the play its meaning. Thus the character who "best embodies" or "is paradigmatic to" this Idea becomes central, no matter how peripheral he may be in the literal structure; and, similarly, the relations and groupings among the characters are determined, not by their literal roles or interactions, but by the way they participate in the Idea. This scheme will also explain the many other kinds of distortion of dramatic fact in these readings, for it requires that the facts be made to conform to the Idea, rather than the other way around. (Sometimes the Idea can even create the facts, as in a study of "the thematic development" of *All's Well That Ends Well* which insists that Parolles must be young, although this "cannot be conclusively proven by any references in the text," because "his youth is nearly a thematic necessity.") Indeed this need not even be seen as a distortion, because in the thematic approach, as in other forms of Platonism, the Idea tends to become more "real"—since it is so much more intelligible—than the multifarious and often recalcitrant particulars which can at best only imperfectly reflect it on the level of sensation or "appearance." From this point of view, therefore, one might say that it is the literal "apparent" structure of the play which distorts the thematic "real" structure, and so must be clarified or brought into line by the right sort of reading.

This Platonic conception of the literary work would also seem to underlie the four characteristics of thematism noted at the beginning of the chapter. (I am not of course implying that these critics are consciously using Plato, but only that they operate, whether or not they are aware of it, within the basic intellectual framework which he articulated so brilliantly; hence their readings can be regarded as imperfect reflections of his philosophy.) Since in this approach the play is viewed as the expression of an idea, it will not be different in kind from treatises or arguments or any other forms of logical discourse with the same purpose, and so will be in competition with them, as it was for Plato himself, in their common effort to ascend the divided line to the True and the Good. Some thematists are quite explicit about this—one of them, for instance, has asserted that "Shakespeare saw drama as moral philosophy," and another that "Jonson's plays preached Christian sermons," and another has written a book entitled *Jacobean Tragedy: The Quest for Moral Order*. And many others have implied as much when they adopt the terminology of abstract reasoning, as we saw in that initial collection of quotations, to describe the play as an "analysis" or "critique" or "discussion" of some general problem, or a "philosophical contribution," or even "one of the greatest essays we possess on the ontology of selfhood." This last claim may sound a little overenthusiastic (especially to students of ontology), but it is perfectly consistent, since if *Volpone* really is about the theme that this critic has found there,[16] or any of the others proposed for it, then it does become a kind of essay and so must be judged against other works of the same class.

Because the play presents him with an intellectual discourse instead of a human action, the thematist will tend to be interested in its characters less as individuals than as examples or symbols of the abstract entities which are his primary concern. We saw that the homogeneous thematic structure must minimize any individuation of character, and even the dialectical structures only permit the crudest differentiation of the dramatis personae into a few general categories, which requires some homogenization of those in each category. In many of these readings the characters do not seem to have any "character" at all, since they have been stripped down to the attitudes or traits which bear upon the central theme, and so have lost their personality. They have also lost any intrinsic significance, for we must remember that in this approach the characters and their actions suffer a double reduction: they are regarded not only as mere symbols of the real subject matter, but also as merely the means to the real end of the play. In the reading of *Measure for Measure* just considered, we are told that "Shakespeare uses the sexual sin" of the characters to bring us to "the realization of [the] concept of universal guilt" (i.e., Original Sin). Another reading explains that "he uses" the love of Florizel and Perdita in *The Winter's Tale* "for the examination of a larger problem—the nature of truth," and so "transforms" their love into one of the "devices for commenting seriously upon the theme of reality and experience"; and yet another finds that in *Coriolanus* "Shakespeare uses both hero and play to conduct an extended exploration of the often precarious correspondence of words and meanings." But if characters and actions are used as devices for some higher purpose, then they will not be important in themselves, and whatever derivative importance they may possess will disappear once they have served that purpose. The Platonic divided line rolls up behind us as we climb it, so that when we finally grasp the central theme of the play, in the heady realm of ideas, we no longer need to be concerned with the particular human actions shown to us way down there on the level of appearances, which we made use of in our ascent. It is not surprising, therefore, that none of the summary statements about the plays, in that initial collection of quotations, points toward any of the people in them.

It is also not surprising that we found no indication in those statements that the plays produced any emotional effect, for this is a necessary consequence of the preceding point. The emotions traditionally associated with the drama, both serious and comic, are of course responses to the characters and their careers in the play, so if the thematist does not really regard these characters as individuals, or even as significant in their own right, we would not expect their actions or fates to evoke any strong feelings in him. Such feelings are not easily aroused by meditating on the playwright's sustained meditation on reality and illusion, or by accompanying him on an extended exploration of the correspondence of words and meanings. Moreover, they would not be relevant to the thematist's attempt to work his way up the divided line, and might even prove a hindrance, as Plato himself thought. And finally, this Platonic scheme will also account for the fourth characteristic of thematism noted at the outset. Since the process of abstraction required by it must necessarily pass beyond the particularities of character and action and emotional effect that distinguish one play from another, it will end up with formulations of theme that are applicable to a great many plays, including ones which may seem, to the rest of us bogged down on the literal level, to be strikingly different.

It is this process of abstraction itself, rather than the specific distortions of fact resulting from it, which constitutes, I believe, the principal disadvantage of thematism. Because of it, this approach will tend to operate at a considerable distance from our actual dramatic experience, from what really affects us—when we are affected—in these plays; for surely, when we say that a tragedy is deeply moving, we are referring to the fate of its characters and not to the outcome of some conflict between ideas. It must be emphasized that I am speaking here of a general tendency, since individual thematic readings can vary considerably in this respect; but we usually find that the more they focus upon the theme, the farther they get from our experience of the play. Just how far they can get may be seen, for example, in those readings which insist that the ending of *King Lear* is not really painful because it represents the triumph of a good abstract entity over a bad one; or in the reading which claims that it does not matter whether Cleopatra submits to Caesar or commits suicide, since "whichever way the decision goes it is immaterial" to the thematic dialectic between the World and the Flesh, symbolized by Rome and Egypt (this is the same one that had her kill herself because of the irreconcilability of these two abstractions). But even the less outrageous conclusions reached by this approach are not part of our dramatic experience; they are thoughts which can occur to people of a certain cast of mind *after* that experience is over—probably long after, for one gets the distinct impression that most of these readings could only have been developed during an extended period of reflection uninterrupted by any directly felt contact with the work itself. Some thematists even acknowledge as much:

> For all its laughter, this is farce raised to a philosophical level. [*Epicene*] is a grimly serious play which exposes moral disease. . . . In gaiety it recalls Jonson's earlier, unreformed comedy. His sympathy for the young men, his general tolerance of high spirits, and his delight in prankishness for its own sake recall the older kinds of romantic drama. Only when we take thought do we see that this play, like *Volpone*, opens the door into darkened, interior chambers of the mind.

Now I am certainly not suggesting that we stop thinking about a play after we have experienced it, which would put us all out of business. But when we think about it afterward, and write about it, we should be thinking and writing about this experience, in all of its concrete particularity—that is, if we claim to be interpreting the play—and not about some general ideas which may later come to us "when we take thought" to ascend from this particularity up the ladder of abstraction. The task of interpretation, surely, is to lead us back into the play, to enrich and refine the experience it was designed to produce, and the greatest disadvantage of thematism is that it leads us away.

The Advantages of Thematism

One of the truisms of critical theory is that each approach to interpretation has both advantages and disadvantages, and so it is only fair that we now go on to consider what seem to be the principal advantages of thematism, which would account for its current popularity. Apparently the most important one, according to the thematists themselves, is that it can discover and demonstrate profundities in the literary work which escape other approaches, since this is a special virtue of the central theme. "It is because of the theme of wit," one of them tells us, "that *Much Ado* rises to the kind of profundity of be found in all great comedies of manners." We have already encountered this claim in our examination of the thematic assumption, where one critic was seen to argue that its theme (which, incidentally, is completely different from the one above) is what makes *Much Ado* a "deep" play, rather than a "trivial" piece "about nothing," and another that Shakespeare's comedies are "thematically serious"—that is, serious because of their themes. And we met it again in some of the quotations illustrating the escalation of "inclusiveness" in the my-theme-can-lick-your-theme gambit: in the assertion that *Volpone* is not merely about avarice but about "the eternal verities," for instance, or that *A Midsummer Night's Dream* is "something more than a slight *divertissement*" because its real subject is not romance but a "larger concern," or that *Romeo and Juliet* "explore[s] problems of larger import" than love. This second argument is in fact simply a logical extension of the first, for if a play becomes profound (or deep or serious) when its subject matter is defined as a thematic idea rather than a human action, then it will become still more profound when its subject is redefined as another idea higher up the ladder. These are just two stages of the same process of abstraction climbing toward the same goal of profundity.

We certainly cannot deny that the thematic approach has this advantage, for it confers instant profundity upon every play it touches (and also upon every critic who touches it, by enabling him to reveal this profundity for the first time). The advantage is inherent in the approach itself, which will always find that the play—any play—is really about some idea of universal import. The simplest farce of mistaken identity can be elevated into an examination of selfhood; any play portraying a courtship or marriage can become a critique of romantic love; any play with a villain can probe the enigma of evil; any play that has people in it can pose the question, Who or what is Man?; and if the people talk to each other, the play can be conducting an inquiry into the communicative process. The literal subject, whatever it may be, must serve a thematic subject which is necessarily larger and higher and deeper and more serious.

The advantage extends even further, since this approach can discover not only that the subject of the play is profound, but also that the play is making a profound statement about it. Not all thematic readings take this second step, however, because there are different conceptions of the nature of the central theme. It is always an abstraction, of course, yet it apparently does not always have to be the same kind of abstraction. In some readings it simply names the general area, usually an aspect of human nature or experience (avarice, folly, etc.), which the play is supposed to be "about," but others formulate it as a general human problem (the discrepancy between appearance and reality, for example) which the play is "exploring," and still others as a general proposition about life which the play is "affirming" (as in the conclusions of the readings of *Othello* and *Measure for Measure* summarized earlier). One would think that such differences in the definition of their basic concept might be a matter of some concern to the thematists, yet they have remarkably little to say about it, either in theory or in relation to the specific works they are examining. Actually these three categories cannot be demarcated very sharply, and it is probably more useful to think of them as arranged on a continuum extending from the first to the third—from the minimum to the maximum propositional commitment. It seems to me, however, that nearly all of the central themes that have been offered to us really translate into the maximum end of the continuum, for the subject matter area usually presents some sort of problem, and the problem usually comes to some sort of resolution. Thus if a critic finds that the theme of a play is "avarice," the play turns out to be saying or showing that avarice is evil or self-defeating or the like; if it is "folly," the play indicates that the activities it portrays belong under that designation; if it is the "problem of appearance and reality," the play warns us that appearances are deceiving, and so on. Even when the critic claims that the play reaches no resolution of its thematic problem, he must at least demonstrate—if the dramatic "exploration" is to be at all convincing—that the problem has received some clarification, which can itself be rendered as a proposition, as can the assertion that the problem is unresolvable. (Sometimes he only means that the dramatist does not state his conclusion, but allows us to infer it from the presentation.) Thus, while some critics may appear reluctant to express their central theme in the form of a general proposition, it is toward such propositions that the approach always seems to be moving.[17]

There are of course many readings that come right out with explicit thematic statements of this kind, often announcing them at the end in the manner of an Aesopian "moral." I have collected a few of them which were discovered by the thematists in the plays of Shakespeare and Jonson, and which can be added to the two we have already seen on the "absolute value" of "trust," and on the need for "maintaining that delicate balance between freedom and restraint." Each quotation, again, is from a different critic:

A.   The play illustrates that a fugitive and cloistered virtue is of equal uselessness with a buried talent, and that noble ideals are supposed to be put into action.

B.   [The play] concludes that freedom and responsibility are linked, that freedom without responsibility is license and, ultimately, bondage.

C.   [The play] demonstrates that happiness lies in process itself—

in experience, growth, maturation. . . . Faith in life itself is essential. Happiness comes from acceptance and courage, as well as
from insight. Courage, experience and insight lead to the
happiness of wisdom.

D.   Both [plays] preach a moral commonplace: the natural order
      provided by a benevolent Providence cannot be violated with
      impunity.

E.   The message . . . brought to us by [the playwright] is, then,
      in the last analysis . . . that man's destiny is not wholly in his
      own hands.

F.   The lesson taught by [the play is] . . . that men are not the
      masters of their own fates. . . . What we intend, and what we
      actually accomplish, are often vastly different.

G.   This guiding and informing principle [of the play] may be stated
      as follows: Every organism or organization, if it is to survive
      and function properly, must achieve and maintian an ordered
      unity.

H.   The play's central thesis [is that] there must be unity in a man,
      as in a state, before the good is achieved.

I.   The moral argument of this play is Platonic. Against the gross
      materialism of society it opposes the saving grace of perfect
      love, which means, of course, disinterested and virtuous friend-
      ship, a friendship which sees in the beloved friend the incarna-
      tion of the highest spiritual ideals.

J.   The right attitude to the world is centered neither in the natural
      wants of the flesh nor in the artificial constructs of the imagina-
      tion, but in a religious awe before the unearned bounty which
      the world bestows on man, an awe akin to man's perception
      of God's grace.

K.   [The playwright] argues that the energy of youth can be con-
      structively and productively incorporated into society only by
      being channeled into the ordered forms of traditional social
      institutions.

L.   Throwing off of bonds of society . . . leads to a lower, animal
      level of existence. Humanity requires society; society requires
      social restraints.

M.   Communication at all levels has a paramount status in human
      life as the essential element on which the entire moral, political,
      and social fabric depends.

N.   An apprehension of what is and what should be are principal
      requirements for the good ruler.

O.   Paradoxically, sex can be a significant sin or a significant virtue,
        circumstances determining which.

These quotations clearly define the kind of profundity which the thematic approach seeks and finds in drama—it is the profundity of philosophy. That is only to be expected, since we saw earlier that this approach
places the play in the same class with philosophic treatises, and so in
competition with them for the same goal. The competition is not very
close, however, because the most obvious point to be made about this
profundity which the critics expect us to admire in these plays is that it is
not profound. The thematic statements that are supposed to embody it
almost always turn out to be banal platitudes and pieties, of which the
above examples are all too typical. Thus we are brought to another paradox of thematism: in attempting to elevate the plays by making them
seem more profound, it has actually debased them, for when the drama,
even the greatest drama, is treated as a species of intellectual discourse,
it becomes a decidedly inferior species. If the meaning and purpose of the
plays really can be found in this kind of general proposition, if *that* is
what they add up to, then it is hard to see why any adult would be interested in them.

Fortunately, however, the second point to be made about this thematic
profundity, such as it is, is that it does not come from the play at all, but
from the thematic structures which the critics impose upon, or substitute
for, the play. This can easily be tested by trying to guess what play is supposed to be affirming each proposition in the list above. I have set up such
a "thematic apperception test" by quoting the passages without the names
of the plays, which are given in the last footnote of this chapter; and I am
prepared to offer a valuable prize—one brand new central theme that has
not yet been discovered in *King Lear*—to anyone who scores over 10 percent. For the connection of these general statements to the plays is as tenuous as that of the themes themselves—the same play apparently makes
very different statements, according to which reading one reads, and very
different plays apparently make almost identical statements.

The connection is so tenuous, in fact, that in most of these statements
one cannot even tell whether the play they allegedly derive from is
serious or comic, and I am offering a second prize—the name of a drama
(a minor one, of course) in which the theme of appearance vs. reality has
not yet been discovered—to those who can get better than a chance score
in guessing that. Anyone familiar with the recent thematic scene will not
be surprised to learn that some of the most solemn and portentous—not
to say pretentious—statements are attributed to comedies, for that has
become a well-established trend, and one more indication of how far this

approach has taken us from our actual dramatic experience. In order to make comedies seem more profound, it has, in effect, decomicalized them. It is now difficult to believe that a Shakespearean critic writing in 1961 (and already quoted on page 18) could complain of the "failure to take the comedies seriously," or that the author of a major book on these plays, published in 1957, felt obliged to apologize in advance for subjecting them to thematic analysis, since they "can appear so light-hearted and capricious, so inconsequential, so beautiful and bawdy . . . that the probing questions of the critic seem ludicrously inapposite. The critic is afraid of taking them too seriously."[18] Just ten years later Paul Jorgensen observed in a review that "most students of Shakespearean comedy have erred on the side of seriousness," and M. A. Shaaber, surveying the current state of Shakespearean criticism, could say, "Comedies are discovered to elicit the same metaphysical shudder as tragedies; anybody who thinks that a comedy is merely funny is shallow and insensitive."[19]

We can get some idea of the effect of this trend upon Shakespearean comedy by seeing what it has done to a single episode, Bottom's soliloquy about his most rare and bottomless dream in IV.i of *A Midsummer Night's Dream*, a play that has been one of the principal beneficiaries of thematic elevation. A few years ago a reviewer welcomed an article for its contribution to "the good work done in recent years in establishing *A Midsummer Night's Dream* as one of the profoundest of the Comedies"; but it could not add much to the "good work" these critics had already lavished upon this scene, which used to be considered quite funny in the prethematic era, and can still raise a laugh in the theater.[20] We were told by one of them that Bottom's speech "is like a glimpse of . . . a higher spiritual reality . . . the awakening, through illusion, of true imagination and faith and therefore of the highest knowledge"; and by a second that it provides "a glimpse of the divine element in human life . . . in what is perhaps the play's deepest, most profound moment"; and by a third (the one who objected to the "failure to take the comedies seriously") that "Bottom's dream is *oneiros* or *somnium*; ambiguous, enigmatic, of high import. . . . Bottom is there to tell us that the blindness of love . . . can be interpreted as a means to grace as well as to irrational animalism; that the two aspects are, perhaps, inseparable"; and by a fourth that it "is the supreme moment of the play," since

> what Shakespeare has caught here in perfection is the original miracle of the Imagination, the awakening of spiritual life in the animal man. Bottom is an ass. If Bottom can be redeemed, matter itself and man in all his materiality can be redeemed also. Democracy becomes possible. Nothing less than this is what this incident implies.

And the same trend has also smothered Jonson's comedies in profound new readings which have transformed the funniest of them, *The Alchemist* and *Bartholomew Fair*, into "ominous" or "sinister" studies of "depravity" and "moral disease" and a whole catalog of mortal sins (including "black magic," a "Black Mass," "diabolism," "heresy," "idolatry," and "sacrilege"), and even of Satan himself and the Antichrist, thereby fulfilling Nicholas Oldisworth's prophecy that "Some future Times will, by a grosse Mistake, /*Johnson* a Bishop, not a Poet make."[21] This process of decomicalization is now so far advanced that further documentation would appear unnecessary, but I would like to add a little garland of titles of articles, all published since 1964, on the works of our two greatest comic playwrights: "The Satanic Nature of Volpone" (which consigns Voltore, Corbaccio, and Corvino to "eternal torment"), "Sir Epicure Mammon: A Study in 'Spiritual Fornication,'" "*Bartholomew Fair* as Blasphemy," "*The Comedy of Errors* Rescued from Tragedy" ("only by the introduction of the two Dromios"), "Das Motiv der Entfremdung in der *Komödie der Irrungen*," "The Darker Purpose of *A Midsummer Night's Dream*," "*A Midsummer Night's Dream*—Fairy Fantasy or Erotic Nightmare?" "Identity Crises in a Midsummer Nightmare: Comedy as Terror in Disguise," "Antonio and the Allegory of Salvation," and "*As You Like It*: The Penalty of Adam" (i.e., Original Sin). My favorite, though, is the title of a new reading of one of Vanbrugh's comedies, "*The Relapse*—Into Death and Damnation."

The relationship between decomicalization and the thematic approach should not be overstated, however; while all the readings I have seen that convert comedy into serious drama are thematic, there are other thematic readings of comedies that do not make this conversion, and there are other factors besides thematism involved in it. The approach, therefore, must be regarded as a necessary but not a sufficient cause of this trend. Yet it bears a heavy responsibility. For one thing, the central theme, by its very nature, does not define any specific emotional response: just as the concept of "bed" can tell us nothing about the color of any given bed, so the thematic ideas say nothing about the tonality or feeling of each play from which they have been abstracted. Indeed the same central theme can be derived from plays of very different emotional textures—thus one critic finds "the issues and implications are much the same" in *Sejanus*, *Volpone*, and *The Alchemist*, and we have seen others who placed all the comedies and tragedies of Shakespeare or of Jonson under a single theme. It is therefore very easy for thematists to ignore the comic effect—to hear merry tales, like Portia's suitor, and smile not. Moreover, since their approach assumes that the particular dramatic actions must always serve a higher "real" meaning, the fact that those actions happen to be comic is irrelevant and so presents no obstacle to a solemn interpretation: "the comic business develops the serious concern of *Twelfth Night*, the fallibility of human communication." But while these aspects of the approach enable the thematists to decomicalize a play, their conception of the play's higher meaning is what provides the motive. That meaning should be profound; and profundity, at least as they define it, is no laughing matter. In order to increase our admiration of a comedy, therefore, by revealing in it this kind of hithertho unsuspected profundity—or, in the words of one of them, "a deeper significance than appears on casual reading"—they will be led to suppress or minimize its comicality.

Although the goal of these new decomicalized readings is very noble, I do not think they have attained it. There certainly is a sense in which great comedy, like all great art, has a profound significance for us, but it cannot be discovered through this type of shortcut that bypasses the play's emotional texture. The search for instant profundity in comedy is self-defeating, because the real profundity of these plays must arise out of their humor, and so must be lost in interpretations that pretend this humor does not exist, or that grudgingly acknowledge it only as a superficial frosting upon some thematic pill (which might be called the "comic, but" tactic). Thus, while these individual readings can seem harmless enough, and even amusing, the trend they represent is not. For if it continues we may eventually witness the death of comedy, at least in our schools and scholarly press, with the consequent sacrifice of the pleasures that the immediate, felt comic experience is capable of imparting. And that, I submit, really will be no laughing matter.

The quest for thematic profundity has had another unfortunate result, which is not limited to comedy. As it continues, there seems to be a kind of competition developing to discover this profundity in more plays where it has not been noticed before, and, in plays where it has, to discover even more profundity than had previously been recognized. In some cases we can trace such an escalation of claims of greater profundity as each critic strives to surpass his predecessors, which is similar (and sometimes related, as we saw) to the escalating claims of greater thematic "inclusiveness" discussed earlier. A reading of *Measure for Measure* appearing in 1949, for instance, made the relatively modest observation that in it Shakespeare produced "a more coherent, a more independent, and in the last analysis, a more Christian piece of thinking on the subject [justice and mercy] than nine out of ten professional Renaissance theologians"; but a few years later someone found in it "one of the most searching studies ever made of the effect of power upon character"; and later still a third critic announced that Shakespeare "here came incredibly

close to encompassing the whole scope of man's moral development."
We may, however, be in some danger of getting too much of a good
thing, for this escalation, like other forms of inflation, can result in a
cheapening of the currency. As more and more plays turn out to be more
and more profound, the term becomes less and less meaningful. If it can
be applied to *A Midsummer Night's Dream* and even to *Love's Labor's
Lost* (we were recently told that the charming song at the end of this play
"presents the totality of human life" and is "an abstract of eternity, the
integer of infinity, the microcosmic icon of human experience"), then
what are we to call *Hamlet* or *King Lear?* Perhaps some kind of profundity control will have to be imposed by an outside authority if the
thematists do not voluntarily exercise more restraint.

A second important advantage of this approach, again according to
the thematists themselves, is that it enables us to discover and demonstrate the play's relevance—a commodity in considerable demand right
now in the academy. And this claim, too, is undeniable, for thematism
can confer instant relevance upon every play it touches, just as it con-
ferred instant profundity. Since the central theme that the play is supposed to be about may be pitched at any level of abstraction the critic
chooses, he can always formulate it in such a way as to bear directly
upon whatever he believes are our most pressing concerns:

> Might it not be better to take single plays more relevant . . . that
> are pertinent to the human situation? *Macbeth* as a study in the
> genesis of evil? *King Lear* as having as its center the most pro-
> found of modern problems—setting aside that of evil—of chil-
> dren and of old age, and "nature" in both? *Coriolanus* as the
> great *exemplum* of the problem of the One and the Many, and of
> the equally modern problem of the soldier in policy and peace?

"But indeed," the writer adds, "this could be done profitably with many
plays; provided only that there is time and the skill." Actually we have
seen that it can be done with *any* play, and with no particular skill, by
the simple technique of the thematic leap—which is just what this writer
describes when he goes on to explain that the revelation of this relevance
calls for "some understanding beyond the surface one of 'plot,' and the
slightly deeper one of 'orthodox' character analysis," and for a critic
"capable of extracting and presenting such aspects of [the human] situation as are latent (*sub specie aeternitatis*) in the plays." (Note again the
standard distinction between the apparent or "surface" meaning of the
play and its real, deeper, "latent" meaning.)

Since the thematic leap is so arbitrary, we would expect it to produce

diverse relevancies in the same play, depending on the critics' predilec-
tions, just as it produced diverse profundities and diverse central themes.
Thus an earlier reading finds the relevance of *King Lear* in a quite
different conception of "the modern problem":

> At an extraordinarily early time Shakespeare got hold of the
> modern problem, got hold of it when the Renaissance had, so
> to speak, barely started it on its way. Lear, in one sense, repre-
> sents the old order, and the play becomes the tragedy of that
> order.

And a later one discovers a quite different relevance in *Coriolanus*:

> In the situation Shakespeare has taken from Plutarch he finds a
> vehicle for a political question as relevant to our democratic
> society as to Roman democracy, ... What is the role of the man
> of principle in politics?

And a fourth critic locates the modern relevance of all of Shakespeare's
plays in yet another problem:[22]

> Shakespeare's statements on order, the order necessary to
> happiness and finally to mere survival, agree very substan-
> tially with what the most influential minds of our own century
> have been concerned to say. "Integration of the personality"—
> what is it but order? The Lawrentian ideal of a full instinctual
> life which renders those who live it immune from the blasting
> and withering of modern industrial civilisation—what is it,
> again, but order? Who are the Organisation Men and the Exur-
> banites and the rest of the damned, but people who are trying
> to live in defiance of wholeness, *i.e.*, of order?

Thematic relevance, moreover, like thematic profundity, can be carried a step further, for this approach is able to show that the plays are not
only dealing with some relevant modern problem, but that they are
making relevant statements about it, or even furnishing relevant solutions. These statements or solutions are of course the general thematic
propositions in which many of these readings terminate, as we saw, and
which can easily be expressed as useful "lessons" for our time. Such
lessons can make the play seem still more relevant to the issues now
in fashion, and so provide a respectable defense for the teaching of
literature, especially since they usually turn out to be the kind of re-
sounding platitudes to which no one could possibly object.

The third advantage which the thematists claim is that their approach can enhance our estimate of the play, not only as a vehicle for profound and relevant ideas, but also as a work of art, by justifying parts or aspects of it that may seem to be defective. This claim (which is shared by the ironic approach) is another characteristic of new readings in general, as was noted earlier. And it has certainly been borne out, because many critics have utilized the concept of thematic unity for just such a rescue operation. In their readings, portions of the play which previous commentators thought irrelevant or inappropriate or disproportionate—the show of the Nine Worthies in *Love's Labor's Lost*, for instance, or the Clown scene in *Othello*—have been salvaged by subsuming them under the play's central theme. And since we saw that one can always find a thematic abstraction which will encompass any combination of characters or events, this strategy cannot fail to vindicate any part of any play. If through some mix-up in Jaggard's shop a scene from *Coriolanus* had been printed in the middle of *Cymbeline*, a resourceful thematist would have no trouble showing how it contributed to the informing thematic structure. Thus upon every play that it touches the approach can confer instant unity, for there is no dramatic component, no matter how refractory it may seem when judged in terms of the play's "apparent" meaning, that cannot be redeemed by being gathered up into the all-forgiving embrace of the central theme.

In addition to this simple technique for transforming apparent defects into real artistic virtues, the approach also provides a critic with an even easier way to make the play seem more successful as a work of art, since it enables him to pass over, if he wishes, any failures in such mundane matters (again, on the "apparent" level) as the characterization or plotting or language, none of which need interfere with the abstract thematic structure he is building above them. This would explain why, now that the approach is moving on to second- and third-rate plays, it is discovering them to be so much better than anyone ever imagined before. For on the thematic level their artistry is indistinguishable from that of acknowledged masterpieces—they are just as plausibly integrated and informed by the central theme, and those aspects in which they are clearly inferior need never enter into the critic's reading. (Of course some thematic readings do point out these deficiencies, but that is not a function of their approach.) This has not been an unmixed blessing, however, because thematic artistry, like thematic profundity, is suffering the effects of inflation. As more and more plays turn out to be more and more perfect, the criteria lose credibility, and we may be led to wonder what is wrong with an approach that cannot make the most obvious aesthetic discriminations. To quote Alfred Harbage, "Evidence of blindness to defects or inconsistencies casts suspicion upon testimony about merits or consistencies. . . . What shall we think of praises of *Hamlet* by one who has raved over *Titus Andronicus*?"[23]

The thematic approach is capable of producing this higher unity not only in individual works but also in the entire canon of an author, and that must be accounted its fourth advantage: it can be used to discover and demonstrate the essential continuity of a literary career. Such demonstrations are, in effect, treating the author's separate plays as parts of one larger composition which must be unified thematically, and so we would expect them to divide into two basic types, the homogeneous and the dialectical, along the same lines as the thematic structures of the plays themselves. In the homogeneous formulation a single theme is found to be central in all of his plays, or in a significant group of them. We have already encountered several examples in the discussion of "all-purpose thematics" at the beginning of this chapter, where we saw critics attempting to encompass Jonson's works under one grand theme, such as "the centrifugal personality" or "the curing of wrongheadedness," and Shakespeare's under the theme of "order" or "appearance and reality." In some of these homogenizing schemes the plays turn out to be pretty much the same throughout the dramatist's career—merely "variations on his principal theme, endless inversions of the same leitmotiv"; but others add something like a dialectical dimension by finding a progressive change in his handling of this one theme, usually in the direction of greater depth or complexity, which is supposed to constitute his "development." This technique has proved especially useful in relating Shakespeare's romantic comedies to his later plays as parts of a single sequence. Thus, according to one critic,

> There are few more fruitful ways of regarding his works than to
> think of them as an account of the warfare between Imagination
> and Chaos. . . . Taken retrospectively, *A Midsummer-Night's
> Dream* seems like the argument of this story, like an overture
> to the vast musical composition which the poet's later master-
> pieces make up.

A second critic finds his overture in another comedy:

> *Much Ado* will lead forward to the "dark" or "problem" come-
> dies of the succeeding years . . . all of which explore the evil
> inherent in society and therefore tend to share the world . . .
> [of the] great tragedies. . . . *Much Ado* and *The Merchant* are,
> then, of considerable importance for Shakespeare's total devel-

opment in that they introduce into his comedy the theme of evil which, after a thorough exploration in the tragedies, will be absorbed back into the comic universe in those final myths of good and evil, *A Winter's Tale* and *The Tempest*.

And a third also begins with *Much Ado about Nothing*, although his development program is entirely different because he believes the theme of that play is "an exploration of the limits and methods of knowledge":

> And finally: "know" reveals the direction in which Shakespeare is moving. Much of the ground in *Much Ado* he traverses again in *Othello* . . . [where] problems of "knowing" are dealt with in much the same way. The other, profounder, questions that relate to "know" are reserved for *Hamlet*. *Much Ado* is a base camp that secures the approaches to the peak.

In a truly dialectical formulation of a dramatist's development, however, the critic finds a different central theme in each of his plays, and then goes on to show how these themes are connected in a larger logical sequence of some kind:

> *Antony and Cleopatra*, dealing with the themes of a man's love for a woman and the ambition of empire, mediates between the themes of *Julius Caesar* and *Troilus and Cressida*, comprehending and in some sense reconciling their moods, their conflicts, and their values; *King Lear*, dealing with the relations of the human family and of human ingratitude, similarly mediates between *Coriolanus* and *Timon of Athens*, comprehends and reconciles them.

A better known scheme has been worked out along very different lines by another thematist, who announces at the outset that his book "is based on the belief that Shakespeare's plays form a coherent whole, that they stem from and express a developing 'attitude to life.'" According to him, "it is surely no accident that one of the first plays in which we recognize the great Shakespeare—the Second Part of *King Henry IV*—is a play of which the controlling theme is time and change. In that play, and in the sonnets on time, we see clearly the beginning of the progress that culminates in *King Lear* and the great tragedies." The next step is the assertion that "a deeply ingrained preoccupation with time almost inevitably brings with it two further allied preoccupations—with death and with appearance and reality . . . and as a consequence an honest and energetic spirit is forced to ask himself what is solid and enduring in the flux." We are then told that *Hamlet* "is a play about death," and *Troilus and Cressida* about appearance and reality. But it seems that

> *Troilus and Cressida* raises a further question, which is simply,
> How do men come to give themselves to appearances? . . . Here
> is indicated the direction that any further exploration is forced to
> take. . . . We are forced to ask ourselves nothing less than, What
> is essential human nature? . . . It is precisely this question that
> *King Lear* attempts to answer.

Of course one might object that the individual themes and the larger
thematic sequence are both completely arbitrary—*Hamlet* is no more
"about death" than about life, or love, or any number of other possible
themes (including time and appearance vs. reality and essential human
nature), and a preoccupation with time does not "almost inevitably" lead
off in any particular direction. But this very arbitrariness is what gives
thematism such an advantage over more exacting modes of dealing with
the problem of artistic development. Someone using this approach need
never worry about recalcitrant historical facts which do not fit his
scheme, for even if the accepted chronology of the plays were to be
altered by new information, he would have no difficulty in accommodating to it by finding different central themes for them, or a different
logical sequence of themes that the dramatist and his readers are "forced"
to follow. This sort of "reading" of an author's career, like the thematic
readings of individual works, is always self-confirming. No one ever
seems to have failed in either undertaking.

The fifth major advantage of thematism (which it also shares with the
ironic approach) is that it enables the critic to discover that the artist holds
the same views, on the basic issues of life, that he does. The thematists
themselves never mention this advantage and apparently are not even
conscious of it. They do not deliberately set out to make such a discovery, but, given the nature of their approach (and of all our egos), it is
almost inevitable. For we saw that the thematic leap permits a critic to
proceed from the play's apparent meaning to any real meaning he wants,
so he would be less than human if he did not find that the real meaning
was what he wanted it to be. M. H. Abrams observed that the distinction between real and apparent meaning is "used as a handy gadget to
replace what an author has said with what a commentator would prefer
him to have said."[24] But this is not quite fair, at least as it applies to the
thematists; their approach assures them that they are revealing the
author, not replacing him, since it assumes that "what an author has
said" can only be learned by abstracting from what he seems to have said
(that is, from the literal or apparent meaning), and furnishes no controls
which might inhibit them from abstracting to their own cherished beliefs.

I have yet to encounter a reading in which the central thematic idea or proposition discovered in the play did not turn out to be one that the discoverer approved of. And we all know of thematists who manage to extract their favorite doctrines from many very different works and writers. One of the earliest and most famous thematic critics of Shakespeare, to take an extreme example, is convinced that the basic ideas expressed in his plays—ideas obviously espoused by the critic himself—also appear in Byron, Dante, Dostoevsky, Goethe, Keats, Tolstoy, Oscar Wilde, and the Gospels. And another thematist tells us that Shakespeare's "view of the world" (which is quite different from that discerned by the preceding critic) is one "he shares with a surprising number of the major writers of the western tradition," including Homer, Aeschylus, Sophocles, Virgil, Dante, Chaucer, Cervantes, Goethe, Stendhal, Tolstoy, and Thomas Mann. But this number is really not at all surprising, for we would expect that an approach which can always find a higher abstract unity to encompass any parts of a work, and any works of an author, will also be able to find one encompassing any group of authors, no matter how diverse they may seem.

I have saved until last what I suspect is the most important advantage of the approach, although this, too, is never mentioned by the thematists. It is very easy—probably the easiest form of criticism now being practiced. To produce a thematic new reading of a play, the critic need not concern himself with the complex particularities of character and action and effect, since he is stationed far above them, on the "real" level of abstractions. All that he has to do is find some central theme which has not yet been proposed for that play, assert its superiority to the themes which have been proposed, and then run it through the text under one of the structures discussed earlier, with success guaranteed in advance. And he does not have to justify or even explain what he is doing, because all of that is automatically assumed. Some years ago G. K. Hunter referred to this sort of operation as "Shakespeare for business machines,"[25] and he spoke more prophetically than he knew, for we now have a paperback Shakespeare series entitled "E-Z Learner Study Texts" which has succeeded in mechanizing almost the entire process by means of something called the "Casyndekan Computerized Concept Index."[26] Alongside each dramatic unit it lists the concepts appearing there (identified by "literary research teams" using the "Casyndekan Universal Set Theory" of all relevant ideas); and it also provides indices, compiled by computer, which enable us to trace every concept or combination of concepts throughout the play. The publisher announces on his book covers that his invention "reduces research time up to 95%," presumably for students, but I see no reason why it should not prove equally useful to thematic critics, and so make their approach even more attractive than it now is.

The Problem of Universality

At this point the reader might begin to suspect that I do not think there is anything to be said on behalf of thematism. But any approach that has achieved such a rapid widespread success and attracted such a large number of critics probably has at least some part of the truth. I would say that this approach has hold of three parts, although in each case it is little more than a fingerhold.

In the first place, it is evident that some literary works really are about an idea or central theme and therefore call for thematic interpretation. Many lyric poems fall into this category (though by no means all of them, as the thematists seem to believe), and it is no accident that in its initial phase thematic criticism was primarily concerned with poetry. Indeed, when the members of this school first turned to drama, they sometimes explained in their introductions that they were subjecting the play to "the techniques of poetic analysis" or even treating it as a kind of poem: "If love is what *Othello* is 'about,' *Othello* is not only a play about love but a poem about love."

One does not have to be a thematist, however, to recognize that "thematic" plays do exist. Probably the most obvious examples are the Moralities, which are without question about a central theme whose identity is equally unquestionable. The theme of each Morality drama is an ethical proposition that is usually stated in the prologue and epilogue and often in the title (*Like Will to Like, Enough Is as Good as a Feast*, etc.), and is always demonstrated directly in the actions and fates of the characters. These characters, moreover, are clearly not meant to be taken as individuals but as symbols of the abstractions designated by their names; and through those abstractions they serve to enact the theme, which constitutes the unifying principle and meaning of the play. This of course is how the thematists describe the later works they are interpreting—in fact they are now telling us that many of them have a "Morality-play structure." It is true that they usually speak of the characters in these works as representatives, rather than as symbols, of the thematic abstractions (although some readings treat the protagonist as an "Everyman" figure, as we saw, and in others characters like Desdemona and Iago are transformed into an allegorized Virtue and Vice), but that is a distinction in dramatic technique—an important one, to be sure—and not in dramatic purpose. In a thematic reading the purpose of the play is essentially the same as that of the Morality, and so is the basic form, since in both the play is organized around an idea, and in both the idea itself is of the same order (for we found that most themes translated into propositional "morals" or "lessons"). The allegorical Morality, in other words, really does have the kind of structure and meaning that the thematists claim to find in the later drama. Viewed through their approach, the greatest plays in our language all aspire to the condition of *Enough Is as Good as a Feast.*

"Thematic" plays are also quite common on the modern stage (and this is surely not unrelated to the history of the thematic approach). In *Waiting for Lefty* and *Waiting for Godot*, to take two clear examples, the subject is obviously an abstract concept rather than a particular human action. Although each of Odets's episodes gives us such an action, they do not form a single, sequential plot but function instead as exempla of a single idea, the need to resist capitalist oppression (summed up in the closing words: "STRIKE, STRIKE, STRIKE!!!"), which the play is about. We may not be so certain of what Beckett's play is about (I have my own theory, of course), but we know it must be an idea, since the characters cannot be interpreted literally but only as symbols of something else. The two plays use radically different methods of presentation, but it is evident that they both use these methods to present a central theme.

Since some plays are about a central theme and some are not, we need a way to determine which kind we are dealing with. The first and most important point is that this is a question which must be confronted for each play—we certainly cannot begin with the thematic assumption that every play, or every good play, has a theme. Nor can we settle the matter by finding some theme which yields a thematic reading of the play, since we saw that this can be done with any play (and with almost any theme). It seems to me that there are two basic criteria for deciding this crucial question—the structure of the play and its effect. We must ask whether the play's organizing principle, which accounts for all of its parts and their order and interrelationships, is a particular action or a general idea, and whether our final response is directed primarily to the fates it metes out to the characters or to a proposition it affirms. There will of course be some disputable or borderline cases that require a careful comparison of the interpretations based upon these two alternatives; but for most plays, I believe, the answer is never really in doubt. It surely is not for the medieval and modern "thematic" dramas cited above, since everyone

immediately recognizes that their subject is an idea. There needs no new
reading come from the thematists to tell us this.

Nor do I believe there can really be any doubt about the Renaissance
plays which have been our concern. For they certainly seem to be literal
representations of individual actions (even the thematists, we saw,
acknowledge that this is their "apparent" meaning), and, so far as we can
determine, they were understood in that way by virtually all viewers and
readers for well over three centuries, until the advent of the new thematic
readings, which otherwise would not be new. In such a situation, I would
argue, the two alternatives cannot be given equal weight, because it is
very much more likely that these plays are what they appear to be, and
what they have been taken to be up to now, and therefore a heavy
burden of proof must rest upon the thematists to show us that they are
not. That of course is just the opposite of the thematic assumption. But
the discussion of this whole question of working hypotheses in interpretation, since it also involves the other approaches still to be considered,
will be reserved for the final chapter.

Even in these Renaissance plays, however, general ideas may have a
very important role, and this is the second partial truth of the thematists.
But again, we did not need them to tell it to us, for it has been recognized
by most literal approaches, which also recognize that the significance of
such ideas will vary from play to play. The mistake of the thematists is
their assumption that these ideas are always the most important component of the play and that they always have the same role—to establish
the play's subject. But ideas may serve other functions in the drama.

The general ideas of the characters themselves, whether expressed
directly or implied in their words and actions, can be a very significant
factor in shaping our attitude toward them, in explaining their choices,
and in defining the meaning of their experiences to them and to us. Such
ideas will of course be more extensive and complex in some plays than in
others, depending largely upon the nature of the characters and of the
issues involved. But even in plays where they are of the greatest importance—in *Hamlet*, for instance, or *King Lear*—they are still the thoughts
of a particular character and not the ideas of the play itself. This distinction is consistently ignored by the thematists, who simply appropriate
these thoughts to their central theme whenever they can be made to serve
that purpose. In fact, one of the best known thematic critics of the
Elizabethan drama has admitted that it does not matter which characters
state the ideas he uses in his readings, since all the ideas (which means all
that he wants to use) are part of the play's exploration of its theme. For

him, and for thematists in general, as we have seen, the characters are not independent dramatic entities—their thoughts, like their actions, do not really belong to them but are merely a means to the higher thematic end.

General ideas, whether expressed or implied, also figure significantly in the play's basic assumptions, both moral and aesthetic. Such assumptions are not "in" the play in the same sense as the characters' thoughts, but they are an essential aspect of it, since without them we would not know how we are meant to respond. Again, the importance (and complexity) of the ideas involved in these assumptions will vary from play to play. And again, we must make a distinction between these ideas and the dramatic subject. A play is not about its assumptions (except in the special case of the "ironic" or "parodic" play, to be discussed in the following chapter); the assumptions provide the context for understanding the actions that the play really is about. But this distinction, too, is seldom observed by the thematist.[27] In the current vogue of reflexive thematics or "metadramatic criticism," noted earlier, the play's aesthetic assumptions often enter into the central theme, which is usually formulated in terms of the nature of art or drama ("the theoretical function of the play itself," according to the statement on *The Revenger's Tragedy* in our initial collection). And in the older and more common version, the moral assumptions of the play are transformed into a problem that it is exploring, or a proposition it is demonstrating, as W. R. Keast pointed out in reviewing an early thematist's book on *King Lear*:

> His method necessitates treating the very premises on which the characterization and action of the play depend for their intelligibility as if they were not premises but unsolved problems . . . . In his view such fundamental questions as whether nature is a moral order in the universe are not determined until the end of the play. . . . [But] the conception of nature as moral order is evident from the first two scenes of the play and is obviously presupposed as a criterion for the assessment of Edmund's soliloquy. . . . The play as a whole presupposes—it asserts as a premise, it takes for granted, it includes among its *données*—that there is a justice, an order. . . . The reader knows from the outset . . . that the view of nature put forward by Edmund is, in all essential respects, wrong.[28]

Finally, there are the general ideas about life which occur to us while we are watching or reading the play, if we are not actively engaged in the dramatic experience, or, more often, after that experience is over. Such reflections are not "in" the play at all, except in the sense that they are generated by it, but they are inevitable and can be very rewarding; for some people, apparently, they constitute the greatest reward that literature has to offer. And they would seem to be the real source of thematic criticism, as I indicated earlier. If one of these critics were to begin his essay by stating, "After seeing a performance of *The Comedy of Errors* the other night, I had the following thoughts about the relationship of appearance to reality . . .," no one could possibly object. It would not be an interpretation, of course, but would be a perfectly legitimate exercise, so long as he did not confuse the play with his later thoughts, and might well prove interesting. But the thematists never make this distinction. Instead of acknowledging that they are treating the play, in Roland Frye's apt phrase, as "a mere point of departure for subjective reverie and reflection,"[29] they insist that their reflections are the subject of the play, its central theme, and then try to demonstrate this by working up a thematic reading. And the obvious objection, also indicated earlier, is that these reflections, although they are abstracted from the play, are not determined by it but by the temperament and interests of the abstractor, and even by his mood, for the same work will produce different thoughts in him at different times. They are not even determined by artistic achievement, since very profound ideas can be abstracted from very inferior plays, or even from a newspaper article, as Marco Mincoff noted in a criticism of thematic readings of *Measure for Measure* which gets to the basic case against this approach:

> Why however must it be assumed that the play is built up
> round an idea at all? If a play is not a gallery of portraits, still
> less is it a philosophical disquisition or investigation. . . . Nat-
> urally we can reflect on his [Angelo's] fall, as we can reflect on
> the report of a murder trial in the papers, but we have no right
> to present our reflections as Shakespeare's meaning.[30]

These general reflections on life are also involved in the third and most important part of the truth that the thematic approach can lay claim to, which turns upon the problem of the "universal" in art. Although I have been arguing that the kind of play we are dealing with presents the particular actions of particular characters, those actions and characters must incorporate some more general component or we could not understand them, much less be moved by them. We would never "recognize" Lear, for instance, if we could not relate his personal traits and thoughts and feelings to general ideas or categories, derived from our past experience (both real and vicarious), which we bring to the play—ideas of kingship, fatherhood, age, rage, love, and many other abstractions, even including appearance and reality. Our response to all literary works depends upon some such interaction between the particular and general (the proportions of the two varying, of course, in different kinds of works), and to that extent the thematists are right.

Their error, it seems to me, is to assume that we reduce or assimilate the particulars to these general ideas—or rather, to one of them, arbitrarily selected as the central theme—so that they function as mere representatives of this idea, which thus becomes the real subject of the play. In other words, they solve the problem of the relationship of the particular to the general in literature by sacrificing the former to the latter. But our actual response to these plays appears to be just the opposite—we use the general ideas to understand the particular actions and characters, which are the primary focus of our attention. For we do not see Lear as the representative of the ideas we bring to bear upon him; although we recognize him by means of these ideas, we at the same time recognize that he is not completely contained under them, that he is something unique in our experience. I do not pretend to understand this psychological process, which presumably involves our capacity to recombine in novel ways the abstractions we have already formed; but we know such a process must take place, or else we could never comprehend a new object (that is, comprehend it *as* new) in art or in life. Of course, this relationship is reciprocal; our particular experience of Lear will later enter into and enrich our prior generalizations which we applied to him. That is how we "learn" from art—at least from this kind of art—not by leaping directly (and thematically) from the characters and events to some universal idea, but by drawing upon their universal aspects in order to grasp them in all of their particularity.

This process has important consequences in our aesthetic judgments as well, since the concept of "universality" is widely employed to account not only for the intelligibility of art but also for its value. We have seen the thematists argue that the superiority of certain plays or certain characters lies in their universality (and the superiority of the thematic approach in its ability to discover this). But the rest of us also use the term to praise plays and characters, so it must point to some significant criterion. The problem is to determine in what this universality inheres. The thematists, naturally, locate it in the central theme which the characters are supposed to represent and the play is supposed to be about; but we found that this created a serious difficulty, because the representativeness, and hence the thematic universality, of an object is inversely proportional to its individuality. In this sense, then, Lear would be much less universal than an Everyman figure or the unnamed Gentleman in his own play, who are defined generically; and for the same reason any work of Shakespeare's would be much less universal than the simplest Morality or melodrama or folktale. That is why the thematists had to strip the dramatic characters of their individuality in order to reduce them to exemplars of the universal thematic ideas. But the individuality of its characters is surely one of the most admirable qualities of this drama. I think we must conclude, therefore, that thematic universality is not really an artistic value at all, but a cheap and "instant" substitute for one, like thematic profundity and relevance, to which it is so closely related.

It seems to me that when we praise the universality of plays or characters we mean something quite different—we are referring not to the inclusiveness of the idea or class they represent, but to the breadth of their appeal. We think they are more universal than inferior characters and plays because they are capable of interesting and moving more people of different cultures and historical periods, which has proved to be true of the best products of the Renaissance stage. And this is not a function of the typicality of the characters, but of their richness, complexity, roundedness, completeness, depth, uniqueness—all the terms we employ to distinguish a successfully individualized character from a class stereotype. Of course, the universality of this appeal will also depend upon the character's relationship to our conceptions of general human nature, as we noted, and upon other factors as well, including the significance of the issues at stake in his actions. But the issues themselves will not determine the play's universality in this sense. That is the thematic fallacy all over again, for we found that it was possible to abstract issues of universal import from *any* play. In the most widely admired of these plays, however, the issues take on their meaning and importance, not in the abstract, but in terms of their very specific relation to the characters who confront them. So even on this count the universal appeal of the play will involve the individualization of its characters and actions. And that individualization, which only great art can give us, is what the thematist sacrifices to get his kind of universality.

Our final judgment of thematism, then, should turn upon this question of what we gain from it and what we lose. We have just seen what is lost in this approach, and the preceding section revealed what we were supposed to gain—a profundity that was essentially bogus, in fact doubly bogus, since it was not really in the play and was not really profound. The profit and the loss were summed up some years ago in Philip Edwards's comment on thematic and symbolic interpretations of Shakespeare's last plays:

There is an appearance (there is certainly a claim) that the depths
are being opened, riches are being revealed. But it is an appearance only. It is a disservice to Shakespeare to pretend that one
is adding to his profundity by discovering that his plots are
symbolic vehicles for ideas and perceptions which are, for the
most part, banal, trite and colourless. The "symbols" are so
much more fiercely active, potent, rich, complex as themselves
than as what they are made to convey. When they are translated, they do not have a tithe of their own magnitude.[31]

And Alfred Harbage made the same point even more succinctly when he
said that this approach asks us to "trade our birthright of great artistry
for a mess of third-rate philosophy."[32] In its quest for the universal profundity of philosophic discourse, which these plays do not possess,
thematism has reduced them to the statement of platitudes, and in this
process it has deprived us of the kind of universality and profundity
which really can be found in the best of them, and is never found in
ontological or deontological treatises, or in Morality dramas or Aesopian
fables. And that is the universally and profoundly moving experience of
the characters, regarded not as symbols or representatives of some
abstract truism, but as unique personalities sharing and calling out to our
common humanity.

Three

Ironic Readings

The term "ironic" has taken on several meanings in the criticism of English Renaissance drama. In its simplest sense, it refers to speeches in which a character says something very different from—usually the opposite of—what he really intends, as when Mark Antony in his funeral oration calls Caesar's assassins "all honourable men." This kind of irony poses no general problems in interpretation, since it is almost always immediately obvious to the audience (if not to the other characters), and so has not been responsible for any of the new readings we are concerned with here. The term is used in another sense to refer to speeches or actions of a character which, because of his misapprehension of the real situation, turn out to have a significance very different from—again, usually the opposite of—what he intends. Thus we say it is ironic that Brutus should assure his fellow conspirators that Antony's oration "shall advantage more than do us wrong," or that, in a larger context, the very actions which he undertook to save the republic actually precipitate its overthrow. This "dramatic irony" (or "tragic irony") is also made obvious to the audience, if not immediately, then certainly by the end of the play, since its effect depends upon our awareness of the character's lack of awareness, and consequently it, too, rarely creates interpretative problems. It has long been recognized as an important aspect of the drama,[1] without the benefit of any new readings to reveal it to us.

The term is now being employed, however, with increasing frequency

78

in a third sense to refer to a dramatic presentation which is not meant to be "taken at face value," since the attitude it seems to call for is very different from—again, usually the opposite of—the attitude we are supposed to adopt. It is in this sense, for instance, that Antony's final tribute to Brutus, "This was the noblest Roman of them all," is said by some recent critics to be ironic—not because Antony does not mean it or wish it to be accepted, but because Shakespeare believed, and wanted his audience to believe, that Brutus was ignoble. In other words, these critics are treating a portion of the play (in most cases, as we shall see, the entire play) as if it were a statement by the playwright which is ironic in the first sense, since what he is "saying" there, in his presentation, is not what he really intends.

This kind of irony, then, differs from the first in that it is attributed to the playwright and not to the speaker, who is no more aware of it than are those he is addressing. And it differs from the second in two important respects. It is primarily concerned not with a character's situation or fate, but with our attitude toward him. And it is never made obvious to the audience, even at the end of the play—indeed it is usually extended by these critics to include the ending (as in the preceding example), and therefore, unlike the errors resulting in "dramatic irony," cannot be revealed to us by subsequent events. Far from being obvious, this kind of irony by its very nature requires the critic to deny the obvious meaning or "face value" of the presentation and to find another meaning opposed to it. Therefore, in contrast to the other two kinds, which are not associated with any particular approach to interpretation, it will generate its own characteristic "reading" of a play. And that will necessarily be a "new reading," because the obvious meaning which it rejects is, by definition, the meaning accepted by virtually all viewers and readers of the play down to our own day (hence these critics often boast that the irony they have discovered was "hitherto unsuspected," or words to that effect). Such ironic new readings of English Renaissance dramas have been multiplying rapidly in recent years and now constitute a major trend—a trend which clearly raises some serious interpretative problems. Our investigation, then, will be limited to this conception of "irony."[2]

The Ironic Scene

We can get a clearer understanding of the nature of this conception and of this trend if we begin, again, with some representative quotations which will illustrate the kinds of conclusions reached by these new readings, and so will serve to introduce us to the present ironic scene. Each statement comes from a different critic, and all have appeared since 1965.

[*Richard III:*] Shakespeare's presentation of Henry Tudor is not without irony.... [It] is far from pleasant. If he is God's avenging angel, he is a most self-righteous, pedantic angel indeed. He simply refers to God too many times to be palatable as His agent.

[*The Two Gentlemen of Verona:*] The fundamental critical error with *Two Gentlemen* is to take Valentine at his own evaluation as an attractive, appealing male lead. He is nothing of the sort. He is ... a "nincompoop." ... [His surrender of Silvia] is a gesture of sublime, fatuous egotism.... On the plane of romantic comedy, the magnitude of Valentine's ego demands comparison with Milton's Satan.

[*Romeo and Juliet:*] Sadly enough, most spectators have also taken at face value ... [the] play's tragic sentimentality.... Audiences are as taken in by Romeo's death-dealing charm as Juliet is. They fail to see that as a hero Romeo lies midway between the surrealist horror of the homicidal Richard III, and the bathos of Pyramus.... Like Richard, also, Romeo is a catalyst of disaster, and something close to a mass murderer.

[*Romeo and Juliet:*] Juliet reveals in unmistakable terms that her love for Romeo is rooted in passion.... She hungers ... violently for Romeo's body (and in the stridency of her imagination comes very close to panting like an animal).... The ugliness which to an Elizabethan audience would have been implicit in the rawness of her sexual hunger is the ugliness which arises from the perversion of her natural capacity to love.

[*A Midsummer Night's Dream:*] The dramatist is deliberately pointing up [Theseus's] perfidy and fraud.... If his first words suggest his reputation for unfaithfulness and unnatural patterns of affection, his later behavior in the opening scene is designed to add to that image of viciousness.... [He] is tyrannically unmerciful ... [and] neglect[s] his duties as a ruler.... The final action of the play, the fairy blessing, ... [is] a ghastly reminder of the fate of the issue of [Theseus's] bride bed.... This scene would have been potentially the most ironic one within the drama.

[*The Merchant of Venice:*] Belmont is as flawed as Venice. Most important, because Belmont's inhabitants are oblivious to their flaws, their festivity is artificial, ambiguous, and highly ironic. ... The rotten core of undiscovered hypocrisy is still present, and

will remain undiscovered and unresolved. . . . [Antonio is]
unbearably self-righteous. . . . [His] charity is also at least doubly
flawed: it is selfish, and it is directed towards only one man, not all
men. . . . [It] brutally dramatizes Belmont's and Antonio's imperfect relationship to the comic and the Christian ideal.

[*Henry V:*] Whatever Shakespeare may say about Henry, in his
heart he regarded him as a murderer. Faced with the demand to
depict such a man as a hero, he took refuge in the irony which
permeates the whole play. . . . [He] equates Bardolph morally
with Henry, who has stolen the peace of England and France. . . .
Henry, Pistol, and the chivalry of France are shown . . . to
move on the same moral level.

[*Julius Caesar:*] Brutus is a dramatic illustration of the
hollowness, presumption, and moral sickness inherent in the
secular concept of virtue-reason's sufficiency. . . . [His mind is]
deranged . . . demented. . . . [His] "constancy" . . . is clearly evil
and results in spiritual death. . . . Brutus commits unmitigated
acts of savagery as a result of his having broken all ties with
humanity.

[*Hamlet:*] [Hamlet is] a soul lost in damnable error . . . a
serpent-like scourge . . . a profane fool. . . . At the play's
ending . . . he becomes himself the minister, rather, of a
poisoned chalice, and in that sense a fellow celebrant with
Claudius in a Black Mass . . . in which Hamlet can . . . help ad-
minister a devilish communion. . . . [He] thus transcends
himself—but only for a demonic self which he makes believe
as heroic.

[*Troilus and Cressida:*] With Hector the appearance may well
blind us to the reality, even as it blinds the other characters in the
play. . . . Yet when we examine Hector's behavior closely and
critically it appears that . . . there are grave flaws in [his]
chivalry. . . . He appears to be a noble, generous, worthy
knight—but . . . beneath the appearance lie pride, conceit, and
self-esteem. . . . His death is the inevitable outcome of his own
foolish, headstrong following of a ridiculous, anachronistic code
of behavior.

[*Measure for Measure:*] The Duke was a fool . . . a face-saving,
hypocritical bumbler. . . . [He is] another Angelo, a public
fraud. . . . It is ironic that the academic theatre and the critics
take the Duke at his face value, and remain caught up in the
whole pretence of "seeming" that Shakespeare attacked. . . . It's
not just the ending of the play that's a charade, the whole
political set-up is.

[*Othello:*] [Desdemona is guilty of] self-righteousness . . . moral
hypocrisy . . . [and a] Platonically proud denial of the body's
claims. . . . [She is] potentially, if not actually, unfaithful to
Othello. . . . She cannot face her own feminine frailty . . . [and]
shrinks from the reality of the whore within her.

[*Antony and Cleopatra:*] Shakespeare's intention [was] to insist
on the gap between what Antony is said to be and what he really
is. . . . [He is] consistently diminished. . . . He has never been
more than an illusory hero—a simulacrum substantiated by the
admiring lookers-on. . . . Everyone (except Enobarbus) is a dupe
of Antony's reputation. . . . Yet even he dies deceived . . . [since]
the Antony we have been seeing is simply not worth . . .
[his] devotion.

[*The Tempest:*] Once we can break free from the mesmerizing
power of Prospero's all-too-often successful attempt to dazzle us
with his halo . . . [we] see how devastating it is to take a stand
with Prospero. . . . Dramatic irony will not allow the audience
to accept these [his professed motives] as the real objectives.
From beginning to end Prospero is bent on vengeance. . . . [He
tries] to paint his foul ends with colors fairer, by focussing
attention away from himself to the evil power of Sycorax. . . .
Prospero would have us believe Sycorax and himself are poles
apart: the play deliberately parallels them.

Although this trend (like most others) has reached its fullest development in the Shakespearean arena, it is by no means limited to his works.
During the same period, for instance, we have been told by still other
critics (a different one, again, in each case) that Frankford, the hero of *A
Woman Killed with Kindness,* is "a beast" who, although he may "appear
to be virtuous," really acts "most hypocritically" with "sacrilegious presumption" and "is not a tragic figure but a despicable one"; that Gerardine's anticipation of a happy marriage to Maria, at the end of *The
Family of Love,* "would seem to be hopelessly optimistic if not thoroughly
ironic," because she "fail[s] to exemplify human love at its highest
level" and is apparently "doomed to become a sharp tongued and deceitful female like the two more mature wives presented in the play"; that
even though "everyone in the play admires or loves" Philaster, he is
really a "satiric portrait" of a "comic fool," in whose actions (which are
"analogous" to those the King and Pharamond) we are meant to "see
much to ridicule and even to despise"; that Lovewit in *The Alchemist* "is
a Falsewit rather than a Truewit" because of his "moral failings," and in
the ending his "sexual bargain-hunting incriminates him" and "seals [his]
condemnation"; that "every time we see" Giovanni, in *The White Devil,*
"we are ominously reminded of his close similarities to his father, Brachi-

ano, and his uncle, Francisco," and at the end "there are implications that
he will be unable to escape his evil heritage"; that there is a "profound
irony" in the "subtly derisive" portrayal of Alsemero in *The Changeling*,
who is "outwardly attractive" but really "pharisaical," "hypocritical,"
and guilty of "fraud" and "dissimulation," since he has "masked" his
"merely lustful" interest in Beatrice by "a fair-seeming exterior," and so is
meant to "suffer by contrast" with Deflores, "whose animality . . . has
at least the merit of being undisguised."

Many more examples could be cited, for by now, thanks to this trend,
just about every major play of the period has turned out to be ironic, and
not a few of the minor ones as well. Like the thematization of the same
body of drama, this result has been achieved largely through the accumulation of individual readings by different critics; but we also find among
them, as we did among the thematists, certain zealots who have taken on
and conquered an entire group of plays. The first quotation comes from a
book on Shakespeare's histories which begins by announcing that there is
a "remarkable prolixity of irony embedded in their structure" and that
"the kings of England portrayed in them are all poor kings." The author
of the second quotation informs us that he "can see only one comic
conclusion" in Shakespeare that is "virtually free from irony." The
assertion that Hamlet is "a soul lost in damnable error" is made in a book
on Shakespearean tragedy, where almost all of the other tragic protagonists are subjected to the same ironic interpretation and also end up
damned. And the quotation on *The Tempest* appears in a book devoted to
Shakespeare's final plays, which was written, its author explains, to
correct "romantic notions of practically all of the leading *dramatis personae* as innocent victims . . . uncorrupted by the evils of the outside
world," by proving that they are actually "hiding behind their masks of
innocence, chastity, purity, benevolence." According to him, if we can
recognize "that these *personae* have been creating the illusion of virtue
for us . . . and that we could easily have been taken in by appearances,"
we will see them for what they really are:

> Pericles is not an impeccable man; Cymbeline is not abused by
> his wicked queen; Posthumus and Imogen are not star-crossed
> lovers; . . . Hermione and Polixenes are not more sinned against
> than sinning; Perdita and Florizel, Miranda and Ferdinand are not
> idyllic youth in all its reinvigorating springtime freshness . . .
> though they all wear this outward mask and try to convince
> themselves and us of its putative sincerity.

Nor have Shakespeare's contemporaries escaped this sort of wholesale
ironization: the author of the quotation on *Philaster* applies the same
kind of reading to *A King and No King* and *The Maid's Tragedy*, while a

second critic has discovered a basic irony in all of Middleton's tragicomedies, and a third in all of Jonson's major comedies, and a fourth in
most of Marlowe's tragedies, and a fifth in much of the repertoire of the
children's troupes, and so on.

Although these examples differ in various ways, they exhibit one
essential similarity: they are all attacks upon a major character in the
play which is being interpreted. In each play—and especially, we shall
see, in its ending—the presentation of this character would seem to
establish very clearly that we are meant to regard him with sympathy
and even admiration, which in fact is how that presentation has been
understood by just about everyone up to the present. And each of these
critics is asserting that this prevailing view is wrong, because the character is actually meant to be antipathetic or ridiculous or both. That will
also turn out to be the basic thrust of all the other new ironic readings we
will examine here—to take a character "ironically," in their sense, is to
take him down.[3]

It is important to realize at the outset that these readings are *not*
arguing that this character is much less sympathetic or admirable than
the playwright wanted him to be. In a few of the cases above, I think, such
a criticism would be justified, and indeed has been made by older
commentators of the pre-ironic era, who accepted "at face value" what
appeared to be the playwright's obvious intention to enlist our sym-
pathies, and yet felt that he had failed to realize it. But the new ironic
readings do not admit the possibility of artistic failure, for they are
designed to vindicate the play (this being, as we noted, one of the general
characteristics of a "reading"). According to them, the playwright did
not fail in his intention to create a sympathetic character because he
really intended the opposite—to create a character who was antipathetic.
And in this "ironic" intention he of course succeeded.

Most ironic readings, to be sure, do not deny that the "face value" of
the play is against them, since it seems to call for a positive response to the
character they are attacking. A number of the quotations even warn us,
implicitly or explicitly, not to be (as one of them puts it) "taken in by
appearances"—by Valentine's pose as "an attractive, appealing male
lead," or Romeo's "charm," or Prospero's dazzling "halo," or those
"masks of innocence, chastity, purity, benevolence" worn by Pericles,
Imogen, Miranda, etc., or by the fact that Hector "appears to be a noble,
generous, worthy knight," or that Frankford may "appear to be virtuous," or that Alsemero has "a fair-seeming exterior." The ironic critic
gets around this difficulty by constructing a distinction between the

play's apparent and its real meaning. We found that this was also the fundamental strategy of the thematists (and was another general characteristic of a "reading"), although they did not develop it in the same way. Their distinction was produced by rejecting the apparent subject of the play (the particular actions represented there) and substituting a real subject of a very different order (the central thematic idea), while in the ironic distinction the critic rejects the play's apparent values, which have "taken in" all previous commentators and would make the character admirable, and replaces them with very different real values, discovered by him, which make the character despicable.

Therefore, even though both strategies create a new meaning for the play (and hence a new reading for the critic), the thematic approach does not require as radical a departure from the apparent meaning. It abstracts from our concrete experience of the characters, yet it can, and often does, leave our attitude toward them relatively intact; in many thematic readings of Shakespeare's tragedies, for instance, the protagonist still remains sympathetic. (Of course, there are other thematic readings—especially those of the homogeneous type, as we saw—which are also ironic.) But the ironic reading involves nothing less than a complete revaluation of our standard for judging the character in question, and so demands a drastic alteration or even inversion of our response to him, and consequently, in most cases, of the overall meaning and effect of the play. For this kind of irony usually turns out to be not only "hitherto unsuspected" but also "pervasive," since we will find that it cannot be applied to a major character without being extended to all the other characters who interact with him, and to all parts of the drama where they appear. In its ultimate implications, then, this trend would seem to pose an even more serious challenge than thematism to the critical enterprise. But we had better reserve our discussion of those implications until later and begin at the beginning by examining the principal strategies employed by the ironic readings to prove what was seen to be their basic (and common) thesis—that an apparently sympathetic character is really presented to us as antipathetic.

Character Assassination

The major strategy adopted in almost all of these readings is to build up a "case" against the targeted character by going through, or at least claiming to go through, his entire career within the play in such a way as to put

him in the worst possible light. A variety of techniques can be used for
this, most of which should be familiar to us since they are the same ones
directed against people in real life, where they have come to be known,
collectively, by a term that is equally appropriate to dramatic criticism—
"character assassination." They do not require any outright falsification
of the facts (although we occasionally find this), but merely the manipulation of them to serve the assassin's purpose. The simplest and most
obvious of these techniques, of course, is selectivity. The critic treats
only those facts which reflect (or can be made to reflect) unfavorably
upon the character, and silently passes over all the others. And since
every fact itself includes many aspects, he can exercise a further selection
by dealing only with those aspects that will submit to his negative thesis.
Moreover, the critic's selectivity makes it possible for him to alter the
proportions of the play by emphasizing relatively trivial facts at the
expense of the important ones which should determine our attitude
toward the character. And it enables him, finally, to take those facts out
of the context established by the playwright to guide our response to
them.

It is difficult to demonstrate this selectivity by brief quotations, since
these "cases" are usually built up at considerable length, and usually
depend upon the cumulative effect of many separate manipulations of
the evidence, some of them quite subtle. But the critic who denounced
Romeo as "something close to a mass murderer" has been good enough to
provide us with a highly condensed version of the technique, in which
the process of selection can easily be seen. He begins by announcing that
he will "examine the action of the play . . . with the forensic precision of
a public prosecutor," and then proceeds to summarize it as follows:

> We have here the supposed case of a well-known young man of
> prominent family who got a girlfriend into such serious trouble
> that her death and his own mother's resulted. He had in fact
> a prior binding commitment to another woman before switching
> to this victim. As a result of a clumsy intervention in a brawl
> this young man also precipitated the murder of one of his best
> friends, and then hastily took fatal revenge on the murderer
> without recourse to law and due process. At the same time as
> all this he was secretly entrapping the fourteen-year-old girl who
> was to be his victim; but he abandoned her shortly thereafter to
> flee his homeland, took up the purchase of illegal drugs (which
> ultimately caused his own death), and finally, while in the act of
> breaking the law, murdered another excellent young man, who
> had properly sought to apprehend him in the execution of an
> assault on private property verging on sacrilege, not to say

necrophilia. This wild youth was directly or indirectly responsible for six deaths and untold suffering.

The critic insists that these "facts" are "exactly true to Romeo's career
as Shakespeare chooses to present it"; yet it is perfectly clear that he
himself has chosen to present only a carefully screened portion of that
career. He selects events which can be used against Romeo and ignores
those which cannot—thus, to take just one obvious example, he never
tells us that Romeo married Juliet. And he selects the aspects of these events
which serve his purpose, as in his account of the fight outside the Capulet
tomb, which explains Paris's motivation but not Romeo's. His selection
also grossly distorts the play's proportions, especially in its transparent
attempt to minimize the importance given to the love of Romeo and
Juliet. And it removes Romeo from the dramatic context. Indeed, the
central element of that context—the family feud—is not even mentioned.
Thus, while each of the facts he cites may be "exactly true," the "case" he
constructs with them is very far from the truth.

The same must also be said of the cases worked out in the other ironic
readings we are considering, although few of them are quite so blatant in
their selectivity, or quite so frank in likening their procedure to that of
"a public prosecutor."[4] (Some come pretty close, however; the author of
the quotation on *Julius Caesar* informs us that his "study focuses on the
moral defects of Brutus.") But they all proceed in this way, since their
purpose is to develop the strongest possible indictment of the character,
and it is therefore obvious that their selection of evidence will be governed by that purpose. It should also be obvious that no person—real or
fictional—can ever be safe from this technique, because one can easily
use such selectivity to build up a completely unfair case against him, if
one wants to, regardless of the facts. That is what the term "character
assassination" means in public life.

This technique is basically unfair in another sense as well: it is not only
false to the dramatic facts (in their totality), but is also false to our
dramatic experience. For when we judge a character in a play we do not
adopt the stance of a prosecutor searching for evidence against him, or
even that of a disinterested juror trying to weigh the evidence. In this
respect drama is very different from life, since the events it presents to us
are not objective facts that we can judge impartially, but are deliberately
shaped by the dramatist to produce the response he desires. He determines
our conception of his characters (if he is successful, of course) in a great
variety of ways—by the manner in which he portrays their actions and
the alternatives he allows them in these actions, by the language he gives
to them, by the comments he has other characters make about them, by

the comparisons he invites us to draw between them, by the standard of judgment he establishes for us to apply to them, and by many other factors of this kind. These are all employed to create our overall impression of each character, with its specific moral and emotional coloring. But this is what the ironic technique of case-building ignores, as it must, since it is directed against the "face value" of the character, which is nothing else but that impression, and also against the traditional view of him, which is the collective impression he has produced upon countless viewers and readers over the years. Thus we know that the critic's summary of Romeo's career must be wrong, because the response which this play really has evoked in almost everyone, from the earliest recorded reactions down to the present, has been very sympathetic to Romeo, and has in fact enshrined him and "the fourteen-year-old girl who was to be his victim" in our cultural pantheon as types of true love. The critic's account, therefore, cannot be "exactly true to Romeo's career as Shakespeare chooses to present it," for if it were, there would be no way to explain that sympathetic response. The general problem which this kind of discrepancy poses (or should pose) for the ironic approach will be discussed later; the only point to be made here is that the selective technique used by this approach to build a case against a character is not controlled either by the actual facts of his career or by the actual impression it produces, and so can be deployed to attack *any* character, no matter how innocent he may be "in fact," or how favorably he may be presented by his creator.

Most of the other techniques used to develop these cases also depend upon some sort of selectivity, but a number of them are more specialized and so can be more easily isolated and illustrated with brief examples. Some, for instance, are specifically directed at one of the dramatic components which affect our view of the character—his actions, his language, and the comments made by others. Since the actions are usually the most important of these components, the ironic critic will attempt, not only to select those which he can employ to discredit the character (as we just saw), but also to treat those he does select in such a way as to make them seem as discreditable as possible. And one of the most common techniques for achieving this is to suppress or minimize the alternatives available to the character, because it is in terms of these alternatives that we judge any action, in drama or in life (the difference being, of course, that the dramatist himself sets up the alternatives for the character in order to determine our judgment).

A nice example of this technique can be seen in the case we were examining, where the critic condemns Romeo for having "precipitated the murder" of Mercutio through "a clumsy intervention in a brawl," which he later goes on to characterize as a "sentimental" and "naive attempt to prevent all brawling in the presence of his own amatory ecstasy." This may sound pretty bad, until we notice that he has been careful *not* to tell us what else Romeo could have done to stop the brawl, or what we would think of him if he had done nothing, for then our critic could as readily have accused him of cowardice, or a sentimental withdrawal from reality, or a callous indifference to bloodshed in the presence of his own amatory ecstasy. (Actually, his decision to intervene was the most honorable course open to him, and was carried out in the most effective way possible; the fact that it resulted in Mercutio's death does not—and surely was not meant to—diminish our regard for Romeo, since we feel that the responsibility for this rests with Tybalt and with "This day's black fate.") And the same tactic is used in an ironic reading of *Macbeth*, where the critic scores a point against Malcolm because in his final action the nobles who aided him "are immediately paid off by being made earls," but never explains how else he could have shown his gratitude, or how we would judge him if he showed none.

In these examples, the failure of the critics to deal with any alternative course of action is certainly understandable, since that alternative would leave the character just as vulnerable to their censure, if not more so. Sometimes, in fact, we find them censuring *both* of the courses available to the character. The critic quoted at the outset who is building a case against Theseus attacks him for not allowing Hermia to marry Lysander in act 1, because this shows him to be "tyrannically unmerciful," and then attacks him for allowing the marriage in act 4, because "there is no apparent reason for his impulsive shift from tyranny to charity," and "this impulsiveness reflects his unreasoned response." Similarly, the critic building a case against Frankford manages to fault him for not forgiving his wife when he discovers her adultery ("that Frankford does not forgive Anne immediately removes him from consideration as a *Christian* gentleman"), and then for forgiving her at the end ("the very fact that he forgives her now . . . shows conclusively the useless extremity of his revenge . . . however, I can see nothing in the last scene which indicates that Frankford realizes his mistake"). The critic building a case against Hector condemns him for adhering to the chivalric code in battle ("he is clearly putting his own reputation before the interests of Troy, for he rejects Troilus's urge to engage in genuine warfare, to fight to kill"), as well as for violating it ("he now pursues his foe without stopping to ascertain whether his opponent is of equal nobility with himself . . . the

vocabulary and feeling are those of the chase, not of chivalrous battle").[5]
And the critic who asserted that Hamlet was "a soul lost in damnable
error" finds one such error in his decision (at V.ii.197–210) to resign
himself to the workings of divine providence instead of acting upon the
"gain-giving in his heart . . . [which may] be the genuine 'divine' he should
be obeying," and another error in his tendency to act "impetuously" on
"decisions made on impulse" or "rash inspiration," instead of awaiting
God's will. Thus poor Hamlet is, quite literally, damned if he does and
damned if he doesn't.[6] But the plight of the other characters subjected to
this technique is much the same. They have no way to escape, for among
the alternatives open to them within the context of the play, there is no
action they can take that the critic cannot attack. In the battle he is waging
against the character, the outcome is never in doubt, because he makes
the rules. And the rules are always "heads I win, tails you lose."

Even actions that seem to exhibit obvious virtues can be turned against
a character in another version of this technique, where the critic argues,
again by ignoring the alternatives, that these virtues are excessive and
therefore really vices. The passage on *Richard III* quoted at the beginning
claims that the portrayal of Henry Tudor is ironic because "he simply
refers to God too many times," as if that in itself were blameworthy. And
the same charge has been levied against Henry V: one reading objects
that "instead of expressing gratitude to . . . his army of yeomen, Henry
characteristically attributes his triumph wholly to God. . . . His reiteration of it becomes psychologically suspicious in the highest degree"; and
another accuses him of "religious camouflage," since "he attributes
everything to God's arm alone, thereby minimizing (and hiding) the hand
which he and his soldiers had in the business." None of these critics goes
on to reveal what could be said against the character if he seemed less
pious, for to do so would cancel out the indictment (presumably he
would suffer the same fate as Othello, who is censured in two new ironic
readings for not mentioning God more often). And none of them considers the possibility that his piety may simply sound overstated to some
modern ears, since the indictment must assume that Shakespeare deliberately overstated it so that the audience would condemn it and the
character. Another critic has discovered a culpable excess of theological
reference and also of the virtue of marital trust in Frankford's protest (*A
Woman Killed with Kindness*, viii.74) that he would "hazard the dear
salvation of [his] soul" on his wife's innocence. Some may have taken
this statement as touching evidence of his love, but not our critic: "Aside
from his certain loss at this wager if he were in earnest, it is interesting that
he bandies about what a Christian gentleman would be loath to lose.

Christian terms are to Frankford little more than bywords with which to measure his faith in his wife." Yet he, like the others, neglects to tell us that the only alternative here—having Frankford show less faith in his wife—would certainly not make him more admirable.

Loving someone in excess of the limits set by the critic can also expose a character to charges of "idolatry," which various ironic readings have brought against Romeo, Juliet, Hamlet, Othello, and Mark Antony, among others. And rationality is another virtue one can have too much of; a critic quoted earlier finds in Brutus the "moral sickness inherent in the secular concept of virtue-reason's sufficiency," and another has found in Othello the "sin" of trusting in the "all-in-all sufficiency" of reason, which is supposed to equate him with Iago (although others have condemned both Brutus and Othello for allowing their passions to overcome their reason). And finally, when all else fails, the character can always be accused of "self-righteousness." We have already seen this epithet applied to Henry Tudor, Antonio, Desdemona, and Alsemero (in the variant form of "pharisaical") in the initial quotations, and many more characters have been disposed of in this way by other ironic critics, including Othello ("to wish to be judged, as he does [at I.ii.17–24], in terms of the law alone is also surely to tempt providence with self-righteousness") and, in one notable reading, the entire cast of *Measure for Measure*: "Angelo is self-righteous, so is Isabella, so is the Duke, so is everyone down to Abhorson the hangman." This last is an extreme case, to be sure, but it shows how easily the charge can be made against almost anyone. And that is equally true of the other charges employed by this technique to condemn the character's actions; it is the technique of fault-finding, and since the finder defines the faults, he will always find them.

Since our judgment of a character is affected not only by the actions he takes but also by the language he speaks, this dramatic component too can be used by the ironic critic in building up his case. The technique here, as might be expected, is to attack the character through his language by discovering in it revealing evidence of various vices. Any alleged defects in the style, for instance, can by this means be made to point to defects in the speaker. (They cannot be in the playwright, since one of the basic principles of the ironic approach, as we shall see, is that he is infallible, so that any apparent failings must be deliberate.) Thus one critic claims that the "artificial, jingling tone" of the Duke's soliloquy in *Measure for Measure*, III.ii.239–60, is meant to suggest the shallowness of his "easy moralizing" there; and another that the strained "Latinate diction and neologism" in Hector's address to Ajax (*Troilus and Cressida*, IV.v.119–38) serves the purpose of showing his "personal disorder" and "debasing" his motivation; and another that Prospero's expository speech to Miranda in the second scene of *The Tempest* is so "tedious" because it is supposed to indicate that he "is tediously striving to justify his actions to himself, to Miranda, and to the audience, and in so doing he metaphorically puts us to sleep. His oration . . . would automatically gain rather than command attention if it were indeed worthy."

An even more popular target of this technique is "commercial imagery," which seems to have become an incontestable proof of the speaker's baseness, and hence of the dramatist's ironical intention. At the end of *Macbeth*, a critic tells us, the victors' "pious exhortations cannot be taken at face value, as many readers and critics take them," because they reveal an "obsession with monetary values and payment" in such phrases as "paid a soldier's debt," "measur'd by his worth," "large expense of time," etc. Another says that Troilus's farewell to Cressida is "betrayed by the ubiquitous imagery of the market-place" in the lines, "We two that with so many thousand sighs / Did buy each other, must poorly sell ourselves / With the rude brevity and discharge of one" (IV.iv.38–40). And another would have us believe that "Claudio significantly betrays his materialism" in his question about Hero: "Can the world buy such a jewel?" (I.i.150). Such imagery is never difficult to find since it is embedded in every level of our language; indeed it would be interesting to see how many biblical passages (that "pearl of great price" in Matthew 13:46, to cite just one example) would turn out to be "ironical" by this line of reasoning.

The same could be said of another favorite target of this technique—the presence in a speech of "sensuous imagery" or any other evidence of the speaker's interest in matters physical, which is also supposed to demonstrate that he and his sentiments cannot be taken at face value. The critic who was so disturbed by Claudio's comparison of Hero to a jewel goes on to argue that his next statement, "In mine eye she is the sweetest lady that ever I look'd on," is "sinister language" and "an outrageous remark in Shakespeare's world, where love should look not with the eyes but with the mind." An ironic reading of *Twelfth Night* (quoted more fully in the next section) scores a similar point against Orsino because, after discovering that his page is really a woman in disguise, he asks her to "let me see thee in thy woman's weeds" (V.i.264); some of us might think this a natural enough request, at least in those days when the sexes dressed differently, but to our critic it is damning proof that Orsino's "concerns are with surface judgments." And there are additional examples in the passages assembled at the beginning of this chapter. Theseus's "first words suggest his reputation for unfaithfulness" since they include the awful word "desires" (he speaks to Hippolyta of "my desires" for "our nuptial hour"); according to the critic, "*desires* and lust were more likely to be equated in the Renaissance mind than were *desires* and love. Unless they were controlled, *desires* were the mark of the man given over completely to concupiscence." Juliet is supposed to reveal the "ugliness" and "rawness of her sexual hunger" in her epithalamium (III.ii.1–31), where she commits the same verbal sin of admitting that she looks forward to the consummation of her marriage. And the evidence that Maria in *The Family of Love* "fail[s] to exemplify human love at its highest level" is her similar speech on the "Elysiums sweet" experienced by "two united lovers" (II.iv.36–41), which, this critic tells us, "conjures up a suspicious vision of a lovers' paradise.... The Bower of Bliss comes to mind, along with Tasso's '*S'ei piace, ei lice*.' ... The pursuit of Love's Elysium ... may well signal moral, spiritual, and social disaster." One would be hard put to name any lovers in the Elizabethan drama, or anywhere else for that matter, whose language could escape the censure of this new ironic prudery.

The critic may also, of course, use his own language to build up his case by restating the character's actions and speeches in a loaded, denigrating vocabulary, as we have seen in a number of the quotations—Malcolm's thanes are "paid off" rather than rewarded, Frankford "bandies about" religious terms instead of using them, Romeo is not wooing Juliet but "entrapping" her, Henry has not waged war but "stolen the peace," and so on. But this tactic (which is also typical of "character assassination" in real life) is too obvious to require any further illustration.

Another dramatic component which often has a major influence in shaping our judgment of a character is the commentary made on him by others—especially by what have been called "choric characters," who, by virtue of their detachment or superior insight or status, seem to speak with a special authority. The technique used by the ironic critic to deal with these comments is very simple: if they are unfavorable (or can be made to sound unfavorable) to the character, he includes them in the case he is building; and if they are favorable, he either ignores them or else explains them away, usually by insisting that the speaker must be mistaken. A clear example of the first tactic is provided, again, by the author of that capsule case against Romeo, for in his later defense of this case he cites Friar Laurence for support on two occasions when he chides the young lover (II.iii.65–80, II.vi.9–11), but never mentions any of the Friar's sympathetic remarks, or his final summary of events, which contains not one word of criticism of "true Romeo" (V.iii.259). And the second tactic can be seen in the passage on *Antony and Cleopatra* quoted at the outset. This reading frequently relies upon Enobarbus's comments to make its case against Antony, since, we are told, "what he says is so often right—not merely intelligent, but accurate too. He usually speaks, in fact, with the voice of the play." Yet when we come to his death scene (IV.vi), where he recognizes how he had misjudged Antony, we are suddenly warned that "we should beware" of accepting his praise of Antony here, because "even he dies deceived."

It turns out, of course, that none of the choric figures in these plays can be trusted, since their final judgment of the character under attack never seems to agree with that of the ironic reading, and hence must not be taken at face value; thus we find one of these critics explaining that his interpretations "make largely ironic the opinions of even the most reliable *raisonneur*." And the same tactic will be deployed against the opinions of most of the other people in the play, because they also fail to condemn the character who is the critic's target and therefore also have to be mistaken, as we saw in the initial quotations: "Everyone (except Enobarbus) is a dupe of Antony's reputation," according to the critic just cited; and Hector's chivalric "appearance," another informed us, "blinds the other characters in the play"; and another acknowledged that "everyone in the play admires or loves" the despicable Philaster (which leads him to argue that their "chorus of undying devotion to Philaster" should "make us question the values of almost everyone in the play"). But this point will be taken up again in the next section, when we consider how these readings cope with the crucial commentary at the end of the action.

Finally, if there is an actual chorus or prologue or epilogue in the play, it too must be mistaken, since, like the choric characters, it never shares the viewpoint of the ironic reading (for if it did, the reading would not be ironic). One might suppose that these extradramatic passages in *Romeo and Juliet* and *Henry V*, for instance, with their very explicit statements of sympathy or admiration for the titular characters (the "piteous overthrows" of "a pair of star-cross'd lovers," "the mirror of all Christian kings," "This Star of England," etc.), should present a problem to these critics, but that would be to underestimate the power of this technique to demolish any commentary that stands in its way. One study of *Romeo and Juliet* settles the matter by asserting that "the perspective of the Prologues . . . represents only the limited vision of Verona's citizenry"; and a study of *Henry V* argues, similarly, that the Chorus is "an abstract of average public opinion" through which "the playwright gives us the popular idea of his hero," which is the opposite of his own idea. But neither of them explains just how we are to make this identification, or why Shakespeare did not make it for us.[7]

Occasionally another tactic will be adopted to explain away a chorus or prologue: instead of transforming it into one more deceived or blinded character, the critic can transform the meaning of its speeches by discovering that they are not supposed to be taken literally. He may find, for instance, that they make their point so strongly that they cannot be believed (another case of too much of a good thing): thus one study claims "the exaggerated gloom of the prologue" to *Antonio's Revenge* is meant to indicate that neither it nor the play should be accepted at face value. (Another critic discounts Anne Frankford's direct address to the audience in *A Woman Killed with Kindness*, xiii.141–44—which certainly seems to function as a choric statement, and directly contradicts his own reading—because it is "such blatant moralizing.") Or the speeches may be treated as a kind of code which must be deciphered to yield its real (i.e., desired) message, as one critic has done with a portion of the Prologue to *Henry V*:

> But pardon, gentles all,
> The flat unraised spirits that hath dar'd
> On this unworthy scaffold to bring forth
> So great an object....
> O, pardon! since a crooked figure may
> Attest in little place a million,
> And let us, ciphers to this great accompt,
> On your imaginary forces work.
>
> [ll. 8–11, 15–18]

According to him, "the real point" of this passage, conveyed through a "lurking dramatic irony" suitably "veiled under choral mask," is "not the inadequacy of the theater (though that is its surface meaning), but rather the likeness of Henry's campaign to a staged play," which carries "an underside of intimation that this warrior may be a crook, his followers moral zeros, and their power largely imaginary, indeed scaffold-bound." This tactic, then, differs from the first in that it regards the chorus or prologue, not as another character who is mistaken, but as the playwright's spokesman who knows the truth, yet prefers (for reasons to be examined later) to reveal it in a very indirect manner. Therefore the two tactics would seem to be incompatible, although one ironic reading of *Romeo and Juliet* allows us a choice between them: "the 'star-cross'd' of the Prologue should be taken in something other than a literal sense, or, better, attributed to the Chorus, not to the poet." Either way, any way, apparently, will do, so long as it is a way to get around the commentary.

The other persons in the play may affect our view of a character not only when they comment upon him, but also when we compare them with him, since our judgment of him is necessarily relative to the "world" in which he exists. These comparisons, then, constitute another important dramatic component which the ironic critics can manipulate to make their case against a character, and they frequently do so by asserting that he has been equated or analogized to someone in the cast whom we are clearly not meant to admire. This might be called the technique of odious comparisons, which is illustrated in a number of the quotations at the beginning of the chapter: Henry V is equated in this way to Bardolph and Pistol, Hamlet to Claudius, Duke Vincentio to Angelo, Prospero to Sycorax, Maria to Mistresses Glister and Purge ("the two more mature wives"), Philaster to the King and Pharamond, Giovanni to Brachiano and Francisco, Alsemero to Deflores. And similar equations have been found between Antonio and Shylock, Brutus and the other conspirators, Hector and Achilles, Othello and Iago, Desdemona and Bianca, Malcolm and Macbeth, the Duchess of Malfi and Julia, Lovewit and the dupes, and so on. We must understand that in each of these examples the critic's point is not merely that he can see the resemblance (which is all that is claimed, one hopes, for the comparison of Valentine to Milton's Satan and of Romeo to Richard III in the initial quotations),[8] but that it has been built into the play by the dramatist, who is deliberately equating down in order to put down. The problem, of course, is that the characters joined by these alleged equations would seem to be sharply differentiated on moral grounds throughout the action and especially in the ending, so that the critic is faced with the task of demonstrating that the obvious differences between them are only apparent or superficial and conceal a more basic similarity.

The task is not very difficult, however, since he has available for this purpose two foolproof tactics. One is to compile a list of parallels between the characters, particular details of action or language or situation which they share and which are supposed to establish their essential likeness. The critic quoted at the outset proves that *The Tempest* "deliberately parallels" Prospero and Sycorax because "each is exiled with an only child; each has exerted influence on the uninhabited island for twelve carefully specified years; each has nurtured offspring in ignorance," etc., and so can conclude that the difference between them "is one of degree not kind." But another critic goes him one better (i.e., one worse) by proving that Prospero is equated with Caliban because of the "salient similarities" in their plans: Caliban's "calls for deposing through murder the present ruler [Prospero], installing a new one [Stephano] in his place, and marrying the new ruler to Miranda"; and Prospero's "appears to have deposed Alonso, set Ferdinand up in his place, and approved of the marriage of the new king to Miranda." The critic who claimed that Philaster is made "analogous" to the King and Pharamond gives as his evidence the fact that all three are "princes" and use "comparably uncontrolled language." Another critic finds a number of these parallels linking Antonio to Shylock: both are "merchants," both practice "economic abstinence," both "avoid the carnal music of this world," and both "hazard all" they have. Another argues that Malcolm is equated with Macbeth at the end of the play because, when the nobles hail him as king of Scotland, we cannot "keep the witches' 'All hail, Macbeth, that shall be king hereafter!' from ringing in our ears." And another tells us there is

> a strange parallel between the wooing-scene, where the Duchess hides Cariola behind the arras and then launches into the declaration of her love, and the scene in V.ii where Julia, the rank whore, proclaims her passion for Bosola and then hides him in her cabinet while she extorts a confession of guilt from the Cardinal: in both cases, a woman's frank avowal; in both, a hidden witness; in both, a woman's triumph leading to her destruction. It is difficult to resist the idea that Julia is meant to provide a comment on the behaviour of the Duchess: they are sisters, Webster hints, in their passions and in their consequent actions.

The trouble with this tactic is that it rests upon two assumptions which never seem to be discussed or even stated, and which are clearly false. It assumes, in the first place, that these lists of parallels will necessarily, in themselves, demonstrate a significant relationship between characters—that is, a relationship intended by the playwright. They will not, since we could easily draw up such a list for any pair of characters by this method. The method itself, which I call Fluellenism, is to be examined in the appendix, where we will see how it can be used to equate any two objects in the universe, by searching through all the facts about them and seizing upon those that represent similarities, regardless of their importance, while ignoring all the rest. The Fluellenist may also bend the facts a little to produce the similarities, as in some of our examples. Prospero never plans to depose Alonso and set Ferdinand up in his place, but only "appears to have" done so, according to this critic, since "he has separated Ferdinand from his father, and Ferdinand believes that his father is dead and he is king of Naples." The only evidence that Antonio "avoid[s] the carnal music of this world" turns out to be his line urging Gratiano to board ship—"No masque to-night. The wind is come about" (II.vi.64). And Julia's "hidden witness," unlike the Duchess's, is not someone she has concealed to observe her wooing a man, but is the man himself, whom she conceals after the wooing to observe an entirely different action. Yet, even if all the parallels were accurately stated, they would prove nothing unless it can also be shown that the playwright made them significant, by dramatic emphasis or juxtaposition or commentary or any of the other devices at his disposal.

Moreover, even if it could be shown that the playwright intended to establish a significant relationship between the characters through those parallels, that still does not require us to accept the second assumption of this tactic, which holds that any such relationship will necessarily, in itself, result in an equation between the characters which debases the more admirable one to the level of the less admirable. That assumption is clearly unjustified, because relations of this sort may also be employed to *contrast* two characters; indeed, the best way to set up such a contrast is to make them comparable by means of these parallels. And it seems evident that this is the effect produced by the alleged equations cited above, whenever they do constitute a significant relationship. If the nobles' salute to Malcolm really causes the witches' salute to Macbeth to ring in our ears, then this must remind us of the striking difference between the initial situation, where sinister creatures hail as king a man who has no legal right to the throne and must commit a horrible crime to attain it, and the final situation, where the legitimate king is acclaimed by his loyal subjects. And if we do compare the two wooing scenes in *The Duchess of Malfi*, then we must see the very sharp opposition between the wooers: the first is a chaste widow, while the second is a flagrant adultress; the first is moved by genuine devotion to a man she has grown to love and respect after a long association, while the second is seized with a sudden passion for a man she has just met; the object of the first is matrimony, while the second seeks only "to kill my longing" by immediate sexual gratification; the first is embarrassed because her superior rank requires her to make the advances, while the second scorns "this nice modesty in ladies" and boasts of her aggressiveness.[9] In such comparisons, then, the result is exactly the reverse of that claimed by the ironic critics—the parallels between the characters are only superficial and so serve to emphasize the much more basic contrast, thus making the "apparently" admirable character appear not less but more admirable to us.

Before moving on we should take another look at the peculiar kind of parallel implied in this assertion that the Duchess of Malfi and "the rank whore" Julia "are sisters," which really cannot be allowed to pass without comment in these days of raised consciousness, especially since it also crops up in two of the readings quoted at the outset. The critic who uncovered "the whore within" Desdemona does so by means of the same parallel: "The presence of Bianca in the play suggests that all women are sisters. Desdemona . . . shrinks from the reality of the whore within her, the potential whore which exists within all women." And since no other reason is given by the critic who predicted that Maria is "doomed to become a sharp tongued and deceitful female like the two more mature wives presented in the play," despite the fact that she is very obviously and very tediously contrasted with them throughout the action, it can only be because she too is guilty of femaleness. The contention in each case, we must remember, is not merely that these characters should be compared because they are women (which would be true in many plays where they are placed in similar situations), but that they should be equated because of this, and equated *down*. Like the Colonel's Lady and Judy O'Grady, their subcutaneous sisterhood is always supposed to assimilate the best of them to the level of the worst, never the other way around. The argument, therefore, is really just another example of the same basic fallacy which was seen to underlie every use of this first tactic, only here it is combined with a second fallacy unique to the illogical masculine mind (all three critics, of course, are men). No one has yet claimed that we must regard Duncan as Macbeth's brother because both are male, and must therefore see in him the reality of the potential murderer and tyrant which exists within all men.

The second tactic used to establish these odious comparisons proceeds in the opposite direction from the first. Instead of descending to a number of particular details or parallels which the two characters are supposed to share, it ascends to a single general abstraction which they are both supposed to exemplify. That abstraction, of course, is our old friend, the "central theme." Often the critic will try to subsume all or most of the other characters of the play under the same abstraction, in order to produce what we called a homogeneous thematic structure. And in the discussion of this structure we noted that it had a special affinity to the ironic approach, since the climb up to the central theme must homogenize the more admirable characters down to the "lowest common denominator" embracing the remainder of the cast, which will have to be something unpleasant.

This result can be seen in the various homogeneous readings of *Mea-*

sure for Measure. The one quoted at the beginning claims that the Duke is "another Angelo" because they both represent "the whole pretence of 'seeming' that Shakespeare attacked" here, and that encompasses—so far as one can tell from the rest of this critic's account—everyone else in the play except Barnardine and Lucio;[10] and another reading states that all of the characters but Barnardine are "seemers." A third tells us that the play "deals with characters who are consumed with self, who have insulated themselves from the world," which is said to cover the Duke, Angelo, Isabella, Mariana, Barnardine, and "even Abhorson"; and a fourth, that they all "reflect the central theme" of the "ridiculousness" of "man, proud man" (this is the one which accused everybody of self-righteousness). The initial quotation on *Troilus and Cressida* is taken from a homogeneous reading of that play, cited in chapter 2, which uses its central theme ("the mistaken conception of honor") to equate Hector with the baser characters, and the Trojans with the Greeks; and in each of the other studies cited there which place these two warring camps under one thematic umbrella,[11] he must suffer the same fate. And this also happens to Brutus in homogeneous readings of his play—one critic, for example, argues for "the centrality of the theme of human irrationality" or "blind folly which pervades *Julius Caesar*" and which therefore joins Brutus with the other "irrational" Romans; while another makes him part of "the pattern of error and misjudgment which is basic to the dramatic structure, involving all the major characters"— namely, "the overthrow of reason and judgment by the passions."

This debasement of the more admirable characters is an inevitable result of the homogeneous thematic structure, although it need not be the critic's main purpose. Most of those who employ the structure seem to be primarily interested in demonstrating the play's "thematic unity," as we found in the preceding chapter, but others are quite explicit about its use as an ironic tactic. The first critic of *Julius Caesar* quoted above says that his interpretation "enhances an anti-heroic reading of the play" (that is, of Brutus); and the second opposes earlier commentators who "isolate the tragedy of Brutus from the rest of the play, instead of relating it" to that "pattern of error and misjudgment," which means reducing him to the same level as "all the major characters." Many more of these readings are also clearly directed toward setting up an odious comparison in order to bring down a sympathetic character; and even when that is not their stated intention, it is their actual effect.

The basic objection to this tactic is that, like the first, it proves nothing because it can prove anything. For we saw in our discussion of thematism that one can always discover some abstraction which will encompass any group of characters, no matter how diverse they may be (just as one can always discover Fluellenist "parallels" between them). Indeed the same group can be accommodated under a number of very different abstractions of this sort, as the above examples show. But in addition to this objection, which applies to the homogeneous thematic structure in general, there is another related more specifically to its ironic use. To force everyone under the single theme, it must dissolve the moral distinctions established by the dramatist, which is always done at the expense of the more admirable or sympathetic characters—Duke Vincentio becomes another Angelo, Hector is no better than Achilles, and Brutus descends to the level of the ignoblest Roman of them all. For these characters turn out to be "apparent exceptions" to the thematic homogeneity, like the similar cases discussed in chapter 2, and in order to prove that their exceptionality is merely apparent, the critic must then attack them by means of the other techniques we have been examining—principally, as might be expected, by his selectivity. He will choose only those facts about the character which can be made to fit the debasing theme, and through these choices will distort the proportions of the character's portrayal and remove him from the context in which he is presented. Actually, the process of thematic abstraction is itself a form of selectivity that inevitably destroys this context: by treating Brutus's decision to join the conspiracy as another example of the generalized "overthrow of reason and judgment by the passions," the abstractor in effect eliminates the particular considerations which individualize this action and so determine its precise meaning in the play. Thus this last technique to be considered brings us back to the first and most basic one, which underlies the others.

These certainly do not exhaust all of the techniques used in the strategy of "character assassination," but they include the most important, I believe, and should be enough to demonstrate how easy it is to build a case against any character in any play, if that is what one wants to do. For this strategy, we found, is not governed by the overall impression of the character which the play creates and we experience. Instead, it deliberately sets out to oppose that impression by launching a full-scale assault upon the character, like the critic who proceeds against Romeo "with the forensic precision of a public prosecutor," or the one whose "study focuses on the moral defects of Brutus," or the author of the initial quotation on *Troilus and Cressida*, who begins by acknowledging that "with Hector the appearance may well blind us to the reality," and then moves on to the attack: "yet when we examine Hector's behavior closely and critically it appears that . . . there are grave flaws in [his] chivalry." In this strategy the critic need not ask why we are blinded by the favorable "appearance" of the character, still less why the playwright should have wished to blind us (a question to be considered later); all he need do is scrutinize the character "closely and critically"—that is, by applying the techniques we have just surveyed—in search of "flaws." And he will be sure to find them, for no character can withstand such a hostile scrutiny. But then, no character was meant to.

Refuting the Ending

A second fundamental strategy of the ironic approach is directed not at the character as such but at the ending of the play, although its effect is also to discredit the character. In almost any approach to interpretation the ending takes on a special importance, because it presents the outcome of the characters' careers as well as the play's ultimate judgment upon them, and so works retroactively to qualify our earlier and more tentative reactions, while shaping the indelible final impression we carry away with us. And for that reason it becomes a major problem to the ironic readings, since in each of the plays we have considered, the concluding action and the concluding judgment seem to call for a very favorable response to the character in question, which would directly contradict the case that the critic has been building against him. A few of these critics try to get around this by ignoring the ending, and a few others try to have it both ways by claiming that the character undergoes a radical reformation late in the play, so that they can attack his "face value" during most of the action, as their case requires, and then accept it at the end (the trouble here is that the playwright never seems to provide us with any clear indication of this reformation or of the complete change in his mode of presentation which is supposed to accompany it). But the great majority of them confront the problem head-on by attempting to prove that the ending itself, like the portrayal of the character up to that point, is "ironic."

We may need to be reminded that they are not referring to the old-fashioned "dramatic irony" involved in the reversal of a character's situation and expectations, for everyone recognizes that many plays of the period end ironically in this sense. They are arguing, rather, that the ending is ironical because it is really intended to mean something quite different from—often the opposite of—what it appears to mean, and what it has been taken to mean up to now. That is why I call their strategy a "refutation" of the ending; the term may not be exactly neutral, but it does accurately describe their goal. They are trying to disprove the conclusion of the play, to persuade us that its author did not want the audience to believe it.

Of course, these ironic readings have also been trying to disprove the rest of the play, as we saw, in constructing their case against the character, so that their attack on him is ultimately not separable from their attack on the ending. Moreover, the techniques employed in constructing that case can be applied at any point in the play, including the ending (hence a few of the examples cited in the preceding section will reappear here), and conversely, some techniques for refuting the ending are not limited to the ending itself. But so long as that is recognized, I think it will be useful to treat this refutation as a distinct critical strategy, because of its crucial importance to the ironic approach. We will begin, then, with some typical passages, published since 1968, which show how three of these critics deal with the endings of three very different plays. Although a few details have been omitted, I have tried to retain all the major points made in each argument, so that we can see what a complete refutation looks like before descending to more fragmentary quotations illustrating the particular techniques.

> The drama ends also with Capulet and Montague burying their
> feud with a handshake. This gesture is noble; yet its motive may
> be little more than their instinctual desire for a self-rehabilitation
> in the public eye. . . . And there is an unmistakable undertone of
> rivalry, with a tinge even of commercialism, as the fathers con-
> tend in promising statues of gold in honor of their dead chil-
> dren. . . . Although Verona achieves a temporary peace through
> the "Poor sacrifices" it makes, we may doubt that these will suffice
> for a long-lasting peace. (Bandello in his account remarks that
> the peace did not last any great while afterwards.) There has
> been attained, as the play's Prologue promised, a burying of
> strife—but not of the human proclivity to one-up-manship. It
> is the Earthly City's peace, useful for its moment of civil agree-
> ment, yet far short of a heavenly peace, which St. Augustine had
> described as a "most harmonious fellowship in the enjoyment
> of God and of one another in God."

> A motif of implicit thematic importance throughout [is] entrap-
> ment. . . . [At the end] Viola's rescuer and Antonio . . . are locked
> forever in the limbo of indefinite incarceration. . . . Orsino's fail-
> ure to grant Antonio pardon is . . . conspicuous. . . . Such sug-
> gestions of entrapment qualify the happiness of the resolution.
> In a world so marked by constriction, marriage may also appear
> as another form of imprisonment, particularly when it is entered

upon in such haste and for such foolish reasons . . . . To the end
[Orsino's] concerns are with surface judgments and self-generated
images of the loved one: before recognizing Viola as a woman he
must see her in feminine dress . . . . Perhaps as testimony to the
precariousness of this union, to the violence that can at any
moment transform Orsino's totalitarian commitment from love to
hate, is the figure of Antonio, whose faithful, vigorous love has
not, like Viola's, been at last rewarded by Orsino's grace. Antonio's fate, we know, can become hers.

Transmutation ends for everyone except, ironically, Lovewit . . . .
If we look at him within the context of the theme of character
transmutation, his appearance at the end of the play acquires new
significance . . . . His new possessions are not unmixed blessings.
First, the petty cash, pots, and pans may not even cover the cost
of cleaning his house; second, the services of Face must now be
constantly suspected and scrutinized, or the clever servant will set
himself up in some new business; and, third, marriage into the
Kastril family (as Kastril's stupidity and his sister's name imply)
is no great achievement. In fact, Lovewit's apparent success may
be interpreted as the final attempt at transmutation in the play.
The circumstances of his life have all changed, and now he must
endure them . . . . Every character in Jonson's play is an alchemist;
but no one, including Lovewit, actually succeeds in transmuting
himself.

It should be evident that each of these critics is waging a kind of war
against the ending on two different fronts: on the level of *plot*, he attacks
its termination of the action of the play, and on the level of *effect*, he
attacks its judgment of that action. And on both, he uses the same basic
strategy by trying to show that the "conclusiveness" of the ending, as a
termination and as a judgment, is only apparent and not real, that it was
not meant to be taken at face value. Although we will find that these two
lines of attack are closely related in most ironic readings, it will be more
convenient to take them up separately, beginning with the refutation of
the terminality of the ending. Now it must be admitted that all dramatic
conclusions are vulnerable on this front, since there are always some
survivors, even in the goriest tragedies, and in their later lives it is always
possible that they will do or suffer something that upsets the resolution
achieved in the play—Rosalind may fall in love with Oliver, Fortinbras
may become a vicious tyrant,[12] and so forth. But if we are interpreting
the author's conception of that resolution—as all the refutations claim to
do—then these future possibilities are obviously irrelevant unless he

intended to have them enter into the audience's final response, and so we must examine the techniques used by the critics to demonstrate such an intention.

The most common technique seeks to undermine some essential component of the resolution, by claiming that the author did not wish us to accept it at face value—that is, to accept it as permanent. If the resolution depends on the repentance or reform of a character, the refuters will try to prove that he is not really sincere. Some of them point us to possible ulterior motives, which are never very difficult to find if one looks hard enough: thus the first passage above suggests that Montague and Capulet are not moved by grief and guilt at the deaths of their children, but only by a concern for the "public eye"; and another critic asserts that in *Measure for Measure* "Angelo's repentance is insincere, for he fears his 'dread' lord's omniscience"; and the same kind of argument has also been directed against Bertram's reform at the end of *All's Well That Ends Well*. Other refuters tell us that if we believe the character there must be something wrong with our sense of humor—

> Claudio's penance [in *Much Ado*], which strikes modern readers as silly in the extreme, I take to be a further illustration of his and his society's superficiality. Readers who are amused by it are, I think, reacting as Shakespeare hoped they would—comically.

or with our savoir faire—

> It would be *simpliste* to regard this statement of total passivity [Kate's closing speech on wifely obedience] at its face value, and as a prognosis. The open end of *The Taming of the Shrew* is Katherina's mind, undisclosed in soliloquy.

One thing they cannot do, however, is cite any statement by any character in the play that supports their attack, for in each of these examples everybody who comments on the reformation—including the play's authority figure, where there is one—accepts it unquestioningly "at its face value." And this is crucial, because it must be remembered that these critics are not claiming that the dramatist failed to convince us of the character's sincerity (which would, I think, be a legitimate objection in some cases), but that he wanted to convince us of his insincerity. To be consistent, therefore, they would have to go on to show that he also wanted to convince us that these other characters who accept the reformation either are very insensitive or else have ulterior motives of their own. Some of them in fact take this further step:

> The Duke . . . is very ready to accept this attitude as evidence of
> true repentance. If Angelo is genuinely penitent, then the Duke's
> plot has been in some measure justified, for Angelo has been
> saved from his soul-destroying pride, but the audience, knowing
> what it does about Angelo, is less likely than the Duke to be
> convinced. The Duke, like all the other characters, believes what
> he most wants to believe.

His argument, it will be noted, ends up by making everyone in the
drama untrustworthy, which we will find to be the logical outcome
of any attempt to refute the ending (and of the ironic approach in
general), although many of the refuters do not go so far, at least so
explicitly. But whether they do or not, it seems to me that they are still
faced with an even more basic problem: since the validity of last-act
reformations was a well-established dramatic convention of the period,
why, if the playwright wished to deviate from it, did he not take the
simple precaution of allowing someone in the play to make this clear,
instead of running the obvious risk of having his meaning misunderstood, as it certainly has been (if these critics are right) in all of these
cases by almost all viewers and readers down to the advent of the new
readings?

   Another application of this same technique, exemplified in the passage
on *Twelfth Night*, is to question the future stability of the marriages
arranged in the resolution (which can involve the preceding point, whenever the success of a marriage depends upon someone's reform). In that
passage the critic forecasts a grim future for Viola's marriage, and apparently also for Olivia's; and we have seen similar predictions for
Gerardine's marriage to Maria in a quotation at the beginning of this
chapter (his expectations "would seem to be hopelessly optimistic if not
thoroughly ironic"), and for all the marriages of *Measure for Measure* in
a reading summarized in chapter 2 ("the balance is precarious. . . . We
cannot assert that there is any great likelihood that the married couples
will live happily ever after"). Another refuter states that at the end
of *All's Well That Ends Well* "there's no certainty that Bertram and
Helena live happily ever after. . . . Whether Bertram did in fact love her
dearly ever is something which is surely made questionable by all we
know of him." According to another, in the closing scene of *The Merchant of Venice* "we are being prompted to see" that the three marriages
it seems to be celebrating may be "followed by the misfortunes of
fickleness or betrayal," while another finds that it "encourage[s] us to
question . . . the quality of love in Belmont." And an ironic reading of
As You Like It claims that "the play extends beyond the curtain," which

casts doubt upon all four of the marriages in its "ambiguous, question-begging conclusion": "Virtually all the relationships manifest a sense of unease, of latent or open hostility. There is little true accord in Arden, prior to the final scene; and the audience is entitled, if it wishes, to its reservations even then."

The justification for these forebodings usually boils down to a complaint that the bride and groom are not properly matched, or that their attachment is something less than perfect love. (The evidence for the latter charge may turn out to be their interest in the physical side of matrimony, as noted earlier; some refuters even clutch at the bawdy jokes, which ritually accompanied the wedding festivities, as an indication of future infidelity.) But while this is often true enough, it is quite beside the point. The issue here is not whether we are to regard the marriage as ideal, but whether we are to regard it as "terminal" in our response to the conclusion. And the contention of these critics, again, is not that the dramatist failed to convince us it was terminal, but that he wished to convince us it was not. Therefore this refutation of the ending is open to the same fundamental objection as the preceding one, because such marriages were firmly established as a final comic solution by one of the oldest and most potent of dramatic conventions, so that if the author really intended to work against our conventional reaction and make us doubt the permanence of the marriage, we would expect him, unless he were hopelessly incompetent, to take special pains to emphasize this in the closing dialogue. But instead we find that, as with the reformations, all of these marriages are accepted as final by all of the characters who comment on them at the end, and no one raises any questions about their future. (The objection would apply still more strongly, I believe, to a special variant of this attack which has recently been deployed against the ending of *Measure for Measure* by some critics, who argue that the marriage of the Duke to Isabella may not even take place, since she never actually accepts his proposal and therefore could reject it.[13] But in this case the comic convention of marital resolutions—reinforced here by the other two marriages arranged at the same time—plus the Duke's authority, both dramatic and political, to manage this resolution, plus the proverbial assumption that "silence gives consent,"[14] all point so unmistakably to her acceptance that, if Shakespeare had intended us to think otherwise, he would surely have indicated this.)

A third application of this same technique is to question the future stability of the reconciliations or final settlements that perform a function analogous to the marriages (sometimes in conjunction with them) in many dramatic resolutions of the period. It may be seen in two of the passages, where we are warned that the trouble is not really over either for Verona or for Lovewit's household ("we may doubt that these will suffice for a long-lasting peace"; "the services of Face must now be constantly suspected"), and also in the reading cited earlier which equates Malcolm with Macbeth, since it tells us that, because of this equation, his accession is "subversively ominous" and "we are ready for the cycle to begin again." But probably the best known and most sweeping attack of this kind was mounted against the endings of Shakespeare's history plays by a critic who found that they dramatize a "Grand Mechanism" which, by its very nature, permitted no conclusive conclusions:

> In each of the Histories the legitimate ruler drags behind him a long chain of crimes. . . . From banishment a young prince returns—the son, grandson, or brother of those murdered—to defend the violated law. The rejected lords gather round him; he personifies the hope for a new order and justice. But every step to power continues to be marked by murder, violence, treachery. And so when the new prince finds himself near the throne, he drags behind him a chain of crimes as long as that of the until now legitimate ruler. When he assumes the crown, he will be just as hated as his predecessor. He has killed enemies, now he will kill former allies. And a new pretender appears in the name of violated justice. The wheel has turned full circle.

He found that this scheme was clearest in *King John, Richard II*, and *Richard III*, and least clear in *Henry V*, but a number of other refuters have been much less merciful to the ending of that play, which they claim is really the beginning of disaster. According to one of them, "there is no warrant for even the chastened and dubious hope at the end, '*May* our oaths well-kept and prosperous be,' or need for the epilogue that reminds us that this glorious episode of the Star of England was only—and inevitably—the prelude to the Wars of the Roses." Another extends this argument to include Henry's marriage to Katherine, which is also supposed to nullify the triumphant conclusion because of its part in what he calls "the grim path from Agincourt to Tewksbury"; "The results of the marriage are to be mad Henry VI, under whom ill-got France was lost, and the Wars of the Roses. From its inception the marriage was as barren of good issue as was Henry V's French war." And many more examples could be quoted, for the ending of this play has become one of the favorite targets of the refuters.

To justify these unhappy predictions the critic may assert—as in the attacks on the reformations and marriages—that the parties to the settlement have hidden ulterior motives or fall short of some ideal (Montague and Capulet, Face, Malcolm); but if the play is based upon history or myth or a story, he can also argue, as we just saw, that its final settlement is negated by later events in the source. The trouble with this argument, however, is that it leaves out the dramatist. For while such a source may have narrowed his options (if it was well known), this does not alter our basic contention that it was up to him, in shaping the audience's response to his conclusion, to decide whether or not he wished them to consider these later events, and up to the critic to take note of his decision. But that is what the refuters fail to do. The author of the passage on *Romeo and Juliet* seems to think he can undercut the reconciliation of the feuding families by pointing to its subsequent breakdown in Bandello's account; but even if we could be sure that the audience had read Bandello, this future "fact" would still be irrelevant since there is no hint of it in Shakespeare's resolution. Similarly, the reading of *A Midsummer Night's Dream* quoted at the beginning of the chapter would have us believe that the fairies' final blessing is "ironic" because it is "a ghastly reminder of the fate of the issue of [Theseus's] bride bed"—namely, Hippolytus, who was to meet such a tragic death. This critic insists that "for an audience aware of the remainder of Theseus' history, the play has not ended"; but we must insist that the remainder of Theseus's history was not meant to affect our view of the ending because the playwright has not done anything there to make us aware of it (if he had, this critic would not be the first to notice that "ghastly reminder"). And the same objection would apply to another critic who attempts to cancel out the Tudor settlement at the end of *Richard III* by noting, "that the Tudor myth was myth indeed is attested by the continuance of the Wars of the Roses, which Henry Tudor was forced to suppress by execution." Such evidence is wholly external to the play and so should be to our final response, if that response is governed by the author's intention. Indeed, the fact that the author omitted events appearing in his source can in itself be a valuable clue to his intention, since there must have been some reason why he chose to do so. (Thus, if we knew that Shakespeare used Bandello's account, we could reasonably infer that he changed it in order to make the reconciliation seem *more* permanent.) But this kind of insight into the artistic process, which has long been regarded as one of the principal contributions of "source studies," disappears in the curious reverse logic of the refuters.[15]

In *Henry V*, to be sure, there is one lonely piece of internal evidence—a single line in the Epilogue—which does point to those future disasters, and which has therefore been seized upon by all of these critics who wish us to see beyond the ending. But the context here makes it perfectly clear that the disasters are not to be blamed upon Henry (unless he can be blamed for dying too soon), and in no way diminish his "glory":

> Thus far, with rough and all-unable pen,
> Our bending author hath pursu'd the story,
> In little room confining mighty men,
> Mangling by starts the full course of their glory.
> Small time; but in that small, most greatly lived
> This Star of England. Fortune made his sword;
> By which the world's best garden he achieved,
> And of it left his son imperial lord.
> Henry the Sixth, in infant bands crown'd King
> Of France and England, did this king succeed;
> Whose state so many had the managing
> That they lost France and made his England bleed;
> Which oft our stage hath shown. . . .

If he had really intended to project the ending of this play onto "the grim path from Agincourt to Tewksbury," Shakespeare (or any playwright of the most minimal competence) could surely have done much better than that.[16] In fact he has done much better, for in those endings where the settlement is to be regarded as ephemeral, he gives us some very clear indication of this (such as Richard's soliloquy in the penultimate scene of *Henry VI, Part III*), which is why we do not need any new ironic readings to refute them. It would seem, then, that with these settlements, as with the reformations and the marriages, there is a kind of "burden of dis-proof" of their finality resting upon the dramatist and hence upon the critics. Since our normal response is to view the settlement, like the reformation and marriage, as terminal, we expect that the dramatist, to avoid being misunderstood, will provide definite signs whenever he wants his audience to look past it to future events which may destroy it, and so should expect that any critic who argues for such an intention will be able to point to such signs. If he cannot, he has no case.

Many of these attacks on the reformations, marriages, and settlements make use of a central theme, which therefore may be regarded as another technique to refute the ending—and an especially effective one, because it can be deployed to undermine either the finality of the action or the finality of the judgment, and often is directed against both. This is illustrated in the passage on *Twelfth Night*, where the theme of "entrap-ment" is supposed to cast doubt upon the viability and the value of the marriages in that conclusion; and in the passage on *The Alchemist*,

where "the theme of character transmutation" is employed to demonstrate that the final settlement achieved by Lovewit is unstable and
undesirable; and in the analysis of Shakespeare's history plays in terms of
a thematic "Grand Mechanism," which dissolves any political settlement
and any moral differentiation of the characters involved. But there is a
more fundamental connection between thematism and these refutations,
for we saw in the preceding chapter that the central theme is frequently
defined as some universal and permanent problem of the human condition which no mere drama can hope to resolve, and which therefore may
be used to negate any dramatic resolution. Thus the marriages in *Measure
for Measure* are in such precarious balance, according to the reading
examined in that chapter, because the theme of the play is "the basic
conflict . . . between freedom and restraint," and "marriage is only one
solution, at best temporary," for this "recurring human problem"; and
the reading of *As You Like It*, quoted above, finds "little true accord in
Arden" because it finds that the central theme here is "the power struggle"
or "the will to mastery," which remains to plague the marriages after the
conclusion (hence "the play extends beyond the curtain"). And many
other endings have been refuted in the same way, since they do not solve
the "problem of human evil" ("Human evil is as powerful as 'anguish,
hunger, or the sea!'. . . There is no progressive feeling that the new
governor, or the new generation, so to speak, will be any more successful
in dealing with the problem of Iago than the old one was"), or the
"problem of human communication" ("Othello himself recurs to the
difficulty in finding the proper words to match elusive reality. . . . [He]
knows that the messenger may not be able to speak of him as he is; and
Iago remains silent, unexplained"), or various other problems of this sort
which are by definition unsolvable. Moreover, since the thematists view
the play as an exploration of these general problems, rather than as the
representation of a particular action, they will tend to regard its conclusion, not as the final outcome of that action, but as a stage or tentative
pause in an ongoing discourse. (This is why we found a number of them
describing a dramatist's development in terms of his continued investigation of the same thematic problem through a sequence of plays.) These
central themes, then, can provide the ironic critic not only with a
powerful technique for attacking the terminality of the ending but also
with a powerful motive for launching this attack.

There remains one relatively minor technique to be considered—the
use of "forgotten" characters or issues, which is exemplified by the
treatment of Antonio and the nameless captain in the passage on *Twelfth
Night*. Now anyone who looks hard enough can find these trivial loose

ends in the conclusions of many plays of this period. Some, no doubt, were the result of oversight, and others of the dramatist's desire to avoid distractions in his concentration upon the fate of the principal characters; but they do not cause any difficulty unless we want them to. (This is quite different from the problem posed by such characters as Shylock, Don John, and Malvolio, who are not forgotten but explicitly excluded from the resolution, since their exclusion is itself part of that resolution and must be taken into account.) We cannot seriously doubt, if we think about it at all, that Orsino in his newfound happiness will pardon the two men who saved his bride and her brother. But we probably do not think about it, if we are actively responding to the presentation, because we are caught up in the rhythm of the ending. This rhythm is unmistakable in most of these plays. The repentances and reformations, the reconciliations and restitutions, the distribution of rewards and punishments, the marriages, the ceremonial dance or feast, and, in the tragedies, the death of the protagonist and establishment of the new order, all operate together very powerfully to create it, and as we get swept along in it we naturally tend to assume—unless there are very clear indications to the contrary—that any leftover details will be taken care of, that the reformations are genuine, that the marriages are permanent (and that those silent women consent to them), and that the final settlement is final. This rhythm is the basic dramatic fact which the refuters of the terminality of the ending consistently ignore, and is the play's most effective defense against them.

If we go on to ask why the refuters ignore this rhythm as well as the various conventions and other factors which were seen to contribute to the terminality of these conclusions, we will find, again, that some part of the blame must be borne by thematism (in those cases where the ironic reading is also thematic). For the preceding chapter showed that this approach operates at such a high level of abstraction that it very easily passes over the particular emotional effects of the play, which are irrelevant to the intellectual formulation it is pursuing. And that would certainly apply to the rhythm of the ending. In fact this rhythm may even be passed over deliberately, as we see in the advice given by a dedicated refuter of Shakespeare's comic conclusions (he is the critic quoted earlier as saying that "only one" of them was "virtually free from irony"), who is also a dedicated thematist:

> We might characterize the matter by distinguishing between the critic and member of the audience—one can be both, but (often) at different times. The playgoer is entitled to yield to the agreeable emotions of the final dance. . . . The critic, who may be the

> same playgoer, has a duty to reflect afterwards on certain
> nuances, on things that were said and left unsaid, done and left
> undone, that he did not fully take in during the performance.
> And he may then arrive at a different estimate of the action. . . .
> Generally, the critic who attends a Shakespearean revel (I say
> nothing of the playgoer) will, I feel, be well advised to follow
> a simple precept: to stay sober.

Few thematic ironists or ironic thematists are so frank about—or perhaps
so aware of—the great distance between their readings and the dramatic
experience intended by the playwright, who, we may need to be reminded, was not writing for critics. Yet it should be obvious that someone who follows the advice "to stay sober" and so remains aloof from the
emotional effect of the ending (which is quite different from soberly
analyzing that effect and its causes) will be able, if he seeks them, to find
things in the ending that can be used to attack its finality—especially
things left "unsaid" or "undone" (such as Orsino's un-pardoning of
Antonio and Isabella's un-acceptance of the Duke's proposal). For this
search is not restrained by what we have called the burden of disproof,
since it fails to take proper account of the response that the dramatist
wanted and expected of his audience, and, consequently, of his need to
make his meaning clear to them. None of these conclusions could withstand such a search, but—as we said of the target of character assassination—none of them was meant to.

The primary responsibility for this refutation of the terminality of the
ending, however, is to be found not in thematism but in the ironic
approach itself—that is, in its need to discover and demonstrate the
"irony" in each play it encounters, which virtually mandates an incon-
clusive resolution. Indeed, many devotees of this approach seem to think
that such a resolution is intrinsically superior to a conclusive one, since it
is supposed to make the play more interesting or honest or profound.
One of them tells us, for instance, that "for a comedy that has depth or
complexity, the ending will be completely convincing only in so far as we
attend to its formal aspects—and to no others. When credible motivation
is used, even intermittently, as for Duke Vincentio, Angelo, Bassanio,
Claudio, and Valentine, the adequacy of the epiphany must remain in
some doubt." And another asserts that "the whole point of a Shakespearean conclusion lies in the questions unanswered, the sense of
problems that are present at, and are not banished by, the feast." But
even when it is not stated explicitly, this belief that "All's Not Well That
Ends Well" (which is the subtitle of one of the articles quoted earlier)
must underlie much of the activity of the refuters, as evidenced by their

confidence that they have done the play—and us—a great favor by proving that it does not end with its ending.

A still more basic explanation of these refutations emerges, however, when we notice what is supposed to happen after "the play extends beyond the curtain," for it is no coincidence that in all the examples cited this projected future is very grim—the reformation will not last, the marriage will come to grief, the political settlement will fall apart. (The same thing can be seen in recent ironic productions of these plays which at the very end add some stage business, unwarranted by the text, to suggest that trouble looms ahead.)[17] I have never seen a refutation which forecast a happier state of affairs than the one presented in the actual conclusion. That, presumably, would not be "ironic," because to take an ending ironically is to take it down, which is just what was meant by taking a character ironically. And the connection between the two becomes clear, once we recognize that the outcome of a character's career in the play is an important determinant of the play's final judgment of him. In order to prove that the character should be taken at less than his face value, therefore, one must also prove that his outcome should be taken at less than its face value. And this appears to be the real motive behind most of these refutations of the terminality of the ending—they are not undertaken for their own sake but primarily as one means of refuting the judgment of the ending.

The judgment of the ending must be refuted, of course, because it directly contradicts the ironic readings. It was noted earlier that the conclusion of every play considered here would seem to indicate very clearly that we are meant to regard with sympathy and even with admiration the character whom the reading is attacking. And since that verdict is rendered through the resolution of the action, which usually brings the character some form of success or reward, and through the commentary of the other characters, which usually states their approval of this resolution and of him, the strategy of refutation will be directed against these two basic aspects of the play's concluding judgment.

The principal technique for refuting the final success or reward of a character is, as might be expected, to prove that it is only apparent and should really be viewed as a failure or punishment. And we have just seen that one way to prove this is to deny that it is final, because each of the arguments *against* the terminality of an ending turns out to be an argument *for* another, later ending which is much worse for the character in question and therefore constitutes a much worse judgment of him. If the marriage comes to grief, that will reflect unfavorably upon one or both of the partners, and sometimes upon a character who arranged it (and who may be the critic's main target). If the political settlements attained at the end of *Macbeth*, *Richard III*, and *Henry V* fall apart, that will in itself be a condemnation of Malcolm and the two Henries (thus the triumph at Agincourt becomes, in the words of the critic quoted earlier, "really defeat, both moral and spiritual"). And if the reformations of Kate and Angelo and Bertram do not last, that will adversely affect our estimate of Petruchio and Duke Vincentio and Helena. (The attempts to undermine the reformation of Montague and Capulet also serve this purpose, since it would have been a kind of posthumous reward for Romeo and Juliet.) Thus, by projecting the action beyond the conclusion of the play, the ironic critic is able to snatch defeat from the jaws of victory, and so reverse the character's outcome and the favorable verdict it provides.

The other way to prove that the character's final success or reward is only apparent and not real is to deny its intrinsic worth rather than its permanence (although the two claims may be closely related). Here a variety of arguments are employed to disparage what he has achieved at the end, or his means of achieving it, or both. One critic impugns Henry Tudor's victory at Bosworth Field because he used "foreign scum" in his army, and another, because his ally, Lord Stanley, was a "time-server" and "we can hardly help feeling that something of his baseness rubs off onto the new regime." Another critic refuses to give Henry V any credit for the victory at Agincourt because it was not really a battle at all but "a massacre or a miracle," since so few English killed so many French (making this one more case where too much of a good thing can get a character into trouble), although he later also objects that the odds were "not nearly as great as they appeared," so that poor Henry must lose his victory either way. Another finds that the Duke's marriage to Isabella in *Measure for Measure* is not a reward but a punishment: "Isabella appears to have learnt nothing from all that has happened; she shows no moral development, and this perhaps makes her proposed marriage with the Duke at the end of the play 'measure for measure' in a truer sense than either of them realizes" (we saw earlier that other refuters of this ending had her rejecting the Duke's proposal, so it would seem that he too loses either way). The passage on the conclusion of *The Alchemist* said that Lovewit only attains an "apparent success" there (or even worse, something "he must endure") because neither the booty nor the new wife which he wins is worth much, while the quotation at the beginning of the chapter said that in winning this wife his "sexual bargain-hunting incriminates him" and "seals [his] condemnation." And we have already seen that some techniques of character assassination can also be deployed against this final success, either by finding fault with the character's actions or speeches connected with it (Henry V and Henry VII thanking God, Orsino asking Viola to put on a dress) or by having it equate him with a less admirable character, often with the one he has just defeated (Antonio with Shylock, Hamlet with Claudius, Malcolm with Macbeth, Lovewit with the dupes). But all such arguments are open to the same basic objection, because in each of these plays the ending itself very emphatically affirms the value of the character's reward or success by presenting it as the fulfillment of his own desires and as the most desirable prize in his world (indeed the ironic critics never seem to tell us what other achievement in this world would impress them, just as they failed to explain what alternative actions the character could have taken to win their approval). And this view of it is also confirmed by the actions and comments of the other characters. The only doubts about its worth come not from the play but from the refuter, who must discredit it in order to justify his ironic reading.

Since the ending so clearly endorses the character's final achievement, any critic who attempts to discredit it has to refer—explicitly or implicitly—to some external standard of judgment which is more exacting than that of the play itself, and which he must impose upon the play. Actually, the imposition of such a standard underlies not only this refutation of the ending but also the strategy of character assassination employed throughout the play, and hence the entire ironic reading, which is generated by the opposition between the play's "apparent" values (i.e., "face value") and the critic's "real" values. But the operation of this imposed standard is most significant in the attacks upon the ending, where its function is somewhat similar to that of the central theme (which is also imposed on the play and is often combined with the standard). Like the central theme, it both motivates the critic to refute the ending and enables him to do so: since the ending does not measure up to his standard, he must prove that it cannot be accepted at face value; and he proves that it cannot be accepted at face value by showing that it does not measure up to his standard. And, again like the central theme, it can be used to refute the finality of the action and of the judgment, as we saw in the readings which denied both permanence and intrinsic worth to the settlement at the end of *Romeo and Juliet* because it falls "far short of a heavenly peace" as defined by Augustine, and to the marriages at the end of *The Merchant of Venice* because of their "imperfect relationship to . . . the Christian ideal," and to the marriage at the end of *The Family of Love* because Maria "fail[s] to exemplify human love at its highest level" (which this critic also takes from a definition by Augustine, although he admits that Middleton "appears never to present an instance of it in this drama").

As the examples show, this kind of attack is very easy to mount, for, unless the character is a saint, one can always find some demanding moral or theological standard which his final situation cannot possibly satisfy (just as one could always find a universal thematic problem which that situation could not possibly solve). The difficulty is that the play itself does not affirm such a standard, or ask us to judge the character in those terms (if it did, his "appearance" would not be favorable, and there would be nothing for the refutation to refute). A not surprising number of ironic critics never face this difficulty, but those who do have two basic recourses. One is to claim that the standard of judgment functions in another work by the same author and therefore should be applied to the play under attack—the unwritten law here being that the author's real attitude is always found in the *other* work and is always negative, so that it can be used against the apparently positive treatment in this one. The assertion, quoted earlier, that Claudio's praise of Hero was "an outrageous remark in Shakespeare's world" presumably means that in some (unspecified) plays Shakespeare expressed his outrage at men who admire pretty women and so must have felt the same about Claudio's remark, even though the scene gives no hint of it. Another critic insists that the cosmic images which convey the love of Antony and Cleopatra must be taken "at less than their face value," since this love could not have been viewed sympathetically by "an author whose horror of sexuality was so immense," and as evidence he produces Hamlet's lines to Gertrude about "the rank sweat of an enseamed bed" (here we have a second unwritten law of this technique: the attitude of any character can be attributed to the author when it suits the refuter's purpose). The critic who censured Maria's speech on "Elysiums sweet" knows that Middleton disapproved of it because "we need only look ahead to" *The Changeling* (written some twenty years later) where "we find the naturalist thinking which informs Maria's lines in II.iv.36–41 changed into a horrible fantasy." And several critics have used Jonson's discussion of comedy in the *Discoveries* (where he says a great deal about instruction and very little about laughter) or his practice in some of his earlier and more didactic plays to justify their imposition of a sternly moralistic standard upon *Epicene* or *The Alchemist* or *Bartholomew Fair* which negates the triumph of the wits in each ending and substitutes for it a solemn "ironic" condemnation of them. The most comprehensive refutation of this kind that I have seen comes from the critic cited at the beginning of the chapter who ironized all of Jonson's major comedies. He argues that the need "to find consistency" throughout the Jonsonian canon requires us to "interpret symptoms of tolerance and moral compromise in the plays as a deliberate exercise in ironic ambiguity," since they conflict with attitudes Jonson expressed elsewhere. And from this it follows, a priori, that "the endings of Jonson's four great comedies leave us with the impression that they do not mean quite what they have said," for "all Jonson's accommodations [in these endings] conceal a conscious irony which ... he expects the judicious to perceive."

One might, of course, even grant this supposed need "to find consistency" in an author and still object that it would have been just as logical to proceed in the opposite direction: Lovewit's final success in *The Alchemist* could be cited to prove that the moral pronouncements in the *Discoveries* "do not mean quite what they have said," and so on. But the real objection to all these interpretations is that we have no right to assume that any author will embody the same standard of judgment in different kinds of works written at different stages of his career, and therefore have no right to refute the endings of any of his plays in order to produce this "consistency."

The second and more common argument for imposing an external standard upon the play is to assert that it was one of the "ideas of the time," and so must have determined the viewpoint of the author and his audience, even though it is not evident in the play itself. Sometimes these ideas are "Elizabethan attitudes" toward (usually against) specific kinds of conduct, which the character under attack is said to violate in his final actions (or earlier), and which can therefore be invoked to deny the "apparently" positive judgment of the ending: the Elizabethan attitude toward revenge has been employed in this way to refute the end of *Hamlet*, the Elizabethan attitude toward suicide to refute the end of *Romeo and Juliet* and *Othello*, etc. And sometimes they turn out to be more generalized "ideals" which the character or his outcome is said to fall short of, so that they too can be invoked to negate the play's final judgment, as we just saw in the readings which drew on "the Christian ideal" or Augustine's definitions of "heavenly peace" or "human love" for this purpose. The discussion of the mode of interpretation based upon these ideas of the time (both specific and general) must be reserved for the next chapter; but even here it should be clear that the objection to the use of the author's attitudes applies still more strongly to them, for if we have no right to assume that a single attitude will govern all the works of any given author, then we certainly have no right to assume that it will govern all the authors of any given period. Moreover, it was noted earlier that many of these ideas or ideals are so demanding that they are beyond the reach of ordinary mortals, which means that their imposition must destroy the ethical basis of most plays by requiring us to condemn the entire cast of characters. And such a wholesale condemnation, which we shall see is a tendency inherent in the ironic approach, points to another fundamental objection to this refutative technique—like the technique of character assassination, it can be directed against *any* character, no matter how sympathetically he may be portrayed or how favorably he may be judged in the verdict of the ending.

We should, finally, mention one other method occasionally employed to impose an external standard of judgment, which is to claim that it actually is presented in the play, but in some unlikely place where nobody thought of looking for it before. One of the refuters of the ending of *Hamlet*, for instance, asserts that this standard (it is, again, "the Christian ideal") is suggested, very indirectly, in "the Christian wit of the singing Gravedigger" and "the mystifying babblings of the deranged Ophelia." But that is by no means the most desperate of these expedients. The critic quoted at the outset of this chapter who equated Duke Vincentio with Angelo finds the standard in Lucio ("I also think that Lucio is a prototype of the fool in *Lear*, and that he tells the truth about the Duke");[18] and the one who called Valentine a "nincompoop" finds it in Thurio ("the only reality-figure who is allowed a voice at the end," whose words "we should take as the final internal criticism of the action"); and a few ironic readings of *The Alchemist* and *Bartholomew Fair* even appeal to the rantings of Ananias, Zeal-of-the-Land Busy, and Justice Adam Overdo: "Ananias (and Jonson) use the epithet with accuracy"; "[when] Busy says, 'the whole Fair is the shop of Satan!' he tells us what we know to be true"; "Overdo's lament . . . provides an epigraph for *Bartholomew Fair*"; "as with Overdo's oration or Busy's tirade, valuable admonitions are here for the listener able to hear or see." Each of these five characters, however, is judged very unfavorably at the end of his play, where he is exposed and ridiculed. Now there are not many certain rules in dramatic criticism, but one of them is that your view of the action had better not coincide with that of a character whom the play has made ridiculous, unless you want to make yourself ridiculous.

The positive judgment that the ending bestows upon the characters attacked in the ironic readings is rendered not only through the outcome of the action but also, as we noted, through the commentary upon it, which may be extremely important, especially in a tragedy where that judgment cannot of course be embodied in the character's final success.[19]

Yet the tragic protagonist usually does win a kind of reward after death in the eulogistic epitaph spoken over him, which dwells, in accents of profound respect, upon his essential goodness and greatness. Almost all of Shakespeare's tragedies end with such an epitaph for the hero, telling us that a rarer spirit never did steer humanity, that he was great of heart, true and faithful, the noblest Roman of them all, who was likely, had he been put on, to have proved most royally, that he shall have a noble memory, and now makes a great decay, the most noble corse that ever herald did follow to his urn, for no grave upon the earth shall clip in it a pair so famous. And in every case this concluding testimony is given by those survivors (usually the hero's adversaries or victims) who will make it most impressive. Therefore, because the testimony is guaranteed in this way, and is never contradicted, and is the play's formal peroration, invested with the solemnity of ritual, it takes on something of a choric quality which establishes the final judgment of the protagonist. And even in plays where the characters win out at the end, we usually find that their victory is accompanied by some admiring commentary of this sort, which is, again, often spoken by their former adversaries and is not contradicted, at least by anybody whose opinion matters to us. (The festive dance or feast closing so many of the comedies can be seen as another form of positive comment upon the main characters, in which the entire society joins in accepting and celebrating their success.) It would seem, then, that anyone who undertakes to refute this aspect of the ending has his work cut out for him.

The ironic critics, however, have proved equal to the task, since they have at their disposal several techniques for canceling out or contradicting this favorable commentary. Some of these even make it possible to create an *un*favorable commentary at the end of the play, where none existed before. This can be done, for instance, by discovering that a speech there which condemns someone else also refers to the character whom the critic is attacking. The author of the passage on *Philaster*, quoted at the beginning of the chapter, asserts that the King's final words acknowledging his own error—"Let Princes learn / By this to rule the passions of their blood, / For what Heaven wills can never be withstood"—apply to Philaster as well, but he never explains (nor do I see how he could) what Philaster tried to withstand or what he learned. And the one who found that Giovanni "ominously reminded" us of his father states that "the lines he addresses to Flamineo when he banishes him from the court [in V.iv] apply also to himself as the inheritor of Brachiano," again without any explanation of what the lines would then mean. Neither critic, it should be understood, claims that the speaker intends this further application, which would be absurd; but another one does seem to argue that Horatio is referring to Hamlet, as well as to Claudius and Laertes, in his lines on "deaths put on by cunning and forc'd cause; / And, in this upshot, purposes mistook / Fall'n on th' inventors' heads" (V.ii. 369–71), although this requires some pretty fancy footwork:

> Hamlet, reciprocally with others in the play, has been the in-
> ventor of a mistaken purpose. . . . He, no less than Claudius and
> Laertes, has shot an arrow of revenge, now fallen, alas, on his
> own head. The put-on cause of the shooting of this arrow has
> been justice, but a justice forced or distorted by rash indignation
> and a blind desire for retaliation. Further, a voluntary cun-
> ning . . . has attended this action. This much Horatio's general-
> ized statement implies, or may be taken to imply.

This last sentence apparently hedges on the question of Horatio's intention, as well it might, since he has never before even suggested such a view of Hamlet.

When no one in the ending makes an unfavorable comment which the critic can turn against the character who is his target, he may use someone's silence for the same purpose. We saw that Isabella's silence at the close of *Measure for Measure* has been interpreted as a rejection of the Duke's proposal, so that it becomes a negative comment on him (and at the same time eliminates one aspect of his final success). A refutation of the conclusion of *A Fair Quarrel* tries to deflate Captain Ager's joyful triumph there by pointing to "the speechless figure" of his mother, whose silence is supposed to "engulf the last few minutes of the play, casting a pall over" the proceedings and reminding us of their "moral irrelevance." And a critic who wishes to undermine Valentine's successful outcome in *The Two Gentlemen of Verona* makes even greater claims for Silvia's silence at the end: "The infallible good taste of Shakespeare renders silent the unfortunate Silvia, a word from whom would have sufficed to blow away the pretensions of the Big Production staged by Valentine and Proteus for their own benefit." But he never explains why Shakespeare, if he meant us to regard Valentine as pretentious, did not have her speak the word that would tell us this. And the same objection can be brought against all such attempts to make a character's silence say what the critic wants to hear.

If the ending does not provide him with any silences to fill in or condemnations to redirect, the refuter with enough imagination can even manufacture an unfavorable comment out of a favorable one by some judicious exegesis. There is a striking example of this in a study of

Antony and Cleopatra which sets out to prove that the two principals are abominable sinners (she is equated to the great harlot of Revelation, and he to the beast with ten horns), and so must reinterpret the praises that accompany their deaths. According to this critic, Charmian's lines on her dead mistress, "Death, in thy possession lies / A lass unparallel'd" (V.ii. 314–15), really mean, "A lover of death, *alas,* can become *possessed* with unparalleled *lies*"; and Eros's speech to his master, just before their suicides, undergoes a similar sea change: "When . . . Eros hails Antony as 'that noble countenance / Wherein the worship of the whole world lies' (IV.xiv.85), is the play merely pleading for us to admire Antony? If we but give the line a double take, do we not recognize that *the world* indeed *lies* in worshipping face?" (Italics in original.) This kind of "close reading" (which is what the critic calls it) can transform any speech in the play, since it is not governed by the ordinary rules of communication or even of grammar. The speaker has no idea of what he is actually saying, nor do his listeners on the stage or in front of it, because his speech is not in the English language but in a secret code through which the dramatist talks directly to the critic, who is the only one to understand it. (Indeed the code seems to be deliberately misleading, since the "apparent" meaning it hides behind is the opposite of its real meaning—which is an important point to be dealt with later.) This is the conception of dramatic dialogue shared by many anti-Stratfordians, who also treat the speech as a coded message sent from the author (Sir Francis) to the cryptanalyst, bypassing the speaker and the other characters and the audience for whom the play was written. And, as the example shows, it can be used to prove anything.

Other refutative techniques are employed, not to create imaginary negative comments in the ending, but to dispose of the positive comments that really are there (the one just considered, of course, manages to do both). One way to accomplish this is by discrediting the commentator himself, either because of his previous opposition to the character he is now praising ("Is the Antony who destroyed Brutus by shattering through innuendo the image of 'The noble Brutus' as 'an honourable man' ideally suited to assume the choric role and speak the formal lines which restore his claim to those proud titles?"; "Aufidius's sudden, inexplicable remorse [in his epitaph to Coriolanus] is so hollow that it seems to me only to add insult to mortal injury. . . . [It] is depressingly ironic"), or because of his own moral failings ("Acton actually praises Frankford's actions, leaving us to consider any judgment praised by a man of this sort"). The first argument is a curious reversal of the rhetorical rule that favorable testimony is more persuasive from a hostile witness than from a friendly one. And both arguments are open to a more general objection, since, like those efforts to condemn a character's action or to disparage his final reward without considering the available alternatives, they never ask who else would be better suited for this role of commentator. The answer is that there is no one, among those present at the end, whose praise of the character could be more convincing; but then no praise of him, no matter who speaks it, could convince a critic intent upon refuting it.

The easiest way to dispose of the favorable commentary, however, is simply to declare that it is mistaken. Most of the refutations finally come down to this argument, although some do not follow it to its logical conclusion. For to be consistent it has to take in a great deal of territory. The "mistake" must include just about all the speakers in the closing scene, since we saw that they agreed in commending the character in question, and it must include not only their attitude toward him but also their view of his career and, hence, of the meaning of the resolution. And it must include the final statements of the character himself, who never seems to recognize the grievous faults or sins that the critic discovered in him (which is understandable enough, because no one around him does either).[20] In the tragedies he remains in invincible ignorance to the end and so is unable to understand the significance of what has happened to him: "Brutus dies with the illusion that 'he only overcame himself' "; "to the end [Othello] maintains his crucial and mistaken allegiance to bad fame"; "Cleopatra's final speech must be seen as a miracle of self decep-tion"; "nothing in the last scene . . . indicates that Frankford realizes his mistake"; and so on. And at the close of the other plays he is not only unaware of his faults but is even under the illusion (shared, again, by everyone around him) that he has been successful. The "self-satisfaction" of "the insufferable Valentine" is "allowed to remain unpunctured," and he is "allowed to strut off stage in the full possession of his triumph." "For Orsino and Olivia, the ending is illusion condoned . . . [they] are not compelled to face reality." "Because Belmont's inhabitants are obli-vious to their flaws, their festivity is artificial, ambiguous, and highly ironic."

As these examples demonstrate, the refutation of the final commentary will carry over to a refutation of the outcome of the action, since these two aspects of the judgment rendered by the ending are so closely related. Nor can it stop there; it must extend back over the rest of the action and the rest of the cast, who also commit the error of admiring the character under attack, as we saw earlier: Hector's "appearance . . . blinds the other characters in the play"; "Everyone (except Enobarbus) is a dupe of Antony's reputation" and "even he dies deceived"; "everyone in the play admires or loves" Philaster, which should "make us question the values of almost everyone in the play." Thus "it's not just the ending of the play that's a charade, the whole ... set-up is." Almost everybody must be mistaken, and almost everything must be viewed "ironically." Not all of these readings go that far, but the tendency is inherent in the basic strategies of the approach; once it is claimed that the play's presentation of a major character cannot be taken at face value, then the other characters who take him at face value cannot themselves be taken at face value, and then still others who take them at face value must also fall, like that row of dominoes, until there is no one left who can be taken at face value. One can therefore sympathize with a devotee of this approach who was led to complain that "when we enter the domain of irony as structure, it is difficult to know where it stops." It is impossible to know where it stops, because the ironic appetite is insatiable and will try to devour anything in the play that might serve as a guide to our response. It leaves us not just with an unreliable ending but with an unreliable play and ultimately an unreliable playwright, who cannot be believed even when he seems to be speaking to us directly,[21] and who may have designed the entire play, we shall later see, as a trick to deceive us. Thus it may be said that the new ironic reading aspires to the condition of total distrust of the dramatic work.

If these readings eliminate all reliable guides to interpretation within the play, we may wonder where we are to find such a guide. There can only be one answer; it must be in the critic himself. We will not be surprised, then, to learn that there are almost as many different ironic interpretations of each play as there are ironic interpreters, for they rarely agree among themselves. But despite these differences, they usually share a very dim view of most if not all of the characters, who emerge in their readings as not merely unreliable but reprehensible. This too seems to be an inherent tendency of the approach, because all the readings reject the play's "apparent" values (however much they may disagree on its "real" values), and therefore will denigrate the most admirable persons in it by the strategy of character assassination, which reduces them to the level of the least admirable. The strategy of refuting the ending has the same reductive effect, for just as the denial of its terminality always seemed to produce a much less favorable future for these "apparently" admirable characters, so the denial of its judgment always seems to produce a much less favorable estimate of their moral stature. And the attack on the morality of one such character, like the attack on his reliability, tends to spread to the others: everyone in Rome is "irrational"; all the inhabitants of Belmont have that "rotten core of undiscovered hypocrisy"; everyone in Vienna is "self-righteous" or "consumed with self" or a "seemer"; the Greeks and Trojans all suffer from a "mistaken conception of honor" or "prideful will and appetite" or "the corruptive spirit"; and everybody in Verona, from Prince Escalus "all the way down the social scale," is guilty of "self-glory" (which of course "is not eradicated even at the end"). Thus it may also be said that the new ironic reading aspires to the condition of total disapproval of the dramatis personae.

"Creating Every Bad a Perfect Best"

Since this approach exacts such a heavy price, it seems only reasonable to ask what it is supposed to offer us in return. On this point the ironic critics themselves seem to be unanimous; like the thematists, they all claim that their readings greatly enhance our appreciation of the play by discovering virtues in it which had hitherto been overlooked. Usually the claim goes even further, since these discovered virtues were not merely overlooked in the traditional, nonironic interpretation of the play, but were actually considered defects. Thus the ironic reading can present itself as a vindication of the play (which we saw was one of the general characteristics of all readings), a demonstration that whatever had previously been condemned in it really should be admired. In the words of Shakespeare's sonnet, the reading is "creating every bad a perfect best."

This ironic vindication, however, can take two distinct forms, so we had better examine them separately. One is directed at parts or aspects of the play which used to be thought artistically deficient. The thematists, we may recall, redeemed these defective components through the all-forgiving embrace of the central theme, which justified their presence in the play and raised them to such a high level of abstraction that any failures in plotting, characterization, diction, and the like tended to disappear. The ironic critics proceed on a very different tack—they argue that the deficiencies are deliberate and therefore are not deficiencies at all, but strokes of consummate artistry designed to ridicule a character whom the play seemed to endorse, or to parody a convention which the play seemed to adopt, or both.

The basic strategy is nicely illustrated in the ironic rescue of the ending of *The Two Gentlemen of Verona*, which had been faulted by many of the older commentators—with, I think, very good reason. The critic who undertakes it (he is the one quoted at the outset of this chapter) begins by announcing that the play "needs to be saved" from them, presenting as an example H. B. Charlton's verdict that "Shakespeare's first attempt to make romantic comedy had only succeeded so far that it had unexpectedly and inadvertently made romance comic."[22] Our vindicator dismisses as "astonishing" the idea that Shakespeare could have done something inadvertently here, and asserts instead that he *intended* to make romance comic, and that Valentine's surrender of Silvia is therefore meant to be seen as "self-evidently a refutation" or "reductio ad absurdum" of "the Romantic conventions," and as a demonstration of his own "fatuous egotism." Thus the very epithet which Charlton had applied to Valentine to indicate the failure of this ending ("but it makes a man a nincompoop") can be taken over as an indication of its success: "He is (and I gladly accept Charlton's term) a 'nincompoop'; and this is the germ of the play."

Essentially the same argument was advanced by another critic back in 1941, only three years after Charlton's book appeared: "By this action Shakespeare is wringing the last drop of silliness out of Valentine's conventions. With the idea of smashing a particularly ridiculous convention, Shakespeare has set out to prove Valentine a fool." Another, writing in 1948, offered a similar defense of *Titus Andronicus*; its excesses and absurdities, he maintained, were supposed to be excessive and absurd, because throughout the play Shakespeare is "disporting himself," "laughing behind his back" while "pulling our leg," deliberately reducing the tragedy "to sheer bathos," and treating it all as "a huge joke." And since then many more readings have attempted to prove, as one of them puts it, that Shakespeare's "apparent flaws" are "consciously contrived ironical effects." This rescue operation has concentrated upon his early works, where there are plenty of apparent flaws to explain away, but it has not been limited to them. The difficulties in the resolution of *Measure for Measure*, which also used to disturb people (also, I would say, with good reason), have been vindicated by another critic as intentional ironies: "There is not a botched-up happy ending, for the mood of the ending is more satirical than happy." And another claims that this ending is unsuccessful because Shakespeare wanted it to be, which therefore makes it successful after all:

> I believe the final effect should be an uneasiness and dissatisfaction, which the spectator never consciously articulates. In addition, if we judge by the radically divided critical response, Shakespeare has succeeded in destroying community within his audience, a destruction that mirrors the lack of community in the weddings at the end of this "comedy."

The sensitive reader will have detected in these arguments more than a whiff of the incense of Bardolatry, for they seem to assume Shakespeare's artistic infallibility.[23] If the very idea that he may have nodded in *The Two Gentlemen of Verona*, one of his earliest and least admired plays, is now viewed as "astonishing," then clearly, unlike his Greek predecessor, he can never nod anywhere. Wherever previous commentators found him dozing off, therefore, he must really have been wide awake, contriving some brilliant irony or parody or leg-pull. Thus the new defenders of the faith have taken over from the defunct disintegrators the crusade to purge the canon of all passages unworthy of the Bard—the disintegrators argued that because the passages were defective they could not be his, and so must have been the product of another artist; the ironic critics argue that because they are his they cannot be defective, and so must be the product of conscious art. They have proclaimed a new gospel of justification by irony which reverses the biblical scheme: before it arrived we had a fallen Shakespeare, capable of artistic lapses—a postlapsarian Shakespeare—but with its coming it has given us a sinless, prelapsarian Shakespeare.

This strategy of ironic vindication, however, cannot be explained as simply the latest manifestation of Bardolatry, for although it has received its fullest development (like most other recent fashions) in Shakespearean criticism, it is now being applied to other playwrights of the period, whose work is undergoing a similar revaluation and is also approaching perfection. Ben Jonson is no longer allowed a dotage any more than Shakespeare is allowed an apprenticeship. Several new readings of *The New Inn*, for example, have asserted that it is not an unsuccessful attempt at romance, as older critics (and apparently its original audience) thought, but a successful parody of romance. They tell us that the "play is nothing if not irony," that "much of what is ridiculous in the play is intentionally so," that it is "almost a later *Knight of the Burning Pestle* in places," and that its ending is deliberately "spoofing romantic comedy," since "the grotesque postulates" of the Frampul family relationships "must, coming from Jonson, be interpreted as a challenge to the audience to swallow a camel if it will."[24] In the crucial phrase "coming from Jonson" we can see the same fallacy of artistic infallibility which underlay the vindication of Shakespeare, for it assumes that the dramatist is a constant, that because he was capable of greatness at one time in his career he is incapable of error at any time. But of course the phrase is highly ambiguous. If those grotesque postulates were "coming from Jonson" during the period of his comic masterpieces (1605–1614), we might have some reason to suspect he was spoofing; but they come from the Jonson of 1629, three years after *The Staple of News* and three years before *The Magnetic Lady*, so it is to *this* Jonson that the argument must apply. And since in both of these plays we find family relationships (of the disguised Pennyboy Canter to his son and brother, and of Placentia and Pleasance to Lady Loadstone) which are no less absurd than those of the Frampuls, the argument from probability points in the opposite direction: the grotesque postulates of *The New Inn*, coming from the same stage of Jonson's career as other plays based on postulates equally grotesque, are not at all likely to be a spoof.

This campaign to transform apparent artistic defects into ironic or parodic virtues is also descending to the lesser playwrights, who as a result are no longer so lesser. It is hard to believe that only nineteen years ago Robert Ornstein considered the possibility of salvaging the much-criticized ending of *Antonio's Revenge* in this way, but held off because the facts of Marston's dramaturgy could not support it.[25] Such heroic self-restraint seems quaintly old-fashioned today. Now the wish is father to the facts, and several ironic readings of the play have appeared which assert that it is meant to end unsatisfactorily. According to the best known of them, "this last scene can only be interpreted as consciously outrageous, flouting with calculated enormity a conventional ending." This critic's argument obviously cannot be based upon the supposed infallibility of the dramatist, but appeals instead to the supposed technique of the boy actors for whom he was writing (it seems they were "consciously ranting in oversize parts," "mimicking rather than simply representing men," "strutting like adults" in "burlesques of adult styles," etc.),[26] yet the conclusion is essentially the same, since it turns out, again, that "much of the so-called clumsiness, nonsense, and bad writing are there for deliberate effect." And the same defense has been advanced, by this critic or others, for Marston's *The Malcontent* and even for Chettle's *Hoffman*.

Thus the list of deliberately-bad-therefore-good plays continues to grow. Within the past twelve years we have been assured by another critic that "*Antonio and Mellida* is not a romantic comedy. It is, rather, a parody of this genre" and "a burlesque of the form rather than an example of it"; and by another that *Antonio's Revenge* is a "parodistic exposure of the amorality of the Kydian revenger," which "deliberately travesties the accepted formula"; and by another that previous interpretations of *Jack Drum's Entertainment* have "managed to mistake burlesque for inept dramaturgy"; and by another that the problems of the ending of *A Mad World, My Masters* disappear if we view the play "as a parody of the moral view expressed in such dramatic satires as those of Jonson"; and by another that Middleton's tragicomedies are all "deliberate parodies," rather than inferior imitations, of "the Fletcherian mode and conventions"; and by another that *Der Bestrafte Brudermord* is a "burlesque creation"; and by another that *The First Part of Hieronimo* is "a full-blown theatrical burlesque of *The Spanish Tragedy*"; and by another that *The Comedy of Timon* is "a law students' burlesque of Shakespeare's *Timon*" which "is most nearly like . . . Beaumont's *Knight of the Burning Pestle*"; and by two critics that *The Old Wives Tale* also belongs to this class—one sees it as "a parody from beginning to end" of "contemporary romantic fiction" and "an earlier *Knight of the Burning Pestle*," so that "all the absurdities of the multiple plots turn into parody"; and the other as a "burlesque [of] both individual poets and the romantic genre as a whole," employing "the same technique used in . . . *The Knight of the Burning Pestle*," which makes it "a satire, the earliest in English dramatic literature."[27] But the year before that claim was registered, a much older and stranger candidate for this special honor had already been discovered in *Nice Wanton*, an interlude of about 1550 which used to be considered a pious and quite perfunctory lesson in the dangers of sparing the rod:

> the more straight-faced it is played the funnier it is. . . . I am myself inclined to regard the play as an entertainment within the tradition of the Feast of Fools and the Lord of Misrule, and thus as a piece of debunking of parental, scholastic and judicial authority at least as deliberate as Shakespeare's treatment of Holofernes and Sir Nathaniel or of Malvolio and Justice Shallow.

All of these readings, we must remember, maintain that they have left the play a better work of art than they found it—indeed, this is said to be the purpose of each reading and its justification. The ironic interpretation of *The New Inn* "open[s] the way to the discovery in it of a complex and intelligent, though imperfectly realized, design." *The Comedy of Timon* "reveals not only some interest but some merit if read as a law students' burlesque of Shakespeare's *Timon*." "Viewed in this light" (that is, "as a parody of *The Spanish Tragedy*") *The First Part of Hieronimo* "emerges . . . as a work of deliberate, comprehensive, and sometimes very deft comic art." "*The Two Gentlemen of Verona* is far more amusing if taken as a burlesque than as serious comedy." And one of those parodic readings of *The Old Wives Tale* concludes that "the best reason for accepting this interpretation is . . . [that it] not only accounts for all the features of the play, but also makes the play far more aesthetically satisfying."

One hesitates to raise any objection to such nobly motivated endeavors, but the fact is, I am afraid, that they do not make the play more satisfying. When they are limited to a particular dramatic component (usually the ending, as we saw), they actually make the play less satisfying, since they create confusion in it and in our response. If, for instance, the conclusion of *The Two Gentlemen of Verona* is supposed "to prove Valentine a fool," then we do not know how to take Silvia's desire to marry him (does that prove her, too, a fool?), or her father's opposition to the match, or any other related event, and so the entire action will become incoherent. And the same result is produced by every reading that attempts an ironic or parodic rescue of one part of a play, because the refutation of a part (which is what these rescues amount to) must call the remainder of the play into question. But we have been through this before.

The situation is somewhat different when a reading claims that the whole play is "a parody from beginning to end," since this in itself would not make the play less artistically satisfying (indeed that would be difficult to do to many of the plays in the list just presented, for our estimate of them could scarcely be lowered). And the claim is at least theoretically possible, because everyone will admit that the dramatists of this period could deliberately write "down" for ironic or parodic effect in portions of their works (for example, in the Pyramus and Thisby playlet), and even in one complete work, *The Knight of the Burning Pestle*, which is appealed to so frequently by these critics. In each of those universally recognized cases, however, we find that the author has provided unmistakable signs within the work itself to indicate his purpose. But no such signs exist in the plays which are the subject of these new readings, because if they did, no new readings would have been required to discover the irony or parody. With respect to their professed motive, therefore, these readings are all self-defeating: if they are correct, we can only conclude that the playwright embodied his intention so ineffectively that it has escaped notice for well over three centuries. And that will not enhance our appreciation of the play's artistic merit.

The absence of any real evidence for these readings should be embarrassing enough, but with some plays there is even evidence against them. The most notable one is *The New Inn*, which, unfortunately for the ironic critics, has come down to us with a very substantial body of authorial comment. We have Jonson's Prologue and Epilogue spoken at the disastrous opening-and-closing performance, as well as a second Epilogue "made for the play in the poet's defense," a Dedication to the Reader, an elaborate Argument, and the "short characterism of the chief actors," all written after the performance, and of course the famous "Ode to Himself" expressing "the just indignation the author took at the vulgar censure of his play." Now, if the ridiculous elements of the play, which presumably contributed to that censure, were "intentionally so" and were "spoofing romantic comedy," as these critics tell us, one would expect Jonson to indicate this, if not in the original Prologue and Epilogue, then surely in some of the later and avowedly defensive material he prepared for publication, where he would have the double incentive of proving the stupidity of the spectators who failed to understand the play, and of ensuring that the readers to whom he was now appealing did not make the same mistake. But there is not the slightest hint of any such intention in all this commentary, or in the verses, also quite extensive, that his supporters composed in answer to the "Ode." Thus, if the ironic readings are right, we must assume that Jonson deliberately chose to keep this vindication of his play a secret, even from the partisans of his own "tribe," and even in the face of the most extreme provocation, and to carry it with him to the grave. And that, from what we know of him, is not very likely.

The New Inn is a special case, to be sure, but a number of the other plays also have some extradramatic components—inductions or prologues or epilogues—where the author is able, more or less directly, to speak for himself, and in none of them can we find any suggestion of the purpose which these readings attribute to him.[28] Of course that does not disprove these readings. They cannot be disproved, because there is no conceivable evidence, internal or external, which could demonstrate that *any* work was *not* ironic (even a direct denial by the author could itself be part of the irony). It is not up to us, however, to prove that they are not ironic; it is up to the proponents of such readings to prove that they are, since the burden of proof rests entirely on them. But this point will be dealt with later.

The actual evidence offered for most of these readings usually boils down to the claim which we saw was their avowed motive and justification—namely, that the play turns out to be a better work of art when its deficiencies are treated as intentional. But even if this were true, it certainly does not prove that they *are* intentional. We have no right to assume that an interpretation is valid merely because it could raise our estimate of the work. That would be absurd, for it would require us to treat all artistic defects in this way, and there would then be no such thing as an artistic defect. In the critical enterprise, wishing will not make it so. Moreover, it simply is not true that these works are appreciably improved if "what is ridiculous in the play is intentionally so." That is not a magic formula which can automatically create a superior play out of an inferior one, and it would take a great deal more than such a declaration of intention by the critic (or even by the author) to transform the "inept dramaturgy" of *Jack Drum's Entertainment* into "burlesque," in any meaningful sense, or "all the absurdities of the multiple plots" of *The Old Wives Tale* "into parody," or any of these plays into "an earlier [or "later"] *Knight of the Burning Pestle.*" Anyone familiar with *The Knight of the Burning Pestle* (or *The Rehearsal* or *Tom Thumb* or *The Critic*) should know that a good parody of bad drama demands considerable skill, and that it is very different from the bad drama itself—and, consequently, very different from these newly discovered parodies, which have been mistaken for their alleged targets down to the present day.[29]

There is a more serious kind of objection to these new readings, for while each of them may be nothing worse than a harmless exercise in wishful thinking, their cumulative impact is far from harmless. Already they are beginning to reinforce each other in a self-sustaining chain reaction (thus one critic is able to support his ironic reading of *The Two Gentlemen of Verona* by pointing to "the supreme example of a thorough-going burlesque" of the "friendship cult" in *The Old Wives Tale*), and there is no end in sight because this strategy will vindicate any play or any part of a play, no matter how flawed it may be. But as more and more of the defects of Renaissance drama are explained away as deliberate irony or parody, the result must be a blurring of essential discriminations. If we cannot recognize the weaknesses in this drama, we will not properly appreciate its genuine achievements—including its achievements in irony and parody. We will not even be able to appreciate the dramatist's own development, if the deficiencies of his earliest work are transmuted into ironic virtues (as we saw the new Bardolaters doing with Shakespeare). Moreover, the interpretative gymnastics required to salvage these plays will probably affect our sensibility, and certainly our credibility. But worse is to come: when we have finally succeeded in "creating every bad a perfect best" we will be in real trouble, for if all bad plays turn out to be burlesques of bad plays, then there will be no bad plays left for them to burlesque. I would recommend, therefore, that we close the open season on artistic defects before they become extinct, and try to conserve what still remains of this endangered species as a valuable and irreplacable part of our cultural heritage.

The other and more common form of ironic vindication of this drama is concerned not with its aesthetic deficiencies but with what might be

termed its moral deficiencies—that is, with attitudes assumed or endorsed in the plays which have now become unacceptable, or at least
seem so to the critic. This rescue operation, like the preceding one, has
been applied most extensively to the Shakespearean canon. And probably the most obvious examples of such attitudes in that canon are those
underlying *The Taming of the Shrew, The Merchant of Venice,* and
Henry V, which would today be called, respectively, male chauvinism,
anti-Semitism, and jingoism. Now it can reasonably be argued, I believe,
that Shakespeare incorporates some qualification of each of these attitudes in the play in question, but that is not enough for the true vindicator. He must prove that Shakespeare is *attacking* them. The only way
to prove this is by constructing an ironic reading which reveals that they
are merely the apparent values of the play and are the opposite of its real
values. And that of course requires the critic to build a case against the
characters espousing these apparent values, who seem to be presented so
sympathetically in each play, and to refute the ending, which seems to
judge these characters so favorably by bringing them to complete
success.

We have already seen how this works. One critic found that Petruchio's domestic conquest could not be taken "at its face value" since
"the open end of *The Taming of the Shrew* is Katherina's mind, undisclosed in soliloquy"; and another that the Christians celebrating their
victory over Shylock harbor a "rotten core of undiscovered hypocrisy";
and another that Henry's triumph at Agincourt is "really defeat, both
moral and spiritual." We need not pause here to ask how we are made
aware of the "undisclosed" contents of Kate's mind, or of that rotten core
of hypocrisy at Belmont if it is "undiscovered," or of the nature of
Henry's "defeat" when the Chorus and all the characters insist it was a
famous victory, because we have already seen that too—those secrets
can only be learned from the critic himself, since his ironic reading has
demolished all reliable sources of information and judgment within the
play. Our present concern, however, is not with the strategies of these
readings but with the motives that produce them and the consequences
that follow from them. Their motivation emerges very clearly in the
program announced by one of the foremost refuters of Shakespeare,
early in his chapter on *Henry V:*

> To think of him [i.e., Shakespeare] as a jingo is as difficult
> as to think of him as a Jew-baiter. Our examination of *The Mer-*
> *chant of Venice* demonstrated, I hope, that he was not the latter.
> The charge that he was the former is equally worthy of
> examination.

And this ensuing examination reveals, not too surprisingly, that *Henry V* is not a jingoistic play at all, but an ironical indictment of jingoism. The point is that this kind of critic feels compelled to clear Shakespeare of any "charge" of mental turpitude. And to accomplish this he must resort to what Clifford Lyons aptly termed "that philosopher's stone of the critic, irony, [which] so readily transmutes unacceptable motifs into golden opinions"[30] by proving that the plays do not really mean what they say.

The same motive underlies the earliest "new reading" of *Henry V* that I could find, cited in chapter 1, for it is surely no accident that this article came from England in 1919, at a time of general revulsion against war and militarism. Since the author feels this revulsion, he wants to believe that Shakespeare did too, and therefore sets out to demonstrate that *"the play is ironic."* And the many other ironic readings of that play and *The Taming of the Shrew* and *The Merchant of Venice* can also be explained in this way. None of these critics seriously entertains the possibility that Shakespeare may have held the wrong attitudes about women or Jews or war—that is apparently unthinkable ("To think of him as a jingo is as difficult as to think of him as a Jew-baiter"), because they all seem to assume that he is morally infallible, just as the other vindicators assumed his artistic infallibility. Thus here, too, we can discern the influence of the new Bardolatry—in fact, the campaign to transform the values of these plays may be seen as an inevitable consequence of idolization. To remain worthy of our worship, the idol's meaning must be changed, like that of our other sacred texts, to conform with current beliefs. That is why we now have an untamed shrew, and a hypocritical and merciless Portia, and a defeated Henry V.

This kind of moral vindication, moreover, is not limited to these three plays or even to Shakespeare, for it would seem to be the motivating force behind most of the readings examined in this chapter. That may not be immediately evident because the attitudes and values of the other plays do not conflict so obviously with the present climate of opinion, yet they obviously do conflict with the critic's opinion, and this is what generates the reading. The older commentators usually felt free to censure the morality of a play (just as they felt free to censure the artistry) when it did not meet their approval, but the new vindicator cannot do this. If he disapproves of the play's values he has to disprove them, by constructing an ironic interpretation which reveals that they belong to the apparent meaning of the play, and that its real meaning embodies values he can approve. Thus all such readings are also based upon the assumption that the dramatist is morally infallible, which can only mean that his morality is identical with the critic's. And it follows, therefore, that the demonstration of this identity will be a vindication of him and of his play.

Although the ironic readings all agree in rejecting the play's apparent meaning, they clearly will not agree on its real meaning, if that is determined by each critic's own moral position. But while there are many individual differences among their positions, most of these critics can be grouped, very roughly, into two opposing camps. On the right are the traditionalists who want to believe that the dramatist upholds the values of an absolute standard derived (as we noted earlier) from the "ideas of the time," especially the religious doctrines, which usually transform the action of his plays into moral exempla on the wages of vice or folly. And on the left are the modernists who want to believe that the dramatist is "our contemporary" and that his plays are challenging the received values or even denying all value, so that their action is usually transformed into some kind of meaningless charade or Grand Mechanism exemplifying our existential dilemma. (Indeed they often seem to assume that the absence of pervasive irony would in itself be a serious failing from which the play must be rescued.) It is highly ironic that these two diametrically opposed camps of ironizers should now be allied in this assault on the meaning and values of Shakespeare and his fellow dramatists. Yet their completely different readings have the same basic purpose—the desire to save the plays by purging them of what the critic considers to be moral deficiencies. And since every play of the period is vulnerable to attack (or salvation) from at least one of these camps, and most from both, we can safely predict that between them they will soon succeed in rewriting the entire body of Renaissance drama.

It seems evident, however, that the actual consequences of "creating every bad a perfect best" in the realm of ethics are at least as unfortunate as they were found to be in the aesthetic branch of this operation. Although the moral vindicators also claim that they are enhancing our respect for the play and its author, the fact is that they also do neither. The play becomes incoherent when we are asked to reject the internal standard of judgment upon which its significance and our response must depend. And the author becomes incompetent when we are asked to accept an intention in his play which it failed to communicate to anyone before. Moreover, these readings not only diminish the play and the playwright but also diminish us. For surely one of the greatest rewards of literature lies in the insights it can give us into different ways of perceiving the human condition. But it can never do this if we go to the work determined to find there a mirror of our own minds. And that is what happens when we try to vindicate the morality of the work, because we are then making it agree with our morality. The ironic approach enables us to produce such an agreement, and this is undoubtedly one of its major (though unacknowledged) attractions, which it shares with thematism. In fact I would have to say of these ironic readings what I said earlier of thematic readings: I have yet to encounter one in which the real meaning discovered in the play did not coincide with the discoverer's own beliefs. That explains how all of these playwrights can become morally infallible, as we just saw. But while this continual confirmation that an author's attitudes and values are the same as ours may be comforting (though it must also be rather boring), it is an almost certain sign that we are misreading him, and consequently cutting ourselves off from the possibility of an enriching and enlarging experience.

The Problem of Reliability

This completes our survey of what might be called the principal offensive strategies utilized by the ironic critics to construct their readings and to support them. But we still have to examine the defensive strategy they have developed to answer the obvious question which must have occurred to anyone trying to follow their arguments here: if the playwright really felt that the character whom they are attacking was so reprehensible or ridiculous, and wanted the audience to share this attitude, why did he not make his intention clear in the play? We know he did not, because this intention has been completely misunderstood by virtually all viewers and readers of the play down to our own day, as these critics themselves acknowledge when they announce their "new readings." One explanation, of course, could be that he blundered very badly; but no ironic critic ever admits this possibility, because they are all committed to vindicating the playwright, as we saw, and so must insist that whatever he did was both deliberate and effective. Therefore, what might have been viewed as a problem of the playwright's ability is transformed into the problem of his (and his play's) reliability: why did he write a play that we cannot trust, a play whose apparent meaning, which it has conveyed to its audiences up to now, is entirely different from the real meaning that the critic has just discovered in it?

A number of the newest new readings do not attempt to confront this problem, which would suggest that the ironic approach has advanced so far, and has refuted so many plays, that it is no longer thought necessary, when introducing yet another candidate for ironihood, to explain why its author chose to conceal his meaning. Some recent critics, it would seem, even assume that such concealment was the normal procedure of the playwrights of this period, or at least of the better ones. This is implied in the reading of *The Two Gentlemen of Verona* quoted earlier, which asserts that Shakespeare showed "infallible good taste" in *not* allowing Silvia to deflate Valentine at the end; we are never told why allowing her to do so would have been in bad taste, but presumably it is because that would have given away Shakespeare's real attitude toward Valentine (that is, the attitude this critic attributes to him). Another critic makes a similar assumption when he argues that "the alleged Christianity" of Henry V is "as suspect in Shakespeare's eyes as is the theology of Dr. Faustus in Marlowe's," although this may not be evident "because Shakespeare, as the more subtle artist, has not so obviously tipped his hand"; and so does another who claims that "to credit Henry V in his public appearances as genuine or pious is to be deceived, and deceived by an author whose grasp of dramatic technique had grown much since Richard III . . . ." For all three critics, apparently, it is simply good artistry (or taste or dramatic technique) to hide one's meaning, even though this will mislead the audience.

Most ironic readings, however, have felt under some obligation to account for the author's unreliability. One possibility is that he was forced to conceal his real (i.e., negative) view of the character in question, and to feign a positive presentation of him, because of public opinion or, perhaps, the censorship. The quotation on *Henry V* at the beginning of the chapter advances this explanation ("Faced with the demand to depict such a man as a hero"), as does a second reading which asserts that Shakespeare had to pretend to approve of this "great national hero" to "get a hearing for his play . . . at a time when patriotism is running high," while a third extends it to include the portrayal of Henry Tudor in *Richard III:* "No doubt the Elizabethan audience, or at least the simpler souls among them, would have taken the future Henry VII as orthodoxy demanded; but Shakespeare, it seems, managed to satisfy his artistic (and perhaps political) conscience while at the same time offering nothing that was explicitly unorthodox or offensive, precisely as he does with that other sacrosanct English hero, Henry V." And a reading of *A Woman Killed with Kindness* states that Heywood wanted us to condemn Frankford for not immediately forgiving his wife, but did not express this attitude directly because it conflicted with contemporary opinion: "He could not write anything approaching a homily on the subject of forgiveness and hope to have his play live to see its second performance."[31]

We might refer to this as the "two-audience" or "two-play" theory, because it finds in each of these works two distinct and contradictory entities—the "apparent" play, sympathetic to the character, which the dramatist had to write in order to deceive the stupid mob (those "simpler souls") or the Master of the Revels (who is presumably supposed to be no less simple); and the opposite "real" play, antipathetic to the character, which he wanted to write in order to enlighten the wiser sort, or possibly just to satisfy himself. Although this theory has exerted considerable influence, it has two basic limitations. It cannot show how the playwright could simultaneously conceal and reveal his two meanings to his two audiences, so that nobody in one audience would respond to the meaning intended for the other. And it can only be applied to a relatively few plays, whose alleged "real" meaning might have antagonized the public or the state.

A second kind of explanation avoids both of these difficulties by claiming that the playwright deliberately set out to deceive his entire audience into admiring the character in question, but that he only did this for their own good, since he later undeceived them, by showing how deplorable the character really is, in order to teach them a lesson from their error. This might be called the "therapeutic deception" theory, which combines the two audiences of the preceding theory into one, and segregates the two meanings (which that theory had juxtaposed throughout the play) in a sequential scheme: first the apparent meaning, then the real one. It is employed by one critic to account for the attractive portrayal of Cleopatra and even extended into a new ironic poetics for all tragedy:

> If under the spell of the moment we allow ourselves to be caught [by "her magic"], our second reflections should awake us to the realization of what salt fish we are. Perhaps the art of tragedy consists in this very temptation to confusion—for the sake of our subsequent recognition of our folly. That is, a tragedy's beguiling heroisms serve to prompt mistaken judgments, so that then we can confess and evaluate our proneness to illusion.

Another critic explains that "if we are made to sympathize with Romeo's commitment, it is only in the end to realize the more emphatically the incompleteness of his awareness of the nature of matured love." And a third seems to be applying the theory to *The White Devil:*

> Webster never relaxes his artistic control to tell the audience how they are to react. The audience is drawn into the dramatic illusion: Webster uses his art to deceive and tempt us just as it

deceives and tempts the characters in the play. We, like them, may be led to make false moral judgments, and though we may recognize these as false when all is said and done, we come away from our experience of the play with a profound awareness of the terrible power of evil.

The argument may be a little difficult to follow, since it fails to explain how, if Webster never tells us the way to react, he can at the same time deceive and tempt us, or how we come to recognize the falsity of our moral judgments when all is said and done, if we do. But this last problem points to a basic weakness of the theory itself. For according to the theory everything depends upon our being undeceived by the ending; the dramatist, who has been completely unreliable through-out most of the play, must become completely reliable there, and present an especially clear judgment against the character and his "beguiling heroisms." Yet in each of our examples we found that the opposite is true—the final judgment of the ending is very favorable to the character whom the critic has been attacking (or at least "appears" to be very favorable), which of course is why the critic must then try to refute it.

Presumably for that reason some of these critics fall back upon a third explanation, a modified version of the "therapeutic deception" theory, in which the final enlightenment does not occur at the end of the play but later, as we pore over the play in the library. (Thus it in effect resurrects the two audiences of the first theory but places them both within the same person: we are the "apparent meaning" audience in the theater, and become the "real meaning" audience when we repair to our desks.) This view is stated explicitly in one critic's refutation of the treason scene (II.ii) in *Henry V*. He begins by admitting that "for anything that appears in the Chorus to this act or on the surface of the story, there is no reason for not taking this scene at its face value: the lucky exposure of three vile traitors"; but he then explains that it should not be taken at face value because these men were really engaged in an honorable attempt to restore the rightful heir, Edmund Mortimer, although this is never mentioned: "The long shadow that the incarcerated Mortimer casts over this play is not visible from a seat in the theater. But it is from the higher vantage point of poetry read in solitude."[32] And the same idea is implicit in another critic's account of how we are first tricked into sympathizing with Romeo and Juliet and then made to realize our error. The purpose of the first Prologue, he says,

> is to engage our sympathy and prompt our pity and fear. But then, while our spellbound emotions are being exercised within this frame, the dramatist weaves into the action archetypal

echoes, through wordplay and emblematic scenes, which offer
for our intellect a deeper significance whenever (either during
or after our moment in the theatre) we are ready to decipher it.

The hedging within the parentheses surely is not meant to be taken at
face value, for the elaborate scheme needed to "decipher" the play, which
is presented in this critic's reading, could not possibly be worked out
during anyone's moment in the theater. But the same must be said of all
the other ironic readings we have seen here; the real meaning (or "deeper
significance") they discover is always sharply differentiated from the
apparent meaning which we directly experience, and so cannot be apprehended during a performance or even an ordinary reading of the play.
Thus they all assume this theory, whether they acknowledge it or not,
because in their approach the play is no longer something to be experienced, either on stage or in print, but something which must be labori-
ously examined and cross-examined, pondered over and wrestled with,
through one of those "unbelievably close" readings, until it is finally
made to yield up its hidden real meaning, like a coded message. Moreover, this message is deliberately misleading, since its apparent meaning
is so often the opposite of its real meaning; hence the play has become
not merely a code or puzzle to be solved, but a trick to be seen through.
Therefore, while this theory has found a way around the problem of the
preceding one, it has raised serious new problems of its own. If such a
prolonged scrutiny of these plays is required in order to uncover their
deception and reveal their true meaning, then it is not easy to explain
why so many of their authors took so little interest in publishing them
(about half of Shakespeare's, for instance, were not printed until after his
death). But even ignoring this embarrassing fact—as all the ironic critics
do—it is obvious that the overwhelming majority of viewers and readers
of the plays have never attempted such a scrutiny and never will. It
would follow, then, that they must always be left with a completely false
conception of the play's meaning, and furthermore that the playwright,
unless he was incredibly naive, must have realized this from the start.

The third theory, therefore, really implies a fourth in which the dramatist is once more writing each play for two separate groups—the general
public whom he permanently misled with his apparent meaning, and the
select few whom he temporarily misled for their own good, since he
could count on their buying a copy of the text (even if he could not count
on its being published) and puzzling over it until they figured out that the
apparent meaning was a trick and that the real meaning was its opposite.
This may be regarded as a combination of the "two-audience" and the
"therapeutic deception" theories; and it is, I believe, the logical con-

clusion of the sequence of explanations we have been considering, and hence the real rationale behind most ironic readings, even though few of them state it explicitly. It is so stated, however, by the critic quoted earlier who claims that the endings of Jonson's major comedies all "conceal a conscious irony which . . . he expects the judicious to perceive." Indeed, he believes that these plays are a kind of test of the judicious, "an inquisition on the audience's critical faculty, a separation of Spectators from Understanders," since they employ "a calculated strategy to tempt the [audience] into false or over-simple interpretations," and that Jonson "is watching us keenly to see if we have taken his finer point." (It seems, though, that "an embarrassing number of Jonson's critics" have succumbed to the temptation and so flunked the test.) And the critic who cleared Shakespeare of the charge of jingoism makes this theory a general principle for interpreting his plays:

> Of course Shakespeare the playwright was writing for audiences. But how about Shakespeare the poet? Drama . . . must make a wide and immediate appeal to a large number of people of ordinary intelligence. . . . The public does not want the truth. It wants confirmation of its prejudices. . . . What the poet is seeking, on the other hand, is the secret of life, and, even if he would, he cannot share [it] with a crowd in a theater. . . . He can share it only with the few, and with them mostly in solitude. . . . And so his greater plays are one thing as drama and another as poetry, one thing on the outside, another within.

The theory is clearly implied, moreover, by the warnings, in the passages quoted at the beginning of this chapter, that the character under attack has very engaging qualities which we should beware of—that Alsemero is "outwardly attractive," that "audiences are . . . taken in by Romeo's death-dealing charm," that Hector's noble "appearance may well blind us to the reality," that we should "break free from the mesmerizing power of Prospero's all-too-often successful attempt to dazzle us with his halo," and so on. Another critic, similarly, cautions that in the love scenes between Antony and Cleopatra "the difficulty is that the speeches are such splendid poetry that we are inclined to be overswayed by them" and to accept them, erroneously, "at their face value"; and another, that "as word music and rhetoric" the Choruses in *Henry V* "are indeed intoxicating," although "we have ourselves to blame if we let them put us in a condition in which we cannot see what is going on." But since the playwright is himself to blame for Alsemero's attractiveness and Romeo's charm and Hector's blinding appearance and Prospero's dazzling halo and Antony and Cleopatra's overswaying poetry and the intoxicating effect of those Choruses, this can only mean that he deliberately set out to deceive his audience—except for those few wise enough to stay aloof from the emotional experience which the play is designed to produce.

The snobbish appeal of such an idea may recall the now discredited practice of explaining away any part of the play which the critic disliked as the dramatist's sop to the groundlings. Actually the new ironic critic is simply extending this tactic: he too explains away whatever he does not like in the play—that is, whatever does not fit his ironic reading—by directing it at the groundlings, but he has enlarged the pit to include all the rest of us. He postulates an elitist playwright who is really writing for a very small minority (sometimes limited to a single member—the critic himself), and is making fools of everybody else. For we must bear in mind that here, unlike the earlier versions of the "therapeutic deception" theory, the great majority of viewers and readers are never undeceived, since they lack the intellectual or moral equipment (to say nothing of the time) required to decipher the code and see through the trick (thus one critic tells us that Shakespeare made the "version of Christianity" exhibited by Henry V "of a superficially attractive kind" which is "capable of beguiling superficial Christians of all ages"). Moreover, unlike the first version of the "two-audience" theory in which the dramatist was forced to conceal his real attitude to avoid trouble, there is here no motive for his deceiving most of the audience, unless it be sheer malicious mischief ("What fun Shakespeare must have had," another study of Henry V states, "making such a fool of his Archbishop, knowing all the while that his audience would swallow his utterances as grave political wisdom"). He is now not writing for his audience but against them, and is willfully leading them into (or confirming them in) very serious error—for the deception is not about trivial matters but his most basic beliefs and values. It is an ugly picture of moral irresponsibility, but, insofar as it is the logical conclusion of this sequence of defensive strategies, it would seem to be the only way to avoid making the playwright a bungler who is unable to communicate his meaning. Thus we arrive at the crowning irony of the ironic approach: its avowed purpose in most of these readings, we found, is to vindicate the playwright's morality; but in order to do this it must bring his artistry into question, and in order to salvage his artistry it must sacrifice his morality.

Whatever its moral implications may be, however, the position itself is irrefutable, which is why it serves as the last line of defense in the sequence we were examining. And any interpretation based upon it is equally irrefutable. It enables the ironic critic to ignore all the evidence against his reading, either in the play (since that must have been part of the dramatist's trick), or in the response which the play has evoked in others (since they must have been taken in by the trick). And all those who object to his reading must be similarly deceived. If we accept this view of the author's relationship to his audience, then there could be no way to argue that he is not being ironic, no matter what appears in his text or even in his extradramatic statements (just as there could be no way to argue that this whole chapter is not itself an ironic exercise whose real purpose is to support the new ironic readings). For he is now not only totally unreliable but actually malicious—to everyone, that is, except our critic, to whom he has revealed his secret.

What principle of interpretation can we offer, then, to find a way out of this circle of self-confirming ironies? It certainly cannot be that non-ironic plays are intrinsically superior in artistry or taste or dramatic technique to ironic ones, which is just as arbitrary and absurd as the contrary proposition. Nor can it be that the dramatists of this period never employed irony, since we have seen some instances of it (including one entire play) that are universally acknowledged, and must admit at least the theoretical possibility that there are others not yet recognized. Surely we must come to each play without any absolute laws of this sort, and try to attend as closely as we can to the experience it provides, aided by whatever relevant knowledge we can obtain about its author, his stage, the dramatic conventions of his time, and the like. But to that general platitude we can add a more specific principle which has been the real basis of this critique of the ironic approach—namely, that the dramatist wanted to be understood by his audience, that he wanted them to grasp his intention and respond to it appropriately, and therefore took some pains to ensure that they would. This of course is the opposite of the ironic critic's conception of the relationship between author and audience, and it will have the opposite consequence, since it means that we can and should trust him and his play.

If we can trust him, then we ought to approach these plays with the assumption that they are to be treated as "straight"—that is, as meaning what they seem to mean—unless they contain clear indications to the contrary. I do not regard this as some convenient rule in a debating game we critics play, for I believe it describes the expectation or mental "set" which audiences actually bring to plays when encountering them for the first time (at least up to very recently), and which dramatists, even ironic dramatists, count on when writing them. And if we begin with this assumption (or working hypothesis), then we are justified in placing what we called a "burden of disproof" upon the playwright. For it gives us the right to expect that, if he wanted his audience to depart in some way from their normal tendency to treat the play as "straight"—if he did not wish them to accept the "face value"of the presentation of a character, or the finality of the ending, or the special authority of a chorus— he would have given them unmistakable signs of this intention. We can be confident that he would do so if he wanted to be understood by them, and possessed even a minimal competence (which is a second assumption we always begin with). And this in turn gives us the right to place an equivalent burden of disproof upon the ironic critic—to demand that anyone claiming to find such an intention in any play will show us these unmistakable signs and so produce an especially strong case against the "straight" or "apparent" meaning, which, until it is proven otherwise beyond a reasonable doubt, we will presume to be the real meaning.

Another important consequence of our principle is that we can and should trust not only the playwright and his play but also the response which this play has evoked in most viewers and readers. For if he wanted to be understood and was at all competent, then their response will correspond to his meaning. It would follow, therefore, that whenever an established interpretation has grown up around a play that has been experienced by many people over many years (which does not apply, to be sure, to all the plays considered here), it is very much more likely to be very much closer to the truth than some brand new reading. We can even restate our original hypothesis in those terms, since the established interpretation has been the "straight" one: we should approach these plays with the assumption that they mean what generations of spectators and readers have taken them to mean (when we have such a consensus), unless there is very good evidence to the contrary. And this, too, gives us the right to place a heavy burden of disproof upon the ironic critic. We have the right, that is, if we are dealing with a reliable playwright and a reliable play. But unless we begin with such a principle, and are willing to accept the restraint imposed upon us by the burden of disproof which follows from it, then anything goes, as it in fact has been going recently in the ironic approach to English Renaissance drama.

There is, finally, one more consequence of this principle, which involves our attitude toward any judgments of these plays that have been established over the years. Such judgments may not call for the same respect as an established interpretation, but they should not be treated lightly. If many intelligent commentators in many different periods have been unhappy with the ending of Measure for Measure and with all of Titus Andronicus, this is pretty good evidence that something really is wrong with these plays, which cannot be set right by asserting that Shakespeare wanted *Measure for Measure* to end unsatisfactorily, or that he was pulling our leg in *Titus*. (The opposite possibility, of an ironic critic attacking a play which was greatly admired in the past, need not concern us, for we saw that this never happens.) The contention that a new ironic reading would "save" the play from such adverse judgments is not evidence for accepting it, as we argued earlier; and our principle would lead to the same conclusion, because it is very much more likely that the established adverse judgment is right than that the established nonironic interpretation is wrong. But we are under no obligation to save all these plays. Indeed, one desirable outcome of the demise of this ironic approach might be the restoration of the critic's duty to criticize—to take note of any artistic defects in the play, rather than explaining them away as deliberate, and of any deficiencies in its moral standards, rather than replacing them with his own. His criteria could be mistaken, of course, but at least they should not interfere with his interpretation of the play, because he would be trying to deal with the play as it is and not as he would like it to be.

Another desirable outcome of this demise might be the rehabilitation of irony itself. I imagine it is quite clear by now that I am no admirer of this ironic approach—in fact I think even less can be said for it than for thematism. (About all that can be said is that it may have helped to correct an earlier tendency to oversentimentalize or overidealize some of the characters in these plays, which is its tiny part of the truth.) But I yield to no one in my admiration of irony; and my principal objection to the ironic approach is that it has given irony a bad name. The most serious damage caused by its wholesale proliferation of hitherto un-suspected but pervasive ironies is not to the individual plays mangled in these readings—the best ones, after all, will survive this fad, as they have survived others, and the rest are not much worse off than before—but to the readers of the readings, who, as Wayne Booth has pointed out, will "learn to live with blurred senses and dulled attention, and deprive themselves of the delights of precise and subtle communication that skillful . . . ironists provide."[33]

Four

Historical Readings

The term "historical" has been applied to the criticism of English Renaissance drama in so many different senses—many more than either "thematic" or "ironic"—that we cannot hope to survey them all here. Historical knowledge of one kind or another is involved in every attempt to interpret these plays. On the most basic level, it gives us the very meaning of the words in our texts. It even gives us the texts themselves, since analytical bibliography is a form of historical reconstruction. And it supplies the facts about the authorship of the plays and their chronology, the sources they drew on, the theater where they appeared, the dramatic or literary traditions and conventions that influenced them, the society they portrayed, and various other aspects of the very extensive context which we bring to bear upon them, often quite unconsciously, and without which we could scarcely be said to understand them at all. To the extent that we do understand them, therefore, we owe an immeasurable debt to the labors of the historical scholars in these fields. But this type of knowledge, essential though it is, does not constitute an approach to interpretation. It is really preinterpretative, since it underlies any informed reading of a play, but does not in itself define the nature of that reading.

If we limit ourselves, then, to the kinds of scholarship which do produce distinctive "historical readings," and so can be considered approaches to interpretation, I think we will find that they are all based upon the contention that the real meaning of the plays is wholly or largely determined by some component of the extradramatic background and can only be apprehended in relation to it. There are several approaches of this sort, which can be differentiated in terms of the increasing particularity of the historical component they employ. On the highest level of abstraction we have the "zeitgeist approach," wherein the play is treated as an embodiment of a very generalized intellectual or emotional atmosphere said to permeate every facet of life in the period. Next come those studies that interpret the play in the light of certain specified attitudes or "ideas of the time." Below them is the "topical" approach to the play, which sees in it a commentary upon contemporary individuals or events. And the extreme of particularity is reached in what I call "occasionalism," where the play is viewed as a kind of private communication directed at a special audience, outside of the commercial theaters, at a special time and place.

This classification should be adequate for our purposes, so long as we recognize that the categories are oversimplified approximations and necessarily overlap. In fact, the lower ones often seem to depend on those above them—almost all occasionalist readings make use of topical references, topical readings frequently invoke the ideas of the time, and many readings based on these ideas derive them from a more general spirit of the age. It would therefore be more accurate to think of these approaches as roughly demarcated areas along a single continuum, with some individual readings falling between two of them or encompassing both. This need not trouble us, however, since we will only be dealing here with two approaches which are not contiguous—the second and the fourth. I have chosen to concentrate upon them because they have become the dominant modes of "historical criticism" in our field. The zeitgeist and topical approaches seem to be less fashionable now, but occasionalism and, especially, the ideas-of-the-time approach are flourishing and bringing forth a bumper crop of new readings which we should investigate.

The-Ideas-of-the-Time Scene

Before beginning our examination of this approach it will be necessary to make another distinction, for the study of the connection between these plays or their authors and the ideas of the time can take two very different forms. In one of them the critic tries to ascertain how the ideas

or attitudes which he finds in the plays are related to the mental climate
of the period. This kind of study has an obvious value in its own right,
and has taught us a great deal about what is usually called "the history of
ideas," and about the dramatist's place in that history—about the ways
in which he followed or modified or departed from the intellectual
traditions he inherited and the intellectual movements of his own day.
However, it is not an approach in our sense, because it is postinterpre-
tative; it relies upon a prior interpretation of the plays and does not (in
theory at least) influence that interpretation. But the study of a dramatist
and the ideas of his time is also commonly understood to refer to another
pursuit which proceeds in the opposite direction, since it does not treat
the plays as independent data to be related to the ideas, but starts with
the ideas and uses them to interpret the plays. And this clearly is an
approach, for we shall see that it determines the principles and methodology and even the conclusions of a certain kind of reading.

It is of course possible to combine these two forms of study in various
ways within the same book or article, but that does not affect the
distinction because they are logically separable procedures. And since we
are concerned with the ideas of the time here only when they are
employed in interpretations of these plays, our investigation will be
limited to the second pursuit. I should acknowledge at the outset, however, that much of what I have to say about it will not be new. For this
approach, unlike the thematic and ironic approaches, has provoked
considerable discussion, and a number of incisive criticisms of it have
appeared, with which I am happy to associate myself, if their authors
will have me.[1] But since the flow of new readings issuing from it has not
perceptibly abated, there would seem to be a need to restate their
position. And I have been able to add some further considerations which
may help to clarify the case against this approach and to place it within
the larger framework of the critique developed in the other chapters.

We will begin then with a convenient summary provided for us in a
survey of the major trends in recent Shakespeare criticism by Patrick
Murray, entitled *The Shakespearian Scene*,[2] which can serve as our
introduction to the ideas-of-the-time scene. Murray calls one of these
trends "the historical approach," and he finds that it has made a "sin-
gularly impressive" contribution "to our understanding of Shakespeare's
plays," because

> it has rescued and brought into the full light of day matters of
> fact as well as patterns of thought; by restoring to view things
> lost or obscured by the passage of time it has provided new and
> productive ways of looking at the plays and . . . has corrected

numerous errors of interpretation and helped to put some of the
wilder theories of impressionistic criticism firmly in their place.

He goes on to supply several examples of this impressive contribution,
from which I have selected three to illustrate the approach. In the first he
explains that "the Elizabethan philosophy of hierarchy described in such
books as Tillyard's *Elizabethan World Picture* and Lovejoy's *The Great
Chain of Being* adds a whole new dimension to one's reading of *King Lear*"
and enables us to appreciate, "in the light of common Elizabethan assumptions," the cosmic significance of Lear's abdication. In the second we
learn that the "examination of Desdemona's role in the light of Elizabethan
courtesy-books and canonical literature suggests that a contemporary
audience would have had stronger reservations than those generally
expressed nowadays about . . . some aspects of her behaviour [such as]
her defiance and deception of her father [and] her breach of matrimonial
conventions." And in the third he informs us that "a proper understanding
of Elizabethan pneumatology" is required to explain the Ghost in *Hamlet*:
"without the insights of the historical approach, without constant reference to Elizabethan theological and philosophical speculations concerning spirits and their discernment, it is difficult to see how a modern
reader can make much sense of . . . the ghost-scenes."

These examples—and most of his others are similar—have several
elements in common that are characteristic of the approach in general. In
each of them the claim is made that certain ideas of the time are essential
to the correct interpretation of a major point in the play, and so must
determine that interpretation. Moreover, this point is not simply a matter
of fact but will vitally affect our judgment of the character involved
(Lear, Desdemona, Hamlet). And it is clearly implied that the result will
be a quite different judgment of this character than the one we adopt
when we do not know these ideas—for if there were no significant
difference, the approach would not be making an impressive contribution
to our understanding of the play. An examination of all the problems raised
in any one of these interpretations is beyond the scope of this chapter,
but that will not be necessary in order to see what light they can shed
upon the approach itself.

The first example should be very familiar by now, since a number of
critics have recently been telling us how Lear's abdication violated the
Renaissance world picture and concept of hierarchy. One of them asserts,
for instance, that "as a king, it was not Lear's prerogative to abandon his
rule . . . he could not abandon his royal obligations without disturbing
the natural order." Another puts this more strongly:

An act of betrayal is also committed by Lear when, in the play's opening scene, he divests himself of kingship and gives up the divinely-appointed duties of monarchy. We must here remember precisely what kingship meant to the Elizabethans, if we are to comprehend the magnitude of Lear's ill-doing. . . . Here is the Lord's deputy divesting himself, most sinfully and criminally, of his divine duty.

And a third is even more vehement:

To understand the enormity of Lear's sin, we must recognize the peculiar position of the king in the highly ordered world which Renaissance Christian humanism carried over from the Middle Ages. Lear's resignation of his throne . . . would have been regarded by a Jacobean audience with a horror difficult for a modern audience to appreciate, for . . . [it was] a violation of the king's responsibility to God, and . . . could result only in . . . chaos on every level of creation. . . . By his resignation of rule Lear disrupts the harmonious order of nature . . . [and the] infinite good of God's order which decrees that the king rule for the good of his people until God relieves him of his responsibility by death.

Now one is immediately led to wonder why, if this idea is so crucial to the play, it is never once mentioned there. Lear's abdication is witnessed and commented upon by a great many characters, but not one of them expresses the least bit of horror at it. Indeed, Kent and Gloucester have apparently been consulted about his decision in advance and have accepted it. Moreover, Lear himself later in the play comes to acknowledge many failings, yet he never acknowledges this one, which is very strange if it is supposed to be his worst sin of all.

There is some reason to doubt, however, that the Jacobeans really would have regarded it as a sin. King James himself presumably would not, for in his *Defence of the Right of Kings* he raises no objection to the idea that kings may "renounce the right of royalty, and of their own accord give over the kingdom."[3] And Herbert Howarth points out that when the Emperor Charles V abdicated in 1555/56 his action was greeted, not with horror, but with admiration.[4] He also points out that King David abdicated in favor of his son Solomon. According to 1 Kings, David did this with the approval and assistance of Nathan the Prophet and Zadok the Priest, and thanked "the Lord God of Israel, which hath given one to sit on my throne this day, mine eyes even seeing it."[5] Nor does the ensuing narrative record any calamities resulting from this disruption of the harmonious order of nature, which ushered in the golden age of Israel's history. And Shakespeare and his audience, as Howarth suggests, were more likely to have read that biblical account than to have read Tillyard. Even if it could be proved, however, that the doctrine of the unresignability of kingship actually was an idea of the time, I would still have to argue that it is not relevant to *King Lear*, for the simple reason that it does not figure in the play.

The second example, Desdemona's marrying without her father's consent, is on a different footing, because we know that the duty of daughters to obey their parents, especially in the choice of a husband, was explicitly affirmed at this time in many of the courtesy books and moral and religious treatises. One critic has assembled some of this material in order "to examine Desdemona's conduct against a background of Elizabethan attitudes" and to demonstrate that "the predictable audience reaction" to her would be unfavorable:

> The conduct of a young lady in the courtesy books is also a far cry from that of Desdemona in her matrimonial arrangements. She marries against the precepts of both courtesy books and canon law, without consulting her father.... In terms of Venetian practice and Elizabethan precept the behavior of the lady is unfilial and unnatural indeed.... [She] is not the ideal young lady of the precept books, and the audience, especially the male members of it, could here be expected to judge Desdemona harshly.

Another asserts on the same basis that her action was "an incredible breach of normal decent behavior," and warns us against the modern tendency to side with her rather than with her father:

> To us at least, his anger that she should have chosen to wed Othello without first asking his leave is unseemly, unsympathetic, and crude. This was not the view in Shakespeare's day.... Brabantio was ... a much-wronged man, and Desdemona was punished, albeit too brutally, for committing a sin against what at that time was regarded as a fundamental decency.

And this kind of evidence has been used to condemn not only Desdemona's marriage to Othello but also Juliet's to Romeo—in fact one critic equates these two "sins" in his discussion of Desdemona: "as with Juliet so here we must allow for the weight given by Shakespeare to the sin of disobedience to parents." Another critic explains that Juliet's behavior would have "shocked" Shakespeare's audience, because of "the fact that in thus boldly asserting her own will she violates a sacred canon of Elizabethan life; namely, that children, and especially daughters, owe

obedience to the wishes of their parents." And another has been quoted
as saying that "a prolonged study of a cache of Elizabethan social
documents" left him "with one overriding impression: that the average
audience of *Romeo and Juliet* would have regarded the behavior of the
young lovers as deserving everything they got."

This alleged "sin" presents us with the same problem as Lear's, however, because it is not condemned in the play itself. The marriages of
both Desdemona and Juliet are judged by the authority figures in their
respective worlds, who do not find their behavior at all sinful. In *Othello*,
I.iii, the Duke of Venice presides over a kind of trial and exonerates
Othello and Desdemona, without any reference to her incredible breach
of normal decent behavior; and in the final scene of *Romeo and Juliet* the
Prince of Verona, after hearing a full account of the events, places the
blame not upon the young lovers but upon their parents, and certainly
never suggests that Juliet deserved everything she got. Apparently neither
the Duke nor the Prince had a chance to study that cache of Elizabethan
social documents.

A further problem arises, moreover, when we try to apply this sacred
canon of Elizabethan life to Shakespeare's other plays, and see what
would happen if all his daughters behaved like the ideal young lady of
the precept books and obeyed their parents in matrimonial arrange-
ments. In *The Two Gentlemen of Verona* Silvia would have to marry
Thurio, of all people, because her father wished it. In *A Midsummer
Night's Dream* Hermia would have to marry Demetrius, despite the
misery this would bring to her and Lysander and Helena. In *Cymbeline*
Imogen would have to marry Cloten. And poor Anne Page in *The Merry
Wives of Windsor* would have to commit bigamy, since one parent wants
her to marry Abraham Slender and the other Doctor Caius. The plays of
Shakespeare's contemporaries provide us with many more examples of
this sort: in *The Shoemakers' Holiday* Rose Otley would have to marry
Hammon, in *Michaelmas Term* Susan Quomodo would have to marry
Andrew Lethe, in *Philaster* Arethusa would have to marry Pharamond,
in *A Chaste Maid in Cheapside* Moll Yellowhammer would have to
marry Sir Walter Whorehound, in *Bartholomew Fair* Grace Wellborn
would have to marry Bartholomew Cokes (here she owes obedience as a
ward rather than a daughter, but the point is the same), in *A Fair Quarrel*
Jane Russell would have to marry Chough, in *A New Way to Pay Old
Debts* Margaret Overreach would have to marry Lord Lovell, and so on
and on. Each of these defiant, disobedient, unfilial, undutiful, unnatural,
indecent, sinful, and sacred-canon-violating young ladies, of course,
rejects the man her father or guardian has chosen for her and manages

(often by deceiving her parent, another form of conduct frowned upon in the courtesy books) to marry the man she has chosen for herself. And in each case her action has the full approval of the play and, presumably, of the audience. Indeed the unsuitability of the suitor favored by the parents could almost be called a convention of this drama. And when there is no such suitor to contend with, many other young ladies defy the opposition of parent or guardian to marry the man of their choice, again with the play's blessing and our own (Maria in *The Family of Love*, Joyce in *A Trick to Catch the Old One*, etc.). We even have plays like *The Witch of Edmonton*, *The Broken Heart*, and *The Miseries of Enforced Marriage* which depict the unfortunate consequences when young people marry in obedience to orders (and to the precepts in those books) instead of following the dictates of their own hearts.

The explanation of this discrepancy between official theory and dramatic practice is simple enough. If a Gallup poll had been taken of the Elizabethan men-in-the-street on the question of whether daughters should obey their parents, no doubt a large majority would have answered yes, because this was a generally accepted idea of the time. But if the audience emerging from the original performance of *A Chaste Maid in Cheapside* had been asked whether Moll should have married Sir Walter Whorehound, surely they would all have answered no. For there was another idea of the time, expressed in many proverbs,[6] that love cannot be compelled, and that it will find a way, despite stone walls and locks and other obstacles set up by the antiromantic older generation. (It must have been a very ancient idea, since it is the basis of most Roman comedies.) The fact that it contradicts the doctrine of the courtesy books does not make it any less an idea of the time; we ourselves can hold contradictory views on many subjects, and there is no reason to believe that the Elizabethans were any different in this respect. One would think that all of this was quite obvious, at least in the plays just cited, yet we find a critic actually insisting that Imogen in *Cymbeline* "would serve the Elizabethans, along with Juliet and Desdemona, as another warning to fair women of the suffering and tragedy which devolve on those undutiful daughters who disobey their fathers." If we remember that obeying her father would have meant marrying Cloten (who is introduced to us as "a thing / Too bad for bad report"), then we can see to what absurd lengths this kind of historical criticism will go to achieve a victory over the plays themselves and over the facts of our own experience.

The third example, the Ghost in *Hamlet*, presents a more complex problem, but I believe the same principles apply to it. A number of critics have sought to determine the nature of this ghost by consulting Elizabethan pneumatology. They certainly have not settled the question, for they reach quite different conclusions, the most remarkable being that it is not really a ghost at all but a demon pretending to be a ghost. This view has now been advanced in several studies, but it will be enough here if we look at the argument of the most thoroughgoing and best known of them, which runs as follows: Protestant theology held that all ghosts were either hallucinations or else angels or demons in disguise. Catholic theology admitted a fourth possibility, that they could be souls temporarily released from purgatory. Now the Ghost in *Hamlet* certainly cannot be a hallucination or an angel. And it fails its purgatorial qualifying test, derived by this critic from two French books on spirits (neither of which, incidentally, had been translated into English at the time of *Hamlet*). According to them, purgatorial ghosts asked for alms, fasts, pilgrimages, prayers, or masses, which this ghost never does; moreover, it asks for revenge on Claudius instead of forgiving him, as Church doctrine required. Ergo, it cannot come from purgatory and so must be a demon.

There seem to be two basic errors in this line of argument. One is the assumption that the ideas of the time about ghosts were limited to what the authorities stated in their treatises—an assumption which leads another critic, for example, to assert that "no Protestant could admit that the spirit of the dead might return, since Purgatory was ruled out and Heaven and Hell were closed to departure." But we have conclusive evidence in the play itself that many must have admitted this, since they believed—in direct contradiction to the authorities—that the spirits of the dead, or at least some of them, did not go to heaven or hell or even purgatory but remained in their graves, to emerge at night or on special occasions. This belief is expressed in Hamlet's first reaction to the Ghost:

> Let me not burst in ignorance, but tell
> Why thy canoniz'd bones, hearsed in death,
> Have burst their cerements; why the sepulchre
> Wherein we saw thee quietly interr'd,
> Hath op'd his ponderous and marble jaws
> To cast thee up again.
>
>   [I.iv.46–51]

And it is repeated later in Horatio's comment, "There needs no ghost, my lord, come from the grave / To tell us this" (I.v.125–26). We also learn in *Hamlet* (I.i.113–16) and in *Julius Caesar* (I.iii.63–75, II.ii.18–24) that on the night before Caesar's assassination ghosts emerged from their graves to walk the streets of Rome. In *Henry VI, Part II* we are told that at night "spirits walk and ghosts break up their graves" (I.iv.18), and in *A Midsummer Night's Dream* that at dawn "ghosts, wand'ring here and there, / Troop home to churchyards" (III.ii.381–82).[7] And one could cite much more evidence of this widespread belief, which still survives in our uneasiness around cemeteries at night. It is not relevant to the Ghost in *Hamlet*, who does not come from the grave, but it does prove that there were more ideas of the time about ghosts than were dreamt of in the official pneumatology.

We have the same kind of conclusive evidence in Shakespeare of another idea of the time about ghosts which is also not found in the treatises, but which is very relevant to *Hamlet*—namely, that the ghosts of murdered men could seek vengeance either by plaguing their killers or by encouraging their revengers. The ghosts at the end of *Richard III* do both (V.iii), and earlier in the play Richard's mother tells him that "the little souls of Edward's children / Whisper the spirits of thine enemies / And promise them success and victory" (IV.iv.192–94). In *Henry VI, Part II* Duke Humphrey's ghost is envisaged as an agent of retribution against two of his murderers, the Duke of Suffolk and Cardinal Beaufort (III.ii. 230–31, 373–74). And Richard II speaks of kings "haunted by the ghosts they have depos'd" (III.ii.158). Caesar's ghost appears twice to Brutus to foretell his doom (V.v.17–20), and Juliet imagines that in her family tomb she will see Tybalt's "ghost / Seeking out Romeo, that did spit his body / Upon a rapier's point" (IV.iii.56–58). It was even thought that these ghosts could torment their kinsmen for *failing* to avenge them: the Duke in *Measure for Measure* asserts that if Isabella should ask him to pardon Angelo, "Her brother's ghost his paved bed would break / And take her hence in horror" (V.i.430–31); and Macduff fears that if Macbeth is "slain and with no stroke of mine, / My wife and children's ghosts will haunt me still" (V.vii.15–16). And these beliefs can be corroborated in the works of other playwrights: in *A King and No King*, for instance, Spaconia says that if Tigranes wrongs her, "when I am dead / For certain I shall walk to visit him" (II.i.295–96); and at the end of *Edward II* young Edward, addressing his dead father, says that "unto thy murdered ghost / I offer up" the head of Mortimer, who had ordered his execution (V.vi.99–100). In fact there are vengeful ghosts who actually appear in a number of plays of this period, including *The Misfortunes of Arthur*, *Locrine*, *The True Tragedy of Richard III*, *The Spanish Tragedy*, *The Revenge of Bussy D'Ambois*, and *Antonio's Revenge* (this one tells us he has come from "his coffin"—III.i.34). Nor can I find any suggestion that any of these ghosts—either those referred to in the dialogue or those presented on stage—are supposed to be demons; they are all regarded as the genuine spirits of the victim, the official pneumatology of the time to the contrary notwithstanding.

The second basic error in this line of argument is the assumption that we can deduce the playwright's meaning in such a crucial matter from the ideas of the time, or from any external source, instead of inducing it from the play itself. For Shakespeare has very carefully established the Ghost's authenticity by twice voicing the demonic hypothesis within the action, and twice refuting it. In I.iv Horatio warns Hamlet that the Ghost may tempt him to the summit of the cliff and there assume some horrible form to drive him mad; but it does not, and Hamlet returns from his encounter to assure Horatio that "it is an honest ghost" (I.v.138). Later, in II.ii, Hamlet himself wonders if it could have been a "devil" operating more subtly, by lying to him about Claudius's guilt rather than driving him off the cliff; but his mousetrap play proves that he can "take the ghost's word for a thousand pound" (III.ii.274–75). And thereafter no doubts about a "damned ghost" are raised by anyone in the play; nor have they been raised, so far as we can tell, by the overwhelming majority of viewers and readers down to the present. Surely, if Shakespeare had wished his audience to regard the Ghost as a demon, he would have tried to make such an important point clear to them, instead of leaving it to be revealed by one of our new readings. I think we must conclude, therefore, that the Ghost is what the play says it is, and not what the ideas of the time, as expounded by these critics, say it should be.

What light, then, is shed by the three examples upon this sort of historical approach to the drama through the ideas of the time? They certainly do not support the claim, quoted at the outset, that it provides a corrective to the vagaries of impressionistic criticism, for we have seen that it is itself highly subjective and selective in its use of historical evidence. It is in fact doubly selective. It chooses which ideas of the time it will apply; from the various beliefs existing then on some subject, it singles out one to be designated as "the Elizabethan attitude" toward that subject. And it also chooses the plays to which it will apply this attitude: the idea that daughters must obey their parents is used against Juliet and Desdemona, but not Anne Page or Moll Yellowhammer; the idea that victims must forgive those who wronged them is used against Hamlet and his father's ghost, but not against Malcolm or Macduff or Lear or Cordelia, and so on.

It is no coincidence, furthermore, that in each of these examples the application of "the Elizabethan attitude" is supposed to make the character involved much less sympathetic than he would otherwise seem to be:

Lear becomes a horrifying sinner before the play begins, and presumably remains one to the end (since he dies without repenting or even recognizing this horrifying sin); both Juliet and Desdemona become unnatural, indecent, sinful, etc.; and Hamlet, in accepting the demon-ghost, will himself become damned. We saw in the preceding chapter that this was the general thrust of any attempt to impose upon the play an external standard of judgment derived from the ideas of the time. For in selecting the ideas that will constitute "Elizabethan attitudes," these critics are almost inevitably drawn to the orthodox pieties which they can confirm in the theological or homiletic literature,[8] and which therefore usually turn out to be some exalted ideal that the character falls short of, or some exacting prescription of conduct that he violates. Thus we found one critic condemning "Antonio's imperfect relationship to . . . the Christian ideal" in *The Merchant of Venice* because, even though he is ready to lay down his life for his friend, his charity "is directed towards only one man, not all men"; and another condemning Montague and Capulet because their reconciliation is "far short of a heavenly peace" described by Augustine; and another condemning Maria in *The Family of Love* because she "fail[s] to exemplify human love at its highest level," which we also owe to Augustine. Another critic censures Romeo for not attaining "true love . . . by Paul's definition"; and another uses Plato's definition for the same purpose: "As Socrates proves in Plato's *Symposium*, love which is not directed toward some demonstrable ideal cannot be said to exist. . . . This is Othello's case (and indeed the case of Claudio and Orsino too)." And, he might have added, of just about every other lover in the drama of this period.

Many more examples of this sort could be cited, in which the ideas of the time, conceived of either as specific rules or general ideals, are invoked to denigrate a character. One critic insists that Frankford in *A Woman Killed with Kindness* removes himself "from consideration as a *Christian* gentleman" when he does not immediately forgive his wife for adultery, since the church taught that "no mortal has the right to withhold forgiveness—only God can judge"; and others have similarly attacked Hamlet (and his father's ghost, as we just saw) for not "joyfully forgiving" Claudius. Desdemona also runs afoul of the Christian ideal (Calvinist section), according to another critic, when she protests that she never trespassed against Othello's love, "Either in discourse of thought or actual deed, / Or that mine eyes, mine ears, or any sense / Delighted them in any other form" (IV.ii.153–55):

> Her reference to her "discourse of thought" and to her "senses" as having been perfectly pure is another example of pride, since the

mind and the senses were notoriously fickle from the Skeptical and Calvinistic points of view.... A virtuous person was expected to acknowledge and thus control his sinful impulses (thought and sense) rather than try to deny them as Desdemona does.

Another finds that Othello's account of his courtship—"She lov'd me for the dangers I had pass'd,/And I lov'd her that she did pity them" (I.iii. 167–68)—is concerned with "bad fame" (reputation among men) rather than "good fame" (glorifying God), a traditional distinction "which Shakespeare's contemporaries would recognize": "Judging from these lines, Othello's love for his wife would seem to be based on her acclaim of his military reputation, and there is no attempt by Othello to offset this by referring his love, on the model of good fame, to God." Other characters have been censured by other critics for failing to maintain the proper subordination of the passions to reason, as orthodox doctrine prescribed (we learn from one of them that "any humanist of the 17th century would have appreciated" this), or for trusting in the sufficiency of reason instead of properly subordinating it to God (the audience, we are assured, "would have understood such a preoccupation with the sin of 'self-sufficiency' . . . [which] every school boy would have known" from his catechism). And one critic has even anathematized Polonius's advice to Laertes on clothes because it violates the biblical admonition to "take no thought . . . for your body, what ye shall put on" (Matt. 6:25).

Still others have argued that contemporary attitudes toward (invariably against) certain specific actions were much harsher than our own, and so require an unfavorable judgment of characters whom we would otherwise regard favorably. The Elizabethan attitude toward suicide has been employed in this way to condemn Romeo and Juliet and Othello; the attitude toward the remarriage of widows to condemn the Duchess of Malfi ("in the seventeenth century the woman who re-married did not escape criticism"); the attitude toward adultery to condemn Antony and Cleopatra ("Elizabethan audiences were more hostile to adultery than the 20th. Century"); the attitude toward magic to condemn Prospero ("within the pneumatological framework of the period, Prospero thus can be seen as a type of Satan");[9] the attitude toward alchemy to condemn Subtle and Face (the play "asks us . . . to shudder at the unleashing of goblins perhaps damned. Because of science and our skeptical habits of mind, we . . . do not feel the tremor that Jonson could count on"); and so forth. It would seem, then, that the marked change in our judgment of the character which this approach is supposed to produce (and on which, we saw, rests the claim that it is making an impressive contribution to our understanding of the play) is always a change for the worse. The ideas of the time have become a club with which to clobber the character.

The Problem of Anachronism

This reductive effect would suggest a relationship to the ironic approach, which also left every character it dealt with much worse than it found him. In fact several of the readings quoted above appeared as examples in the preceding chapter,[10] for the two approaches can be employed together. But they are theoretically distinct. While some ironic readings enlist an idea of the time in their attack upon a character (since it is so easy to find one severe enough to condemn him), others do not; and there are ideas-of-the-time readings which never allude to irony or explicitly challenge the "face value" of the play, because their rationale is quite different. They are not claiming that the playwright deliberately concealed his real meaning; on the contrary, they will insist, if they consistently follow the principles of the approach, that this meaning seemed perfectly obvious to him and to his original audience ("Shakespeare's contemporaries would recognize," "every school boy would have known"), and is not obvious to us only because the ideas of our time are not the ideas of his. Thus instead of the ironic critic's distinction between the hidden real meaning and the deceptive apparent meaning, they distinguish the true historical meaning from the anachronistic modern meaning. But while this is an important difference in theory, the result is much the same, since both approaches ask us to reject our felt experience of the play and to substitute for it an interpretation which we have not experienced—specifically, as we saw, to regard with antipathy a character whom we found sympathetic. In practice, moreover, if the historical critic tries to confront the facts of the play, he almost always has to resort to methods of the ironic critics in order to negate them, since in each of the examples these facts are clearly ranged against his interpretation (if they were not, there would be no need to invoke the ideas of the time and he would not have a "new reading"). The distinction between the two approaches, therefore, may seem to be more a matter of their rhetoric than of their actual procedure.

Although these historical readings often employ some strategies of the ironic approach, they do have one that is uniquely their own—the parading of the "authorities" endorsing the particular idea (or ideas) of the time which they intend to apply to the play. These are the contemporary theologians and philosophers and moralists, or earlier ones who influenced contemporary thought, and they serve as the principal weapons of this approach. The critic scores points against the character by citing the authorities who would disapprove of his conduct, and the more of them he can cite, the better for him and the worse for the character. In order to convict Othello of addiction to "bad fame," for example, the reading just quoted draws upon Augustine's *De Civitate Dei*, Boethius's *De Consolatione Philosophiae*, Petrarch's *Africa*, Erasmus's *Enchiridion Militis Christiani*, and Vives's *Introductio ad Sapientiam* and *Christi Jesu Triumphans*. And the reading referred to in chapter 3, which undertakes to prove that Hamlet is "a soul lost in damnable error," is able to muster an even more formidable battery against him, including Agrippa, Aquinas, Augustine, Boethius, Calvin, Dante, Peter Lombard, Francis de Sales, Nicholas Trivet, and Ludovicus Vives, along with seven books of the Old and New Testaments. With all those impressive voices proclaiming Hamlet's damnation, who will hear Horatio say, "Good night, sweet prince,/And flights of angels sing thee to thy rest"?

This type of historical critic will not hear those words, because he is not listening to the play but to the ideas of the time, which will settle the matter for him a priori. The deductive inevitability of his conclusion is in fact built into the typical organization of these readings, which is explained to us in the introduction to the study of the Ghost in *Hamlet* discussed earlier:

> The reader will retrace the path taken by my own investigation, and take the same steps in the same order: first, defining conventional attitudes toward revenge in Shakespeare's day; next, ascertaining audience attitudes toward revenge in the plays of Shakespeare and his contemporaries; then testing the Ghost according to criteria familiar to both Protestants and Catholics; and, finally, analyzing the play itself in the light of some surprising discoveries.

We begin, in other words, with the ideas of the time (as defined by those "authorities"), which become the unquestioned premises of the argument, and so when we finally get to "the play itself," the analysis of it "in the light of" these ideas will necessarily be determined by them, as the conclusion of a syllogism is determined by the premises. It is therefore not at all surprising that this critic's discoveries about contemporary views of revenge and pneumatology should be mirrored in the play and should require the condemnation of both the Ghost and Hamlet. And numerous other historical readings proceed down this same path—first establishing "the Elizabethan attitude" toward some aspect of life, and then censuring the character for failing to measure up to it.

Sometimes these Elizabethan attitudes are employed to determine not only the judgment of a particular character but even the form and overall effect of the play. The reader will have noticed that the interpretations produced by this approach regularly transform the tragedies of the period, with their sympathetic and pitiful protagonists, into a kind of villain-hero drama where we are supposed to watch with grim satisfaction the punishment of sinners "deserving everything they got." But such a conception of tragedy has itself been deduced from the ideas of the time, by certain historical critics, and then used to deduce the need to apply other ideas of the time in order to prove that the characters are sinful. The earliest example of this double argument that I could find appears in an influential book on Shakespearean tragedy published in 1930, which is presented in three parts following an irresistible logical progression. The first section deals with "the purpose and method of tragedy" as "Shakespeare's contemporaries thought" of it, and demonstrates, through extensive quotation of the authorities, that they saw tragedies as "*exempla* by which men are taught the lessons of moral philosophy" on "how to avoid ruin and misery." The second section surveys "moral philosophy in Shakespeare's day" in order to show, again by extensive quotations, that this philosophy found "in men's passions . . . the cause of the evil which they bring upon themselves." And the third examines Shakespeare's major tragedies and discovers that they "made concrete" the "philosophical teaching of the period," since in each of them the protagonist's downfall is caused by the excess of a particular passion, which instructs us to avoid it. Trapped within this two-pronged historical necessity, Hamlet, Othello, Lear, and Macbeth are thus reduced to "slaves of passion," and their tragedies to edifying lessons in how not to behave. *Quod erat demonstrandum.*

The principal objection to the use of the ideas of the time in all these readings is the same one that we raised in the preceding chapter to the illegitimate use of sources (which is not strange, since these ideas are treated as a kind of source)—namely, that it leaves out the artist. For he becomes nothing more than a conduit through which the ideas (or sources) are transmitted from the historical "context" or "background" to the play. And it is assumed that this transmission must occur regardless of what he may do or not do in the play itself, because he presumably is unable to ignore or modify that context (if he could, then it would not be possible to deduce his meaning from the ideas of his time). This assumption emerges very clearly at the end of a thematic reading of *Troilus and Cressida* quoted in chapter 2, which found that each of the main characters is an "exemplum" of "the overpowering of Right Judgment by Passion." The author asserts that this was the "entirely traditional" and "orthodox" moral doctrine (for his reading is one of those where an idea of the time is made the central theme of the play), and so concludes that to interpret the play in any other way "is to take the work out of its context—out of which it may mean anything." One could of course counter that when the work is put into such a context it may mean anything, or anything the critic wants, since he chooses the ideas which define the context. But leaving that point aside, it is evident that if this context determines Shakespeare's meaning in *Troilus and Cressida*, it must also do so in his other plays; thus the author finds that the same "orthodox" doctrine informs *Measure for Measure, Othello, Lear, Macbeth, Antony and Cleopatra,* and *Coriolanus*. Nor can we stop there, for the historical context which governed Shakespeare had to govern his contemporaries as well, and the result must be that all of the works of all of the writers of the English Renaissance will embody the same set of ideas and attitudes and therefore will have the same meaning.[11] That is the logical conclusion of this approach, and its reductio ad absurdum.

I hope it is not necessary to argue that this is absurd. It should be obvious, for instance, that very different judgments of revenge are called for in *Hamlet, Antonio's Revenge, Hoffman,* and *The Atheist's Tragedy* (which were all written in a space of twelve years), and that no monolithic "Elizabethan attitude" toward revenge, however it is formulated, could be applied to these plays without distorting some of them beyond recognition. We even encounter very different attitudes in the canon of one playwright—the morality of *Volpone* is certainly not the same as that of *Bartholomew Fair*. In fact very different attitudes can function within a single play, for we often find that one standard of judgment is being applied to the main action and another to the subplot, especially when it centers around a clown character (as may be seen, for example, in the treatment of Faustus's and Robin's dealings with the devil). And there would be no possible way to account for all of these differences if the artist were controlled by the ideas of his time. He therefore must have been able to choose, within fairly wide limits, the specific ideas in terms of which he wanted the action to be judged, and he also must have been able to establish them within the play itself.

The establishment of such an internal standard can be a very complicated and subtle process, one which I have never seen satisfactorily explained (and which I could recommend as an area of investigation likely to yield far more valuable results than the production of another new reading). But fortunately we do not need to understand its mode of operation in order to respond to it. And the fact is that in most of these plays we do know how to respond—we know whether a character is meant to be sympathetic or antipathetic, whether we are to laugh at him or with him, and so on. We know this without the benefit of any of those historical readings based upon some idea of the time (indeed such readings can only confuse us, since we saw that they set out to refute our actual experience of the play). And this must mean that the playwrights, or at least the best of them, have been careful to incorporate into the play the relevant ideas and attitudes which are to guide our reaction. And if they have, then the critic's task is clear—that is, if he seeks to interpret the author's intention. He must induce each play's standard of judgment from that play, and not try to deduce it from the ideas of the time or any other external source.

The same evidence would indicate, moreover, that the assumptions of this approach grossly oversimplify the audience's activity as well as the artist's. For if we adopt different standards of judgment in different plays, our response cannot be determined by the kind of logic which was seen to underlie the methodology of these readings. We do not decide how to regard Hamlet by plugging him into a preconceived categorical syllogism:

> All revengers are evil.
> Hamlet is a revenger.
> Therefore, Hamlet is evil.

And we may be sure that the Elizabethans did not either, if they were human beings and not machines. Spectators and readers—then or now— do not automatically apply some universal principle to a character, because they do not see him merely as a member of a general class ("revenger") but as a particular individual in a particular situation within the particular kind of "world" created by each play. All of these factors enter into the audience's response, and since they are all under the dramatist's control, he could, if he were at all skillful, shape their attitude for or against the revenger (which is still true today, as anyone familiar with the movies or television can testify). And this will hold not only for revenge but for all other actions or aspects of life. Therefore no idea of the time—no matter how many authorities endorsed it—can tell us how the Elizabethans judged any given character, or how we should judge him, unless it can be shown that the idea actually functions within the play to that end. But this is just another way of saying that the standard of judgment must be induced from the play itself rather than deduced from the historical "context."

Their treatment of that "context" raises another type of objection to the ideas-of-the-time readings, since they betray a basic misconception not only of drama (with respect both to the dramatist and his audience) but also of history. This historical approach ascribes to the English Renaissance a kind of uniformity which no reputable historian could ever accept. Such a uniformity cannot be found in any period—even those that may seem relatively stable and conformist, such as the Middle Ages, will reveal considerable diversity upon closer inspection. And it certainly cannot be found in the Renaissance, which was, after all, one of the major turning points in Western civilization, marked by great ferment and change in all areas—religious, political, social, economic, scientific, and aesthetic. The most cursory study will confirm that the people of this time held many very different and often contradictory views. We have no right, therefore, to assume that there was a single "Elizabethan attitude" toward abdication or filial obedience or ghosts or revenge or love or forgiveness or fame or clothes or the remarriage of widows or magic (black or white) or the role of reason and passion and sensation or any of the other questions which are settled so facilely in these readings.

Furthermore, even if there were a predominant attitude on some subject, it could never be discovered or demonstrated from the kind of authorities upon which these readings rely. For all of those sermons and courtesy books and moral and theological treatises were written to tell people how they *should* think, not to describe current thought.[12] Some of their doctrines in fact represent ideals so demanding that they are beyond the reach of mere mortals in real life or in the drama. (This is even acknowledged by a few of these critics: the one who accused Antonio of failing to live up to "the Christian ideal" adds that his "depraved" state is shared by "every other human being"; the one who attacked Desdemona's "pride" explains that her faults appear in "all mankind," and so form part of what he calls the "universal guilt in *Othello*"; and since the one who censured the reconciliation of Montague and Capulet for falling "far short of a heavenly peace" gives as his reason their retention of "the human proclivity to one-up-manship," it would seem that the only way they could satisfy this ideal is by transcending their humanity.) And the constant reiteration of other doctrines in this contemporary homiletic literature may well indicate the presence of very powerful popular feelings opposed to them. Just to take one example, the study of the Ghost in *Hamlet* discussed earlier seeks to prove that the Elizabethans condemned

revenge (and so would have regarded the Ghost as demonic) by pointing
to the "progressive intensity of the propaganda campaign" in which,
"throughout the last half of the sixteenth century, Church, State, and
conventional morality fulminated against private revenge in any form";
but there obviously would have been no need for all of that intense
fulmination unless many Elizabethans believed in private revenge. We
might even argue, then, that the more "authorities" of this sort who can
be found urging the adoption of a particular attitude, the more probable
it is that the attitude was *not* generally accepted. At least this would be
very good evidence that the contrary attitude existed.

There is much better evidence, however, in the drama itself, for in each
of our examples the attitude endorsed by the play contradicts the doctrines of the "authorities" cited by the critics, and that attitude must have
been, by definition, an idea of the time. Moreover, since most of this
drama was aimed at a large audience including many segments of society,
the ideas and attitudes embodied in it are more likely to represent deeply
felt beliefs at the heart of the culture than are the ideas and attitudes
promulgated in the homiletic literature. Of course some caution must be
exercised here; because various dramatic conventions, and the dramatic
experience itself, produced a "distancing" from reality, we cannot assume
that every attitude which the audience accepted in a play would also be
accepted by them in their everyday lives. Yet even with this qualification,
the popular drama still remains one of our best sources of knowledge
about the popular mind of the period. It is from such primary evidence
that any generalizations concerning the contemporary climate of opinion
must be derived, so if the attitudes in the plays conflict with some
scholar's construction of the Elizabethan "world picture," then so much
the worse for that world picture. For in this area the plays are a better
authority than the "authorities," and I would therefore suggest that they
can tell us more about the ideas of the time than the ideas of the time can
tell us about them.

This approach is also open to another important objection on historical grounds—it does not take into account the actual response which
these plays have evoked down through the centuries. In every case dealt
with here that response, as far back as we can trace it (and for many of
the plays that goes back to the seventeenth century), has been favorable
to the character whom these critics are attacking, which is acknowledged
by them when they present their discoveries as "new readings." But it is
then difficult to understand their claim that the new readings are based
upon the ideas of the time, if those ideas were, presumably, compatible
with the old readings which the new ones controvert.[13] Indeed, there

would seem to be a contradiction in the very notion of a new historical reading, since it can be new only if it rejects the interpretation given us by history. The view of Romeo and Juliet as essentially innocent victims deserving our sympathy and pity is the historical one, established by a very long and very well documented tradition; therefore we would have to conclude that the so-called historical restoration which views them as a pair of sinners "deserving everything they got" is really a modern anachronism. So in this sense, too, the historical approach we have been examining turns out to be unhistorical.

Despite all of these objections, however, something may still be said for this approach. It is at least theoretically possible that a dramatist assumed (perhaps quite unconsciously) certain ideas or attitudes which should determine the proper response to his play, but which we are no longer aware of. There are some plays of the period—I would nominate a few in the Beaumont and Fletcher canon—whose standard of judgment is very difficult to ascertain, and this may well be the reason (although it may, of course, be the result of the playwright's own confusion or irresponsibility). In dealing with such problems the critics of this school could be helpful. But they will not help us by citing a list of authorities who expounded the idea they wish to apply, since the mere fact that an idea existed at the time cannot prove that it operated as a standard in any given play. They must show that it does operate in this way, and that it enables us to make sense out of a work which, without it, will not yield a coherent meaning. To this possibility, I believe, we must always remain open.

It seems to me, though, that these problems arise in a relatively small number of plays of the period. For the great majority, and certainly for the best of them, we do know how to respond, and that must be, I have been arguing, because the ideas and attitudes necessary to guide our response are established in the plays themselves. Is there any major English Renaissance drama where we would go seriously wrong in our interpretation without a special knowledge of some idea of the time? I will go out on a limb and admit that I cannot think of any, although I am prepared to be corrected on this. Historical research into the contemporary intellectual climate can of course enlarge and enrich our understanding of the ideas embodied in these plays, and it can, as we saw at the beginning of our investigation, place the plays within this climate, and within the context of "the history of ideas." It may also furnish us with suggestions of what to look for in the plays, and may even help to corroborate our findings. But such research cannot substitute for the inductive interpretation of each play in its own terms. Nothing can.

The Occasionalist Scene

The second historical approach to be investigated, which I call occasion-alism, interprets the plays as compositions directed at a special audience, outside of the commercial theaters (both "public" and "private"), at a special time and place. This approach is not a recent invention, for suggestions of it can be found as far back as the eighteenth century; but during the past few decades it has been enjoying a kind of vogue, which has reached its fullest development, like all the other vogues we have examined, in Shakespearean criticism. Most of the old claims have been revived and refurbished, and many new ones have been staked out, so that the number of occasional plays in his canon seems to be increasing at a remarkable rate. The most popular species is the "court play," allegedly written for a royal performance, which now includes *Love's Labor's Lost*, *The Merry Wives of Windsor*, *Twelfth Night*, *Othello*, *Measure for Measure*, *King Lear*, *Macbeth*, *Cymbeline*, *The Winter's Tale*, *The Tem-pest*, and *Henry VIII*. Second largest is the group of "nuptial plays" which were supposedly commissioned to celebrate various noble wed-dings at various noble houses; *The Two Gentlemen of Verona*, *The Taming of the Shrew*, *A Midsummer Night's Dream*, and *As You Like It* have been placed in this class, but so have several of the "court plays" just listed, since the occasionalists, like the thematic and ironic critics, often disagree among themselves (even those who agree that certain plays were written for noble weddings will differ on which wedding was the occasion for which play). We have also been told that *The Comedy of Errors*, *Troilus and Cressida*, and *Timon of Athens* were composed for feasts at the Inns of Court, and *Hamlet* for Oxford or Cambridge. And two of his possible collaborations, *Edward III* and *The Two Noble Kinsmen*, were granted tentative occasional status in a recent study, which asserts that the former "could have been used at a great house in compliment to a great lady" and the latter "was perhaps only commis-sioned to provide a setting" for a court masque.

The roster thus already encompasses a majority of Shakespeare's plays (a very substantial majority if we exclude the histories, which, except for *Henry VIII*, have so far been neglected), and it has probably grown since these lines were written, because there is nothing to stop the application of this approach to the rest of the canon. As the trend continues, then, we will soon have to exchange the reconstructions of the Globe and Black-friars in our textbooks for pictures of some of those "great halls" in the

royal or noble residences for which his plays were actually designed. And
we will have to revise Ben Jonson's famous encomium in order to explain
that his gentle Shakespeare was not of an age, still less for all time, but
for the privileged few invited to the wedding of the Earl of Derby to
Elizabeth Vere at Greenwich Palace on 26 January 1595, and a similar
group assembled at a Garter investiture in Westminster on 23 April
1597, and another at Whitehall on 6 January 1600/1 to honor the Duke
of Bracciano, and another at Hampton Court on 7 August 1606 for the
visit of Christian IV of Denmark, and so on.

This occasionalist scene, like the others we have surveyed, is in large
part the cumulative result of individual critics working on individual
plays. But there are some enthusiasts who have found occasions for
several plays, and even those who limit themselves to a single work will
frequently endorse the discoveries of their fellow laborers as part of their
own demonstration, since the approach has reached the stage where it
can feed upon itself, and the "fact" that some Shakespearean plays were
aimed at a special audience is now being used to justify the same claim
for others (and for some of the plays of his contemporaries, to whom the
vogue is spreading). The study quoted above, for example, argues the
occasionalist case for *Edward III* in this way:

> *Love's Labour's Lost* and *A Midsummer Night's Dream* were very
> possibly written for private performance. The first was regarded
> with especial interest by the Southampton family; it has been
> suggested that *A Midsummer Night's Dream* was composed for
> the remarriage of the Dowager Countess of Southampton. If
> she presided over her son's fortunes during his minority, she
> might well be the further object of compliment in a play written
> for his circle.

A second critic cites different precedents to support his occasionalization
of *Othello*:

> It is becoming increasingly clear that at least two of the plays
> written by Shakespeare during the early years of the new reign
> were probably intended to reflect James I's opinions and tastes.
> *Othello*, acted at court on 1 November 1604, seems never to
> have been considered in relation to Shakespeare's new patron. I
> want to suggest that, like *Measure for Measure*, *Macbeth*, and
> possibly other plays written during these years, *Othello* was also
> designed as a work appropriate to the chief dramatist of the
> King's Men.

Another envisages a Shakespeare who presented annual gifts to the King:
"Since the play [*Macbeth*] is so clearly written for King James, it is

tempting to see it as the dramatist's offering of 1605/6, as *Measure for Measure* was in 1604/5, and *Lear* in 1606/7." And another has announced that *Cymbeline*, *The Winter's Tale*, and *The Tempest* all "bear the unmistakable hall-mark of court commission, with the Blackfriars in mind by way of hard-cash earnings from a wider public, and with transfer to the Globe as a subsequent possibility rather than a certainty."

Of course the claim that a play was intended for a certain occasion does not in itself constitute an interpretative approach; it becomes one only when it is used to generate a reading of the play. Some of the critics who advance these claims never take this further step. One of those referred to below, for instance, who argues at length that *Measure for Measure* was written for a court performance, believes that this adds an interesting "historical dimension" but "cannot radically alter our sense of the inherent dramatic design of the play." But others invoke this occasion to explain specific speeches or events, such as the sentencing of Lucio: "In a play given before King James," one of them tells us, "it would never do to let the slanderer of a sovereign go unpunished." And still others insist that it is the essential key to any true understanding of the play, and so have given us several complete "occasionalist readings," including a book entitled *"Measure for Measure" as Royal Entertainment*. (*The Royal Play of "Macbeth"* is another book-length reading of the same sort.) In most cases, I believe, the claim that a play was occasional has produced an interpretation of the play in terms of the occasion—if not by the person who first made the claim, then by someone following after him. This is what we would expect, since the arguments brought forward to support such a claim are usually based upon the contention that parts or aspects of the play would have a special (and often hidden) meaning— personal, topical, allegorical, etc.—for the particular audience for whom it was supposedly written; and that contention will in turn make this audience (and the occasion of their assembling) the principle for inter- preting the meaning of the play, which then becomes a kind of private communication to them. The reasoning is entirely circular, to be sure, but that has not troubled the occasionalists. (Some have even used the alleged special nature of the alleged special audience to justify their rejection of the play's literal meaning—one of the thematic readings of *A Midsummer Night's Dream* quoted in chapter 2, for instance, argues that "if we think of the original audience, courtly and cultured and demand- ing in its art the intellectual stimulus of symbolic meaning, we must look upon the play as something more than a slight *divertissement*, interesting mainly for its charm and innocent humour on the foibles of lovers"; and other examples of this logic appear below.) I think we can conclude, therefore, that most occasionalist claims carry within themselves the seeds of occasionalist readings; but even if they do not, it is obvious that every such reading depends on such a claim. And since the entire approach must stand or fall with this assertion that certain plays were composed for certain occasions, we will focus our investigation upon it.

The recent proliferation of Shakespeare's occasional plays described earlier should seem all the more remarkable when we realize that it has been achieved without the benefit of anything that could be called factual corroboration. Over fifteen years ago Alfred Harbage pointed out, in a protest against this vogue, that "there is no supporting external evidence to prove that any regular play performed by any regular company, juvenile or adult, was originally written for a special occasion during the whole reign of Elizabeth and lifetime of Shakespeare,"[14] and his declaration, so far as I know, has never been challenged. Moreover, as Harbage went on to argue, this absence of external evidence is itself important evidence against the occasionalists, because if plays were commissioned for these special performances one would expect to find that circumstance recorded in household accounts, on title pages, and the like (as in the case of royal or civic entertainments or court masques, which really were occasional). In fact, all of the external evidence we do possess points in the opposite direction, for it shows that the dramas presented at court and the Inns of Court and the "great houses" of the aristocracy were, as a matter of regular practice, selected from those already in the public repertories of the theatrical companies[15] (although they may have undergone some alterations to make them more "convenient" for the occasion). A very striking proof of this can be found, as J. M. Nosworthy has noted,[16] in the list of fourteen plays produced at court during the festivities attending the marriage of Princess Elizabeth to the Elector Palatine, since every play on the list that we can identify had previously appeared on the public stage. Indeed a surprising number were quite old, and an even more surprising number exhibit none of the features which the occasionalists are so quick to seize upon as evidence of a "court" or a "nupital" play. Therefore, if no plays were specially written for such a celebration, which must have been one of the most elaborate and extravagant of the entire period, it seems highly unlikely that they would have been written for less important events. (It is, incidentally, all too typical of the present state of occasionalism that we see critics arguing that *Henry VIII* was designed for these festivities, even though the play does not appear on this list.)

This conclusion, furthermore, is just what the economics of the situation should lead one to expect, from the standpoint of both parties. The dramatic companies would wish to avoid all the trouble and expense involved in having a play assigned, composed, approved, rehearsed, and mounted for a special production (even if enough time were available for this, which could itself be a major problem), and the celebrants would find it much more costly to commission a tailor-made play than to accept a ready-made one from the repertory. All this of course does not preclude the possibility that an occasional play may have occasionally been written, but it does place a very heavy burden of proof upon anyone who wishes to convince us that he has discovered such an exception to the normal theatrical practice of the time, since he must establish a positive case for that play which is impressive enough to outweigh these fundamental general objections.

The "King James Version" of *Measure for Measure*

The investigation of these positive cases presents a problem, however, since occasionalism, we must remember, is the most particularized of the historical approaches, and the tactics of its practitioners vary so greatly from play to play that they cannot easily be surveyed and illustrated by the kind of sampling process used up to now. I thought it would be more appropriate, therefore, to concentrate upon the case that has been made for a single play, which will allow us to examine that complete case in considerable detail, and so match the approach's extreme of particularity with our own. For this purpose I have selected what might be called the "King James Version" of *Measure for Measure*—the contention that this play was specifically designed for the performance which we believe took place before the King at Whitehall on 26 December 1604.[17] It seemed the obvious choice, because it is the strongest occasionalist case for a Shakespearean play, supported by a greater number and variety of arguments than any other, and because it has won the widest acceptance (with the possible exception of the similar case for *Macbeth*).[18] Moreover, this acceptance is based entirely upon a group of studies which appeared within the past twenty years and so are representative of the new occasionalist vogue. On all these counts, then, it should provide the fairest possible test of the approach as a whole.

The idea that *Measure for Measure* had some connection with King James is not new. It was apparently first suggested by Thomas Tyrwhitt in 1766, was noted by George Chalmers, Charles Knight, and a few others during the eighteenth and nineteenth centuries, and was developed

at length by Louis Albrecht in 1914.[19] But the present status of the play as
an acknowledged occasional production, which Shakespeare planned
and wrote for his royal patron, really dates from the late 1950s. Since
then we have had six studies devoted primarily or largely to establishing
this status (including, we saw, one entire book), and at least six more
which have given it further support. And the success of their collective
undertaking can be judged from the opening sentence of an article
published in 1970, where we are referred to the "series of scholarly
studies which enable us to say with confidence that *Measure for Measure*
was acted before King James and that its chief purpose was 'to flatter,
entertain, and please the King.'"[20] The authors of these studies are not in
complete agreement; they do not all present the same kind of evidence
for their occasionalist thesis, nor do they all (as we just noted) attach the
same degree of importance to it. In the examination that follows, however, I have ignored these differences and treated all the studies together,
since I am concerned only with the nature of their arguments, regardless
of who stated them. Nor have I felt it necessary to include every minor
point of every critic, but have focused instead upon the arguments which
they themselves regard as most significant.

The great majority of these arguments turn on a special relationship
which the critics find between King James and Shakespeare's Duke Vincentio, whom they variously describe as a "flattering portrayal" or
"idealized image" of the King, made "in the mold of James's ideal prince"
with "features that were obviously drawn from James," whose "whole
character . . . was created . . . to please and flatter the King."[21] And the
proof of this relationship is derived primarily from the *Basilicon Doron*,
James's book of advice to his son, Prince Henry, which was published in
London in 1603. According to one study,

> evidence that Shakespeare created a Duke of Vienna whose
> views would seem appropriate ones to James lies in Shake-
> speare's demonstrable use of the King's book on statecraft,
> the *Basilicon Doron*, or "Kingly Gift," as a source of the Duke's
> ideas. . . . The accumulation of such echoes [of this book in the
> Duke's words and actions] finally defeats skepticism, and forces
> us to realize that Shakespeare carefully mined the *Basilicon
> Doron* to dramatize the intellectual interests of his new patron.

And a second describes Shakespeare's (and Vincentio's) indebtedness to
this book in even stronger terms:

> He makes the Duke voice the King's principles of government
> as set forth in the *Basilikon Doron*, and attempt to put them

into practice. . . . He is dramatizing the *Basilikon Doron*, making a play of it. . . . He is the King's scholar, his puppet.

Let us look then at these "echoes" which force us to such conclusions.

The largest group consists of general moral or political observations expressed by the Duke which seem to resemble those in the King's book. Most frequently cited is the parallel between the Duke's speech to Angelo—

> Heaven doth with us as we with torches do,
> Not light them for themselves; for if our virtues
> Did not go forth of us, 'twere all alike
> As if we had them not.
>
> [I.i.33–36]

and James's admonition:

> For it is not enough that ye have and retain, as prisoners within yourself, never so many good qualities and virtues, except ye employ them, and set them on work. [P. 105][22]

Then the Duke's sentiments in his soliloquy at the end of act 3—

> He who the sword of heaven will bear
> Should be as holy as severe;
> Pattern in himself to know,
> Grace to stand, and virtue go;
> More nor less to others paying
> Than by self-offences weighing.
>
> [III.ii.239–44]

are said by one critic to be "an echo of the sense of many passages in the *Basilicon Doron*," two of which he quotes:

> As your company should be a pattern to the rest of the people, so should your person be a lamp and mirror to your company, giving light to your servants to walk in the path of virtue. [P. 137]

> He cannot be thought worthy to rule and command others, that cannot rule and danton [subdue] his own proper affections and unreasonable appetites. [P. 25]

A second critic asserts that "this soliloquy turns King James's concept of kingship into tetrameter verse" and "lightly echoes" the King's introductory sonnet, the relevant lines of which seem to be

> Observe the statutes of your heavenly King,
> And from His law, make all your laws to spring,

> Since his lieutenant here ye should remain,
> Reward the just, be steadfast, true, and plain,
> Repress the proud, maintaining aye the right,
> Walk always so, as ever in His sight. [P. 5]

Another parallel has been found between a later soliloquy of the Duke's—

> O place and greatness! millions of false eyes
> Are stuck upon thee; volumes of report
> Run with these false and most contrarious quests
> Upon thy doings; thousand escapes of wit
> Make thee the father of their idle dreams
> And rack thee in their fancies.
>
> [IV.i.58–63]

and James's statement in his address "To the Reader":

> For kings, being public persons by reason of their office and
> authority, are as it were set (as it was said of old) upon a public
> stage, in the sight of all the people, where all the beholders' eyes
> are attentively bent, to look and pry in the least circumstance
> of their secretest drifts. [P. 12]

And some critics note another between the Duke's complaint against slander—

> No might nor greatness in mortality
> Can censure scape. Back-wounding calumny
> The whitest virtue strikes. What king so strong
> Can tie the gall up in the slanderous tongue?
>
> [III.ii.170–73]

and the King's—

> Unto one fault is all the common people of this kingdom subject
> ... which is to judge and speak rashly of their Prince, setting
> the commonweal upon four props, as we call it, ever wearying
> of the present estate, and desirous of novelties. [P. 93]

while the last clause of this sentence has also been compared to the Duke's remark to Escalus:

> Novelty is only in request, and it is as dangerous to be aged
> in any kind of course as it is virtuous to be constant in any
> undertaking.
>
> [III.ii.206–8]

In addition, we are told, both Duke and King are in favor of chastity
(*MM*, III.ii.112–13; *BD*, p. 123), moderation (*MM*, III.ii.217–19; *BD*,

p. 139), piety (*MM*, II.iii.3–39; *BD*, p. 81), and sobriety (*MM*, III.ii.118–20; *BD*, p. 169), and there are a few other minor parallels of this general type.

I am afraid it would have to be a very weak skepticism indeed that could be defeated by an "accumulation of such echoes." For it should be evident that in every one of them the observations of the Duke and of the King are the platitudes of traditional wisdom which Shakespeare could have found in any number of books of the period or of the past, if he needed to find them in books at all.[23] And since the ideas are of this nature, the fact that the Shakespearean passage "lightly echoes" a passage in the King's book—or, in the words of another critic, is a "loose paraphrase" of the book—does not establish any connection between them. For it does not meet the basic requirement which has long been understood to govern the employment of "parallel passages" in source or attribution studies, namely, that any parallelism, to be considered significant, cannot be limited to a general idea (especially if that idea is a commonplace), but must also include its specific mode of expression.[24] These "echoes" could demonstrate Shakespeare's indebtedness to James, therefore, only if they showed similarities in the language, or the imagery, or the illustrative examples, or something else that pointed uniquely to the *Basilicon Doron*. But not a single similarity of this kind has yet come to light, and since so many of these critics, and Albrecht before them, have obviously combed through the two works very carefully without discovering any, their series of scholarly studies does "enable us to say with confidence" that none exists. Indeed, the first alleged "echo," which several of the critics seem to regard as the most impressive, actually exposes the invalidity of this method of parallel-hunting, for James in his marginal notes here cites Plato, Aristotle, and Cicero as his authorities, while Shakespeare's simile suggests a biblical origin.[25] And further evidence against the method has appeared in two recent articles which use it to locate the source of the ideas of *Measure for Measure* in two other works as different from the *Basilicon Doron* as they are from each other—the Gospel of St. Mark and John Mush's *Dialogue betwixt a Secular Priest and a Lay Gentleman*.

One of our critics acknowledges that, "though many of the views on Justice and Good Rule in the *Basilikon Doron* find fairly exact parallels in Shakespeare's play, these are of too commonplace a nature to prove indebtedness in the absence of close verbal echoes." But others adopt various strategies to get around this embarrassing fact:

> One cannot claim, of course, that either the Duke of Vienna
> or James Stuart was startlingly original in the choice of attitudes

and ideas they have in common. Nor could one assert any connection between these two on this basis were it not that the date of *Measure for Measure* coincides so nicely with that of the *Basilicon Doron*, and with James's entry into England.

The circularity of this type of argument, which assumes the very relationship that it purports to prove, can be seen even more clearly in the reasoning of another critic:

> It is not that the ideas of princely duty expressed in this book are unusual. On the contrary, parallels to the Duke's utterances have been cited from Cicero, Erasmus, Sir Thomas Elyot, and even from Machiavelli. King James sprinkled his margins with citations of classical authorities. What makes it so certain that Shakespeare was deliberately echoing the *Basilikon Doron* is that this is the book he could be sure his audience would recognize, and therefore allusions to it would be effective.

In another argument the absence of any verbal parallels is explained away as a deliberate choice of Shakespeare's:

> One of the most amazing and puzzling achievements of this play is the echoing of the King's expressed principles of rule . . . without suggesting impersonation, since that would certainly have given offense. . . . The person of the Duke and his manner of speech should not, and need not, in any way echo the person and speech of the King. . . . Even when he is echoing the *Basilikon Doron* there is no hint of paraphrase or parody of the style.

I call this the "heads-I-win-tails-you-lose" strategy, since it can treat any differences as well as any likenesses between Duke and King as positive evidence for connecting them—the latter demonstrate that Shakespeare was "echoing," and the former that he was avoiding "offense" (although why James would be offended at a "hint of paraphrase" of his book is never made clear). And yet another defensive strategy is to take the offensive by shifting the burden of proof:

> In fact, since it must be assumed that the audience was already familiar with the *Basilikon Doron*, the burden of proof rests on anyone who denies that Shakespeare was deliberately alluding to it.

I do not pretend to understand the logical relationship between these two clauses, but the tactic is a shrewd one, because there is of course no possible way to prove that Shakespeare was *not* alluding to this book, or to any similar book for that matter. This is precisely the trouble, as can also be seen in another attempt to shift the burden of proof:

> Indeed, it would be difficult to find *any* comment in this play
> concerning the "properties" of government and "sufficiency"
> in office which did not agree rather narrowly with James's per-
> sonal convictions as of 1603–04.

That may well be true, but it would be equally difficult to find any
comments of this sort in the play which did not agree with many other
political treatises of the time (or conversely, to find any other "good
ruler" in the drama of the time whose comments on government did not
agree with the *Basilicon Doron*). This crucial objection is in fact admitted
by one of these critics in defending Shakespeare's sincerity:

> An acceptance of the belief . . . that the views on Justice and
> Good Rule which [*Measure for Measure*] expresses are closely
> similar to those found in the political writings of the King, in
> no way compels one to see the play less as an expression of
> Shakespeare's most personal and sincerely held convictions.
> For . . . Shakespeare's own views on these matters seem to have
> been in close accord with those of the King and other humanist
> writers of his day. . . . They are views held by humane and
> enlightened men in all ages.

The defense undermines the entire position, however, since if a view is
held by many writers, its presence in any two works cannot prove any
connection between them.
    There is, finally, one last-ditch defensive strategy, which is to claim a
special exemption from the criteria for source studies:

> In rebuttal, alternative sources have been suggested for many
> of the principles expressed by the Duke; and the importance
> of the *Basilikon Doron* has been denied because the enormous
> popularity of this little book in 1603 and 1604 has not been rec-
> ognized, and its relation to the play has been treated from the
> point of view of source, rather than as material for familiar allu-
> sion. . . . It has been treated as a source for ideas rather than as
> what it was, a basis for multiple allusions easily caught by a
> majority of the audience.

But this defense undermines the position even further, because it really
means that the requirements for identifying parallel passages should be
applied not less but more stringently than in an ordinary source study.
These critics, we must remember, are contending not merely that Shakespeare borrowed his Duke's principles from the *Basilicon Doron*, but also
that he wanted this borrowing to be perceived by the court audience,
since its whole purpose was "to flatter, entertain, and please the King."
As one of them explains, "James is a writer, and Shakespeare, the

professional, knows that the flattery to which every writer, and especially the amateur, is most susceptible is the echo of his own composition." If this was his purpose, therefore, one would expect his borrowings
to resemble the King's book even more closely than if it had simply been
a source in the usual sense, because he would have had every reason to
make them as obvious as possible, and no reason at all to confine them to
"light echoes" or "loose paraphrases" and thereby run the risk that they
would escape notice. For the critic's assurance that such echoes would be
"easily caught by a majority of the audience" (or another's that "to
audiences of 1604 the Duke's initial advice to Angelo . . . must necessarily have recalled the king's precepts") seems best explained as a kind
of optical illusion produced by staring too long at these two texts. It is
very unlikely that an audience would have recognized—and still more
unlikely that Shakespeare would have counted on their recognizing—
that a few scattered speeches of the Duke, containing quite conventional
thoughts, were somewhat similar to a few equally scattered and equally
conventional passages in the King's book. The only way to ensure this
recognition would be to follow the procedure that the critics must have
adopted—to place the *Basilicon Doron* and *Measure for Measure* side by
side on a desk and pore over them long enough for the "echoes" to
appear.

The same basic objection applies to a second group of "echoes" of the
King's book which these critics have discovered in the Duke's actions,
rather than his speeches. They tell us that the Duke not only voices the
principles set forth in the *Basilicon Doron* but also "attempt[s] to put
them into practice," and that the Duke's "behavior as a ruler . . . followed patterns which the King had publicly advocated," and even that
one of the principles in the King's book "sums up the Duke's behaviour."
But when we examine these royal precepts that are supposed to govern
the Duke's conduct they turn out to be the same sort of platitudes we
have already seen, exhortations in favor of virtue and against vice, which
are found in any number of other treatises, and which are followed by
any number of other sympathetic rulers in the contemporary drama.
Indeed it would have been impossible to portray such a ruler who did not
put into practice many passages of the King's book. But one searches in
vain in that book for anything that might even suggest the particular
course of conduct of Shakespeare's Duke—his handing the government
over to Angelo, his return in disguise to observe the results,[26] his arrangement of the bed trick, and his staging of the final trial. And without such
particular connections, the alleged echoes of the *Basilicon Doron* in the
Duke's actions are no more convincing than those discerned in his
speeches.

There is, however, one echo in this second group which seems more specific than the others, and which is for that reason cited by almost all the critics as a major piece of evidence. It involves James's advice to his son to give the laws "full execution" at the beginning of his reign:

> For if otherwise ye kyth [practice] your clemency at the first, the offenses would soon come to such heaps, and the contempt of you grow so great, that when ye would fall to punish, the number of them to be punished would exceed the innocent; and ye would be troubled to resolve whom-at to begin, and against your nature would be compelled then to wrack many, whom the chastisement of few in the beginning might have preserved. But in this, my over-dear bought experience may serve you for a sufficient lesson. For I confess, where I thought, by being gracious at the beginning, to win all men's hearts to a loving and willing obedience, I by the contrary found the disorder of the country and the loss of my thanks to be all my reward. [Pp. 63–65]

This passage, they claim, is drawn upon and alluded to in the Duke's speech to Friar Thomas:

> We have strict statutes and most biting laws
> (The needful bits and curbs to headstrong steeds),
> Which for this fourteen years we have let sleep;
> Even like an o'ergrown lion in a cave,
> That goes not out to prey. Now, as fond fathers,
> Having bound up the threat'ning twigs of birch,
> Only to stick it in their children's sight
> For terror, not to use, in time the rod
> Becomes more mock'd than fear'd; so our decrees,
> Dead to infliction, to themselves are dead,
> And liberty plucks justice by the nose.
> . . . .
> Sith 'twas my fault to give the people scope,
> 'Twould be my tyranny to strike and gall them
> For what I bid them do. For we bid this be done
> When evil deeds have their permissive pass
> And not the punishment. Therefore, indeed, my father,
> I have on Angelo impos'd the office,
> Who may in th' ambush of my name strike home,
> And yet my nature never in the fight
> To do it slander.
>
> [I.iii.19–29, 35–43]

But the two situations are not quite as similar as these critics would have us believe (one of them says of James's account that "it is just this experience which, as the Duke explains to Friar Thomas, has motivated his abdication"). The King's excessive clemency was limited to the beginning of his reign, while the Duke's has persisted for fourteen years (nineteen, according to Claudio in I.ii.154). Their reasons for this clemency are not the same. And they see the problems of ending the disorder resulting from it in very different terms. James's point is that his son would find it painful ("against your nature") to punish so many, but he never suggests that this would be "tyranny," a term he usually reserves for usurpers. In fact, immediately before this passage he tells his son that he should feel free to give the laws "full execution" precisely because he will not be "an usurping tyrant": "For since ye come not to your reign *precariò*, nor by conquest, but by right and due descent, fear no uproars for doing of justice" (p. 63). And he would scarcely approve of the Duke's plan to avoid public censure by placing the onus upon Angelo, which runs counter to the whole spirit of the *Basilicon Doron* and sounds much more like something one would expect to find in *The Prince*.[27]

Another kind of difficulty arises when we try to relate this claim that the Duke is here drawing upon the King's book to the occasionalist thesis which the claim is supposed to support, since it is not easy to see why Shakespeare would expect to "flatter, entertain, and please" his royal patron by reminding him of a serious mistake of his youth. And we are confronted with another difficulty when this claim is related to the conclusion of the play, because there the Duke seems to forget the need to revive those sleeping statutes and tempers his final justice with a very generous infusion of mercy—a procedure which is recommended in other passages of James's book, but in this context completely undercuts his argument that a ruler who fails to give the laws "full execution" at the outset will be forced to be even more severe later on. But there is a still more serious problem, for the character in *Measure for Measure* who does insist upon a "full execution" of the laws at the beginning of his reign is none other than Angelo, and the justification he gives for doing so, when he rejects Isabella's plea to spare Claudio, comes closer to this argument of the King's than anything said by the Duke:

Isab.   Who is it that hath died for this offence?
        There's many have committed it.
        . . . .
Ang.   The law hath not been dead, though it hath slept.
        Those many had not dar'd to do that evil
        If that the first that did th' edict infringe
        Had answer'd for his deed. Now 'tis awake,
        Takes note of what is done, and like a prophet

> Looks in a glass that shows what future evils—
> Either new, or by remissness new conceiv'd,
> And so in progress to be hatch'd and born—
> Are now to have no successive degrees,
> But, ere they live, to end.
> Isab.   Yet show some pity.
> Ang.   I show it most of all when I show justice;
> For then I pity those I do not know,
> Which a dismiss'd offence would after gall.

> [II.ii.88–102]

We are thus faced with the embarrassing fact that, in a drama which was allegedly written to flatter King James by exemplifying the principles set forth in his book, the character who most clearly attempts to put this particular principle into practice is not the "idealized image" of James but the villain of the piece.

Several of these studies do try to relate Angelo to the *Basilicon Doron*, but they of course go to other material from that book since they wish to place him in direct opposition to James's portrait of the good ruler, and so demonstrate "that if Shakespeare had created a Duke to seem particularly appealing to James, Angelo as Deputy . . . was created to seem particularly evil." Their case centers upon three passages, two of which are supposed to show that "Angelo's behavior agrees with the conduct attributed by King James to a tyrant":

> An usurping tyrant, . . . counterfeiting the saint while he once creep in credit, will then, by inverting all good laws to serve only for his unruly private affections, frame the commonweal ever to advance his particular. [P. 57]

> An usurping tyrant . . . would enter like a saint while he found himself fast underfoot, and then would suffer his unruly affections to burst forth. [P. 61]

We are told of the first statement that "this is exactly what Angelo does," and of the second that "this is the pattern set by Angelo," but the facts are otherwise. Angelo has no ambitions of this sort; he is reluctant to accept the position of Deputy from the Duke (I.i.48–51), he surrenders it willingly when the Duke returns, and in the interim he makes no attempt to aggrandize his power. Nor does he counterfeit saintliness in order to advance himself; on the contrary, he seems to be completely sincere at first in his professions of virtue and is then completely astonished to discover his passion for Isabella (II.ii.162–87). Moreover, the context of the second passage indicates that to "enter like a saint" means to be lenient in enforcing the laws, for the next sentence reads: "Therefore be ye contrary, at your first entry to your kingdom, to that *Quinquennium Neronis*, with his tenderhearted wish, *Vellem nescire literas*, in giving the law full execution against all breakers thereof" (p. 61); and this is followed by the passage quoted earlier urging Prince Henry not to "kyth your clemency at the first." Therefore, in his initial strict application of the law, Angelo's conduct is exactly the opposite of that which King James attributes to a tyrant, and is in agreement, as we saw, with the conduct James recommends to his son. There is no way to equate him with James's tyrant without a serious distortion both of Shakespeare's play and of the King's book.

The third passage from the *Basilicon Doron* is employed by these critics to set Angelo in opposition to the Duke as well as to the King:

> For laws are ordained as rules of virtuous and social living, and not to be snares to trap your good subjects; and therefore the law must be interpreted according to the meaning, and not to the literal sense thereof. [P. 141]

One of them quotes this sentence to prove that "in picking out the statute against fornication to enforce literally, [Angelo] ran counter to James's basic premise," and another says, "This is the principle of the Duke . . . but it is entirely neglected by Angelo in his dealing with Claudio" (another claims that it "sums up the Duke's behaviour"). But Angelo is not trying to "trap" Claudio when he sentences him for fornication; he is simply executing the law, which is just what the Duke intended him to do, and what the Duke blamed himself for not doing years before, as was shown. The Duke changes his attitude in the resolution, to be sure, but he never criticizes Angelo for his original sentencing of Claudio. So here too the attempt to relate Angelo to the *Basilicon Doron* requires a distortion of his character and role in the play.

Some of the critics also connect Angelo to this book by equating him with the Puritans who are castigated there, since "the drama of the exposure of a proud Puritan by a ruler would be one of considerable appeal to James." But if Shakespeare wished to please the King by exposing his enemies in the person of Angelo, one can only ask why he did not make that clear. There was certainly no need to be coy about it, since the Puritans were fair game in the drama of the period, and were openly attacked by Jonson and Middleton, among others. Shakespeare, therefore, would have had no reason to conceal Angelo's Puritanism and every reason to exploit it, so it is safe to assume that, since he did not identify him with this sect, he did not expect the audience—royal or otherwise—to do so either. (Actually, the closest he came to Puritan-baiting was in *Twelfth Night*, which is pre-Jacobean.) The fact that some modern critics can find "Puritan traits" in Angelo proves nothing, for we just saw that they found "tyrannical traits" in him as well, and it is amusing to note that the study referred to earlier, which located the source of *Measure for Measure* in Mush's *Dialogue*, uses this same kind of reasoning to equate Angelo with the Puritans' arch-enemies, the Jesuits.

The only other character whom these critics relate to the *Basilicon Doron* is Lucio, and they do this by claiming that he "provides a comic representation of the type of person who libels his ruler as King James complained of being libeled" in his book. The trouble is that Lucio does not in the least resemble any group that James complained of in this connection, and his libels are not at all like any actually directed against the King; but the occasionalists get around this with various versions of the "heads-I-win-tails-you-lose" strategy. Thus one of them explains that

> James I's over-sensitive reaction to calumny, and his desire that
> the laws should be put into execution against "unreverent speak-
> ers," are matched in the Duke's . . . exceptionally severe rebukes
> to Lucio in the last act. With inverse effect, Lucio's slanders
> about the Duke's sexual morals form a ridiculous contrast to the
> king's earnest warnings against the sin of fornication.

And another, that

> Shakespeare is tactful in keeping his parallels at a distance from
> reality. . . . Lucio's accusations against the Duke were the op-
> posite of the truth. So far as women were concerned King James
> was, and was reputed to be, a model of virtue. . . . Shakespeare
> has kept safely away from the King's person, in representing
> the Duke as abused by false report. While appealing to the King's
> experience with slanderers, thereby invoking his sympathy, he
> has avoided the indiscretion of personal allusion.

A third critic, however, does not require this kind of argument, or any other, since he knows exactly how James responded to Lucio, and even knows that Shakespeare would have known it in advance and timed it down to the split second:

> James would be the first to recognize and relish the comedy,
> appropriate in a court with its usual contingent of braggarts,
> know-alls, and whisperers. It would please his pride in his own

shrewd insight into human foibles. He would mutter how
he knew a score of Lucios, the gallants who affected one thing
to his face, another behind his back; and next moment he would
hear Shakespeare confirming his thought: "No might nor greatness in mortality," etc.

But the rest of us, who have not been blessed with such omniscience,
must surely be allowed to ask once again why, if Shakespeare wanted the
King to recognize his own detractors in Lucio, he did not make this
evident. For in the portrayal of Lucio there is nothing specific that points
to them, and the manner in which this character exposes himself un-
wittingly to the Duke is after all a stock comic situation that Shakespeare
had used in Falstaff's encounters with Prince Hal, written some years
before James and his book crossed the border into England.

There is, finally, one more kind of "echo" of the King's book discovered by these critics, not in the particular characters or events of
Measure for Measure, but in its central theme, which they claim is based
on some idea in the *Basilicon Doron*. The problem with such central
themes, however, as we saw in chapter 2, is that so many of them can be
abstracted from any play, and it is therefore not surprising that the critics
cannot agree on the passage or doctrine from James's book which
Shakespeare's play is supposed to be about. One of them in fact finds
three different central themes for the play in this book: the first is the
sentence quoted earlier describing how a tyrant would "enter like a saint"
(p. 61), which he says "might well be a statement of the plot of the play";
but he later tells us that "the whole play indeed revolves round James's
advice to his son [on p. 73] that in order to be the readier to govern his
subjects he must act like a good physician"; and later still he asserts that a
passage on using justice with moderation (p. 139) "might almost be the
summing up of *Measure for Measure*." Another critic claims that "the
thematic question in *Measure for Measure*" is "the proper relationship
between mercy and justice," which he connects to "James's theoretical
analysis of this relationship in the *Basilicon Doron*." And another pieces
together several of James's statements advocating temperance and concludes, "There could hardly be a more apt comment on the attitudes of
the Duke, Angelo, and Isabella in Shakespeare's play." But there is no
way to limit the number of commonplaces of this sort which could be
made the theme of *Measure for Measure*, and no way to demonstrate
that any of them need have come from the *Basilicon Doron*.[28]

Another one of these critics, however, has discovered a theme which is
certainly much more unusual in itself and in its alleged relationship to
James's political creed:

> Upon assuming sovereignty ... Angelo's virtue turns at once into deep-dyed villainy.... Critics cannot explain this sudden change in him, but it is a natural corollary of the theory of Divine Right: a ruler may not give a common man the mantle of God's Anointed any more than Henry VIII in his will could change the heaven-directed order of royal succession.... In short, the major action in the plot illustrates the need of a Divine Right ruler.... For two centuries and more, this bitter comedy has puzzled critics ... but, if one takes it as a problem play on Divine Right, the parts fall into place.

And another also says "the larger design of the play" shows that "Angelo's failure is symbolic of the failure of anyone ruling who was not born to do so," since "someone not born to rule cannot be trusted in a sovereign position." But if this is the real cause of Angelo's downfall, it is a pity that no one in the play ever bothers to tell us, or him, or poor Escalus, who is no less a "common man" and yet is permitted to depart under the illusion (encouraged by the Duke's praise at the end) that he has done pretty well while wearing "the mantle of God's Anointed." It is even more of a pity that no one bothered to tell King James about this "natural corollary" of his favorite theory, since from October 1589 to May 1590 he too left his realm in the hands of unanointed deputies while he tarried with his new bride in Scandinavia. We might suspect, therefore, that this corollary (along with the doctrine of the unresignability of kingship discussed earlier, which was also apparently unknown to James) has been invented for their own purposes by modern historical critics, who, like the new convert "more Catholic than the Pope," are considerably more absolute in their interpretation of divine right than the divine right monarch himself. And we might also observe that Shakespeare's most forceful statement of the theory of divine right is found, not in this play, but in some of the speeches of *Richard II*, composed long before James became his king.

This, then, concludes our survey of the "accumulation of echoes" of the *Basilicon Doron* which have been discovered in *Measure for Measure*, and I think it must be acknowledged that they do not establish any significant connection between them. It is of course possible that Shakespeare read the King's book and took some ideas from it—there seems to be no way to prove or disprove this hypothesis, which is in any event irrelevant to our understanding of his play. But these critics certainly have not demonstrated their claim that he "carefully mined" the book or "dramatized" it, much less that he deliberately called attention to this in order to flatter the King. For even if we pass over the distortions of the play or the book revealed in some of their arguments, we are still left with a case based on nothing more than a collection of isolated and vague similarities of the sort that could be produced throughout the literature of the period. None of the similarities is unique to these two works—we noted that some alleged echoes of the *Basilicon Doron* in *Measure for Measure* also appear in other plays of Shakespeare written before he could have seen the King's book, and it would be easy to find them in many more Elizabethan plays that could not be echoing James, and, conversely, to find James's ideas, which Shakespeare is supposed to be echoing, in many other treatises. And we have not even mentioned the dissimilarities between these works. It should be obvious that large portions of *Measure for Measure*, including the major central scenes built around Angelo, Isabella, and Claudio, cannot be related to the *Basilicon Doron*. Moreover, there are aspects of Shakespeare's Duke which place him in direct opposition to dictates of James's book. Without making anything like a systematic search, I have come upon the following:

1. James throughout his book attacks the "Papists" and the "Popish Church"; but the Duke poses as a friar throughout most of the play, and professes to have come from the Pope (III.ii.201–3), and even hears confession (II.iii.19–39, IV.ii.192–93, V.i.522).

2. James is in favor of marrying early ("defer not then to marry till your age, for it is ordained for quenching the lust of your youth" [p. 127]); but the Duke has not done so.

3. James believes the ruler should find a wife of his own rank ("if he marry first basely beneath his rank, he will ever be the less accounted of thereafter" [p. 131]); but the Duke proposes to Isabella, who is basely beneath his rank.

4. James urges his son "to eschew the opinion that ye love not to haunt company, which is one of the marks of a tyrant" (p. 165); but the Duke says, "I have ever lov'd the life removed / And held in idle price to haunt assemblies / Where youth and cost and witless bravery keeps" (I.iii.8–10). (Note that the verbal connection between these passages, in the words "love" and "haunt," is closer than in any of the parallels which the occasionalists have turned up; perhaps we should conclude that here Shakespeare is deliberately contradicting the King.)

5. James includes "willful murther" among the "horrible crimes that ye are bound in conscience never to forgive" (p. 65); but the Duke pardons the murderer Barnardine (V.i.475–80).

6. James says the ruler should make a special effort to ensure that the members of his court obey the laws by "punishing the breach thereof in a courtier more severely than in the person of any other of your subjects; and above all suffer none of them, by abusing their credit with you, to oppress or wrong any of your subjects" (p. 119); but the Duke punishes Angelo, who tried to use his official position to oppress and wrong Isabella, less severely than Lucio, an ordinary subject.

7. James would have the ruler "use a natural and plain form" in his speech (p. 179); but the Duke does not.

And I am confident that more such "dissonances" could be found by anyone willing to comb through the *Basilicon Doron* seeking them as diligently as these critics have sought their "echoes."

This does not quite complete the occasionalists' case, however, because they also try to make some connections between Duke Vincentio and King James which do not involve the *Basilicon Doron*. All but one of these can be disposed of briefly, in no particular order.

It is alleged that the Duke's comment on Barnardine, "How came it that the absent Duke had not either deliver'd him to his liberty or executed him? I have heard it was ever his manner to do so" (IV.ii. 123–25), is intended to parallel and to compliment the King's "insistence that prisoners either be punished or pardoned rather than left to rot in jail." But the evidence for this "insistence" turns out to be a single incident at Newark on 25 April 1603 where James ordered the immediate execution of a cutpurse and pardoned all the prisoners in the Castle. There is no reason to believe that this was "ever his manner," or that the prisons of England were any less crowded in December 1604 than they were under Elizabeth.

It is alleged that the Duke's opening speech—

> Of government the properties to unfold
> Would seem in me t' affect speech and discourse,
> Since I am put to know that your own science
> Exceeds, in that, the lists of all advice
> My strength can give you.
>
> [I.i.3–7]

is addressed to the King, and in it Shakespeare is "flattering his royal patron" (or making "an obeisance" to him) by implying "that one among the gathering is the supreme expositor of the science of government, and no dramatist or actor should presume to speak of it in his presence." But the text clearly indicates that the Duke is speaking to Escalus:

Duke.   Escalus.
Escal.   My lord.
Duke.   Of government the properties to unfold. . . .

It would surely be a violation of the most elementary stage logic (to say nothing of good manners) for the Duke to call Escalus and then, as soon as he responded, turn and address someone else. Moreover, a little later in this scene the Duke pays a similar gracious compliment to Angelo— "But I do bend my speech / To one that can my part in him advertise" (ll. 41–42)—which could scarcely be directed at the King. Indeed we might think that the two speeches ought to embarrass these critics, since if the play was written to flatter James, the character who is his "idealized image" should not acknowledge that others know more about government than he does. But that would be to overlook the occasionalist's privileged insight into the reactions of the original audience. It seems that at the outset they saw Vincentio and James as separate entities,

> but as the play proceeds, the Duke begins to coalesce with the King. A court audience would be alive to potential resemblances and cooperative in welcoming them, though it would not press for consistency and would forget them if the action of the comedy required—so that identifications in a play of this epoch are likely to be intermittent, now sharp and bright, now in recess.

Here we have another example of the kind of circularity noted earlier, where an interpretation presented as evidence to support the occasionalist thesis (that the play was written for a special audience) itself depends upon the thesis (the special nature of this audience) which it is supposed to support. Of course, if a critic is allowed to turn his topical identifications on and off at will with such an argument, and to invent whatever stage business suits his purpose, regardless of the text,[29] he can prove anything he likes about any play.

   It is alleged that the Duke's defense of himself to Lucio, "Let him be but testimonied in his own bringings-forth, and he shall appear to the envious a scholar, a statesman, and a soldier" (III.ii.132–34), is really a "compliment to King James" because it alludes directly to his erudition and his writing ("bringings-forth," we are told, "was another word for publishing"), of which he was so proud, so that "few people in the audience could have failed to be reminded of James." But "bring forth" had no special reference to publication, according to the OED, and is not used in that sense in any of its other appearances in Shakespeare. Moreover, James was not a soldier and would not have been likely to enjoy being called one, for he wished to be known as a peacemaker.[30] And in any event this triad (with the statesman demoted to a courtier in the case of nonrulers) was a conventional Renaissance ideal of masculine accomplishment: in *The Merry Wives of Windsor*, for example, Ford praises Falstaff as being "generally allow'd for your many warlike, court-like, and learned preparations" (II.ii.204–5); Ophelia says that Hamlet was formerly "the courtier's, soldier's, scholar's, eye, tongue, sword" (III.i.151; Q1 reads "courtier, scholar, soldier"); and in Tailor's *The Hog Hath Lost His Pearl* we even get a comic version:

> I wonder who did at the first invent
> These beds, the breeders of disease and sloth,
> 'A was no soldier, sure, nor no scholar,
> And yet 'a might be very well a courtier.
>
> [V.i.1573–76][31]

There is no reason then to believe that James would have taken this sentence as a compliment, or that it would have reminded anyone else of him.

It is alleged that the Duke's use of disguise is meant to recall the King's grandfather, James V of Scotland, who went among his people incognito as "the Goodman of Ballengiech," and so serves "as another channel for the gratulation of the King which was the wellspring of this play." But the "disguised ruler" mingling with his people was a very common and ancient folk motif, going back at least as far as the legends of Caliph Haroun al-Rashid and the Emperor Alexander Severus, as various studies have shown.[32] And in the English drama at this time there was a vogue of these figures, who appear in a wide range of plays, including *Friar Bacon and Friar Bungay, Fair Em, Mucedorus, George a Greene, A Knack to Know a Knave, Sir John Oldcastle, Edward IV, Part I, When You See Me You Know Me, Law Tricks, The Malcontent, The Phoenix, The Fawn, The Fleer,* and *Bartholomew Fair,* some written before and some after James's ascension to the English throne.[33] In fact Shakespeare had already employed this role in both parts of *Henry IV* and in *Henry V,* which are of course pre-Jacobean. To establish a relationship to James, therefore, the occasionalists would have to show that in some significant respect the Duke resembled the Goodman of Ballengiech more closely than he did these other disguised rulers of the old legends and the contemporary stage, but they have not done so.

The last of these alleged connections is viewed by some of the critics as their most telling point. It involves two passages in the play, one where the Duke explains why he prefers to leave the city "privily"—

> I love the people,
> But do not like to stage me to their eyes.
> Though it do well, I do not relish well
> Their loud applause and ave's vehement;
> Nor do I think the man of safe discretion
> That does affect it.

[I.i.68–73]

and the other where Angelo describes the rush of blood to his heart:

> So play the foolish throngs with one that swounds—
> Come all to help him, and so stop the air
> By which he should revive; and even so
> The general subject to a well-wish'd king,
> Quit their own part, and in obsequious fondness
> Crowd to his presence, where their untaught love
> Must needs appear offence.

[II.iv.24–30]

Both of these are said to "reflect in a flattering way a publicly known distaste on James's part of displaying himself before shouting, unruly London crowds," which became evident during his visit to the Exchange in March 1604 when he was greatly disturbed by the mob gathered around him. But I think it is necessary to distinguish between the two speeches. The first is part of the Duke's self-characterization (compare the remark quoted earlier on his having "ever lov'd the life removed"), and its emphasis is not so much on his dislike of crowds as on his distrust of rulers who "affect" cheap popularity—a perfectly conventional idea of the time that Shakespeare had already developed at much greater length in *Henry IV, Part I*, III.ii.39–84, and *Henry IV, Part II*, I.iii.87–108, some years before James came to England. Furthermore, the Duke later does deliberately "stage" himself to the people's eyes by arranging to have the final trial take place at the city gates, a very unusual and very public setting for such a scene, which Shakespeare is at some pains to underscore (IV.iii.90–93, IV.iv.4–9, IV.v.9, IV.vi.10–15, V.i.14). If then James had taken the first speech as a complimentary reference to himself, this change of the Duke's attitude would presumably have cancelled out that compliment and produced the opposite effect on him, which is a pretty good reason for doubting the occasionalists' view of the first speech.

The second speech is different since, as several critics point out, its comparison seems quite strained, with a very tenuous connection to Angelo's character or state of mind, and this would suggest that it may have been tacked on here for some special purpose, such as a topical allusion. But we should note that it has nothing to do with the Duke, or hence with his alleged flattering relationship to King James.[34] Moreover, it does not focus on the ruler but the crowd, whose behavior it in part excuses ("well-wish'd," "obsequious fondness," "untaught love"). Thus if it really was an allusion to the incident at the Exchange, and if James's reaction to that incident really was as "publicly known" as these critics claim, then I fail to see why this passage would not have been at least as appropriate for the Globe audience as for the one at Whitehall. There is of course a possibility that it (and perhaps the first passage as well) was added later for the court performance,[35] but that would not mean the play was written for the King—in fact, it would mean the play was *not* written for him. And if one or both of the passages were in the original text, that also, we saw, does not require an occasionalist explanation.

We have now completed our examination of all the significant evidence which has been presented to demonstrate that *Measure for Measure* was designed for the court, and I do not see how any impartial judge could conclude that it is impressive enough to outweigh the general objections to occasionalism with which we began. If, then, this is the strongest occasionalist case yet made for any play written by Shakespeare or his contemporaries, we can be spared the trouble of investigating the others. They all must fall with the "King James Version" of *Measure for Measure*, and so, too, must the entire approach, since this is the best it has to offer. Unlike the other approaches we have considered, there would seem to be nothing that can be said in its favor.

The case for an occasional *Measure for Measure* is so feeble, in fact, that one can only wonder why so many critics have espoused it (to say nothing of the even feebler cases for the other plays). I think, however, that the answer to this lies not in the nature of the evidence itself, but in the mental set that led them to seek such evidence in the first place. For virtually all of them start by assuming that Shakespeare would have been likely to write a play for the King, as can be seen in the following passages, each taken from one of their introductions:

> *Measure for Measure* seems to have been the first play that Shakespeare wrote after the King's accession; and since James' one claim to the English throne was Divine Right by his birth, one might expect to find this theme in a play written right after Shakespeare's company had been made the King's Men.

> It is not surprising if, meditating a play to be given at Court for a King who had not long been on the throne and whom the plague

had made an infrequent visitor to the capital, Shakespeare recon-
noitered the pages of the *Basilikon Doron*.

In 1604 Shakespeare's company enjoyed royal patronage. The
players had had a subsidy and other favors. If they did not have
a new play ready and suitable for the Christmas revels at court,
they were remiss in their duty; and if their chief playwright did
not produce a comedy especially for the occasion, he must have
been in a very dark mood indeed.

The greatest asset of his acting company in 1603–1604 was its new
status as the King's men. As one of the principal directing members of this company, Shakespeare undoubtedly wished to foster
its recently acquired royal sponsorship and to encourage, if possible, a direct personal attachment of the King for the royal
players. Shakespeare, indeed, may even have felt under obligation to identify his first Jacobean comedy with the ideas of the
new ruler.

And similar statements appear in many of the studies which stake out an
occasionalist claim for other plays of the period.[36]

Having begun with such an assumption, it is then inevitable that these
critics will search through *Measure for Measure* for any possible connections to King James; and having undertaken such a search, it is inevitable
that they will discover some (just as they would discover connections to
Queen Elizabeth, or the remarriage of the Dowager Countess of South-
ampton, or any other person or event, if that is what they were looking
for). But this brings us back to our own introduction, where it was
shown that, on the basis of all the available evidence, the critic should
begin with the opposite assumption—namely, that Shakespeare and his
contemporaries would have been very unlikely to write a play for a special
audience. There is no other way to stem the occasionalist tide, because
almost every play of the time has something in it that would be appropriate to at least one of these occasions, and usually to several: if it
contains students or philosophical discussions, it could have been composed for a university; if it deals with love, for a noble wedding; if it has
a sympathetic ruler, for the court; if it has an unsympathetic ruler, for
the Inns of Court—and any inappropriate elements can easily be ignored
(the usual practice), or misread, or explained away by one of the strategies we have observed.

We still have to ask, finally, why so many critics adopt this occasionalist assumption. Why do they want to find that these plays were designed
for special audiences? The answer they give is the same one we encountered in the other approaches—that this is supposed to increase our
appreciation of the plays, to make them more interesting and more

admirable. But since these special audiences always turn out to be at the upper end of the social register, we may suspect that a more subtle influence is at work. Behind many of the studies, apparently, lies the unstated (and perhaps unrecognized) belief that the value of a play is coordinate with the value of the people for whom it was intended, so that when one elevates these people, the play has also somehow been elevated. (This belief is implied, I think, in the titles of some of the studies cited earlier: *"Measure for Measure" as Royal Entertainment, The Royal Play of "Macbeth," "Middleton's The Phoenix* as a Royal Play.") There would seem to be a powerful appeal, at least for certain minds, in the idea that the dramatist (especially if he is Shakespeare) was not really catering to ordinary folk, that he was connected to aristocratic circles and was conducting, through his plays, a kind of private conversation with his monarch (and even, according to some of these readings, offering him advice). It is the same appeal that is responsible for the legends that Queen Elizabeth asked Shakespeare to portray Falstaff in love, and that King James sent him a personal letter.[37] And it must also motivate the anti-Stratfordians, whose surrogates for "Shake-speare" are invariably of a much higher social standing. The occasionalists have not, of course, made the Bard a member of the nobility, but they have done the next best thing by making him write for them.[38]

Even if we accepted their claim that these plays were occasional, however, I do not see how this would enhance our estimate of them as works of art. For the sort of interest it adds to them is entirely extra-artistic, on the level with gossip about the author or the actors or the alleged real-life original behind some character. In the case of a play like *The Phoenix*, which could use all the additional interest it can get from any source, this may be harmless enough. But that is not true of the better works, for there the arguments employed to establish the occasionalist claim, and the readings resulting from it, may do considerable damage. As can be seen even from our one example, this approach tends to distort the plays so that they will fit the preconceived thesis, and to substitute external for internal interpretations of their components and overall meaning, and to distract us, for the sake of a specious historical particularity, from their universal aspects which have preserved them as an important part of our cultural heritage. But it would be naive to think that aesthetic considerations of this kind, any more than the logical ones upon which we have concentrated here, will deter someone intent on discovering yet another royal play or nuptial play or the like, and we can therefore expect in the future to see new claims being advanced for new occasionalist readings based on much less evidence than the "King James Version" of *Measure for Measure*.

Five

Some Modest Proposals

If the major trends in the current reinterpretation of English Renaissance drama are producing the unfortunate results which our investigation has revealed, it would seem appropriate to consider what we can do, either individually or collectively, to improve this situation. But we should be modest in our expectations, for it is obvious that no magical remedies will be found. Each of the approaches examined here was seen to have its own special and powerful appeal to many critics, and so will undoubtedly be with us for some time to come. Moreover, there must also be more general forces at work to account for the widespread popularity of all three and of the "new reading" itself. Certainly the most pervasive of these has been the process of social change which has profoundly affected our outlook on various aspects of life. If each age tends to interpret the literature of the past in its own image, it is not surprising that the relativistic and skeptical "modern sensibility" should seek to infuse into these plays the qualities it admires, and to purge them of the qualities it does not. This tendency is largely responsible for what we called the left wing of the ironic approach, with its distrust of the heroic or romantic or hierarchic values embodied in so many plays of the period. The critics of this school, and the directors of the recent productions influenced by them, have quite understandably tried to make Shakespeare and his fellow dramatists our contemporaries, like the eighteenth-century "improvers" and the Romantics and Victorians before them. The tragedies become existential, the histories absurdist, the comedies black, and all turn out to be "problem plays" in a very modern sense of the term.

Although it may seem paradoxical, this same modern sensibility is probably also at least partly responsible for the growth of the opposite school of ironic critics. Several commentators have suggested that the decline of faith in religious and moral absolutes in our day has led some people to seek them in great works of literature (especially those of Shakespeare), which then come to function as a kind of substitute scripture. Such an impulse is apparent in the right wing of the ironic approach, and in the closely related ideas-of-the-time approach, for we saw that they both attempted to impose upon these plays a theological or ethical orthodoxy. And it would help to explain the attraction of the thematic approach, which so often reveals that the plays are making profound "statements" endorsing these pieties (although we found other thematists demonstrating that the same plays were conveying typically modern messages about the unreliability of language, the impossibility of communication, etc.). It has also been an important influence in the recent trend (to be discussed in the appendix) to discover "Christ figures" in these plays, where earlier, more religious ages had no need to look for them. And if those "Christ figures" are a reaction to our secularism, perhaps the occasionalist vogue of "royal plays" and "noble wedding plays" may be seen as a similar reaction to our egalitarianism. There is no way to prove such speculations, of course, but since we observed that both the thematic and ironic approaches allow each critic to make each play mean whatever he wants it to mean, it is evident that they have been very useful in these efforts to transform the plays either to mirror the modern sensibility or to serve as a bulwark against it. Both of these tendencies, then, would account for some part of the general appeal of the two approaches.

Another, more proximate cause which has contributed to the reinterpretation of English Renaissance drama has been the triumph of the New Criticism in virtually all areas of literary study. Although I have said very little about this movement in the preceding chapters, primarily because it is so difficult to define or pin down, it has obviously had a major role in the proliferation of new readings of these plays. Indeed the ten characteristics of the reading with which we began could be taken as a generic description of the practice of most New Critics, to whom we owe the very term "close reading." And this practice is often associated specifically with the ironic or thematic approaches. Many of their readings are devoted to uncovering some hitherto unnoticed but pervasive irony in the work (although not always in the sense employed here), and many of them turn upon a central theme.[1] One of the earliest and most influential books of this movement, in fact, is an exercise in what we called reflexive thematics, since it discovers that each of the poems it deals with is really presenting a statement about poetry (and since each statement proclaims the superiority of poetry to modern science as a repository of the higher truths, this may be viewed as another example of the tendency just noted to treat literature as a surrogate scripture—a tendency which is also associated with several of the original New Critics). And it is surely no accident that the period in which these approaches have flourished coincides exactly with the ascendancy of the New Criticism in our universities, from which almost all of the readings considered here have emerged.

The relationship of these readings to the university, moreover, must itself be regarded as another general and very important influence upon them. We are now so used to the near-monopolization of literary criticism by professors of literature that we may sometimes forget that it is a relatively recent phenomenon, yet it will inevitably affect the nature of this criticism. The most obvious such influence is the pressures which the conditions of their employment exert upon the professors to produce the criticism, and which we all realize, in our franker moments, is a major cause of this profusion of new readings. The command to "publish or perish" may not be as sternly applied as the public seems to think (just about every English department contains some people who have done neither), but it is undeniable that many university teachers, particularly the younger ones, are powerfully driven to seek the rewards of publication—raises, promotions, tenure, fellowships, released time, invitations to speak, recognition by professional associations, and the like. And they know that their interpretations are not likely to be published unless they say something about the work that has never been said before, which all too often means, if the work has already accumulated a substantial body of criticism (as have most of those treated here), that they must say something very strange. There is an inherent absurdity in the idea of inducing a large number of people to set out deliberately every year to conceive new interpretations of these plays, for the resultant annual crop will always include a large proportion of monsters. Of course one might object that they do not have to write interpretations, since there are many other forms of publishable research in the field. But most teachers are apparently not suited, either by training or inclination, to undertake such research (some of which also requires resources not readily available to them), and they could argue, with some justice, that interpretation is the primary purpose of the study and teaching of literature, and, presumably, of these other kinds of literary research. They are thus placed in a cruel dilemma—a choice between publishable novelty and unpublishable credibility; so it is not surprising that many of them opt for the first alternative. And if they do, then the approaches we have been examining should seem especially attractive, since we found that each one provides a guaranteed and easily mastered method for discovering and demonstrating a new reading of any play.

The widespread if tacit recognition of this situation, it seems to me, goes a long way toward explaining the attitude of laissez-faire described in the opening chapter. Because each critic must keep busy producing his own publications, and knows that his colleagues must do the same, he tends to regard their work with amiable tolerance; he does not interfere with them, nor do they with him. (A similar atmosphere prevails in our professional meetings, even in most of the so-called panels, where each speaker in turn presents his self-contained paper and then politely sits through the other equally self-contained papers.) This attitude has made it possible for us to live with the babel of conflicting new readings (for which it is partly responsible), but at the expense of any real dialogue between the critics. As a result, their tolerance of other interpretations comes to look more like indifference, if not downright cynicism. It does not seem to matter very much what gets published, so long as it does get published, and thus the "Shakespeare industry" and all the allied industries continue to churn out their quota of new readings year after year.

The influence of the professionalization of literary studies, moreover, is not limited to this pressure to publish. Having served now for four years as a referee of all papers in the field submitted to one of our leading journals, I can testify that what we see in print is only the tip of the proverbial iceberg. For every new reading accepted for publication, there must be at least ten still more dubious readings which make the rounds of the journals without finding a home. And for every one of those, there must be many others even more dubious (to judge from the reports one hears) which are never written up but are taught in our classrooms. It is not pleasant to contemplate what goes on in some of those classrooms, where the critic-as-pedagogue is in absolute control, and his interpretations are not subject to even the minimal accountability that publication provides. We are not concerned here, however, with the eccentricities of individual teachers, but with the effect of teaching itself upon the interpretation of this body of drama. One such effect, I think, is that we tend to regard the play as something to be "studied" rather than experienced. It becomes an assigned problem which we must get our students to work out, and this work must have its own justification. The play, therefore, cannot be merely enjoyable or moving; it has to yield some rewarding ideas or message in order to qualify as an appropriate object of "study." We have already seen this conception in the thematists' search for instant profundity and instant relevance; and it is clearly related to the other approaches as well, since they all assume that the meaning of the play is not found in our direct experience of it but in an elaborate intellectual operation quite separate from that experience. Such an assumption is implicit in the distinction, basic to all three approaches, between the play's apparent meaning, which is immediately available, and its real meaning, which is revealed, as one of the critics put it, "only when we take thought." Because of that distinction, then, these approaches lead to the "study" of the play, in this sense, and the classroom "study" of the play in turn leads to these approaches.

There is another, more subtle appeal that the approaches we have examined may hold out to the teacher: each of them gives him a secret key to interpreting the play—the central theme, the hidden irony, the idea of the time, the special occasion—which he knows and his students do not (and which is also a consequence of the distinction between real and apparent meaning). Anyone who has ever faced a class can appreciate the value of such a key. In almost all other disciplines the professor's role depends upon his possession of a body of expert knowledge, and until recently this was also true of the professor of literature. In the not too distant past, when the literature taught in college was Greek and Latin, his expertise was philological, as it continued to be during the early period of "English Studies," which concentrated upon Anglo-Saxon and Middle English. Later, when more modern authors were introduced into the curriculum, the emphasis was primarily on literary history and bio-graphy, and his expertise was in those areas. But the revolutionary shift in the orientation of our English departments from this historical scholarship to analysis and criticism has left him, for the first time, without any special knowledge to "profess," except for odds and ends of information about prosody and figures of speech and the like. It is easy to understand, therefore, how he might be attracted by the promise of that secret key which these three approaches offer, and which would help to explain why the popularity of these approaches coincides with this revolution. But it is an illusory promise, so far as his classroom role is concerned—many students are quickly turned off when they discover that their interpre-tations are always wrong, because the work never means what it seems to mean, while those who catch on to the teacher's mode of operation treat the whole thing as a game of guessing what he has in mind. And outside the classroom it has contributed to the widespread impression that critics have made literature a private preserve not accessible to ordinary mortals. This, too, may be seen as a result of the professionalization of literary studies, since every profession wants to have its own "mystery," and consequently as another source of the appeal of the approaches we have been investigating.

If this account of the general causes underlying the current proliferation of new readings of English Renaissance drama is even partly correct, it is clear that nothing we can do will produce any sudden or radical change in the situation. But this does not mean that we can do nothing, and I have two modest proposals to present—one concerning our individual behavior as critics, and the other our collective behavior as a profession—which could, I think, help to bring about some improvement, or at least start us off in that direction. The first involves the procedure we should adopt when we set out to interpret one of these plays. I stated in the opening chapter that it was not my purpose in this book to promote a particular approach, and I am not going to do so now. There is not and can never be any one correct approach to interpretation. No approach, no matter how good it may be, is capable of bringing all aspects of the work into equally sharp focus; and conversely, no approach, no matter how bad it may be, is incapable of illuminating some aspects of the work. But the recognition of this truism should not allow us to lapse into complete relativism, because it is also true that there are better and worse approaches to interpreting a play, and I believe they can be distinguished in terms of one of the most fundamental assumptions in any interpretation—the assumption we make about what kind of thing that play is.

Of course, one might object that the critic should not make any such assumption, but should remain open to all possibilities. Yet in actual practice we find that we have to start off with some hypothesis about the object we are interpreting. Since every approach must begin in this way, we would expect the better ones to be those which begin with the most reasonable working hypothesis, although the critic must obviously be prepared to modify or abandon it if it does not work. And the most reasonable hypothesis about a play of this period, I submit, is that, unless proven otherwise, it is in its primary aspect what it appears to be, and what it has been taken to be by the overwhelming majority of viewers and readers down to the present—namely, a literal representation of particular characters engaged in particular actions. It would follow, therefore, that the contour of these actions constitutes the basic form or structure of the play, and that the response they evoke will constitute the dramatic experience which the play was designed for. This assumption, I am sure most readers have realized by now, has been applied throughout our investigation of the thematic and ironic and historical approaches, but it is not itself another approach. It is only a working hypothesis, or, more accurately, a hypothesis about such hypotheses, which is the starting point of several different approaches and, I believe, of most of our best criticism of English Renaissance drama.

It is certainly not the starting point, however, of the three approaches examined here, for they begin with very different assumptions which in effect deny the one I am proposing. The thematists, we saw, assume that the play is not about what it appears to be about—the particular actions of particular characters—because it is really about a general idea. Consequently, the characters and events are no longer significant in their own right, but as exemplars of the idea, which is supposed to be the object of our response. And since in the abstractness of that idea the specific structure or physiognomy of the play is inevitably lost, the tendency of this approach is to lead us away from our actual dramatic experience. Therefore, if we believe that the primary meaning of the play is to be sought initially in that experience of the particular human actions presented to us, we will not accept the thematic assumption that the play is some form of intellectual discourse about an idea which the critic has to abstract from those actions.

If we should not assume that the play is a kind of treatise which the critic must abstract, still less should we assume that it is a kind of code or puzzle which he must solve. Some of the more extreme thematists may sound as if they were working from this hypothesis, but it is more typical of the historical approach, as we defined it, and of several others—typological, myth and ritual, Marxist, Freudian—not dealt with in our investigation. Each of these begins with the assumption that the characters and events cannot be understood in themselves but only in terms of some body of knowledge external to the play. They become, in other words, a collection of clues supplied by the dramatist, consciously or unconsciously, which the critic can use in his deciphering operation, provided, of course, that he is properly equipped with the essential knowledge of Elizabethan political theory or Jacobean court gossip or patristic theology or structural anthropology or the class struggle or whatever the approach is based upon. The deciphered meanings that emerge, therefore, will usually be at an even greater distance than most thematic readings from our dramatic experience, and hence from the starting point I have proposed. If we begin by looking for the play's primary meaning in this experience, then we will not assume that the literal representation which evokes it is a form of code or puzzle requiring some special lore to unlock.

Finally, I would argue that if we are not to assume that the play is a code which must be broken, still less are we to assume that it is a trick which must be seen through. Although some code-breakers seem to treat the play as a trick, this hypothesis is specifically associated with the ironic reading, which, we saw, frequently warns us not to be "taken in" by the dramatic presentation and the emotions it arouses. In such a view, then, the human actions portrayed are not even clues to the play's meaning, because they set up false trails intended to divert us from it. Thus this approach goes a step beyond the others, since the interpretations it constructs are not only divorced from but directly opposed to the actual experience produced by the play. But we cannot accept this if we believe the meaning of the play is to be sought initially in that experience, for then we will not assume that it is a trick designed to deceive everyone except the elite few who refuse to participate in it.

Although this elitism is most obvious in the ironic approach, as we saw, it is implicit in the others as well, since it is another consequence of the distinction they all make between the play's apparent and real meaning—in each approach the former is equated to the immediate impression derived by ordinary people, while the latter is always a delayed discovery resulting from the kind of "close reading" that can only be undertaken by the elect (i.e., the practitioners of that approach). And it is the opposite of the stance required by the hypothesis I am advocating, which calls for an attitude of humility toward the critical tradition that has grown up around the play, and toward the concrete facts of character and action in the play itself. These two actually amount to the same thing, because the critical tradition has been formed by generations of viewers and readers responding to those dramatic facts, without the intervention of any of the three special assumptions just discussed— indeed, it is the intervention of these assumptions which has been responsible for almost all of the "new readings" that depart from this tradition. The same humility, moreover, will also lead the critic to entertain the possibility that the values and attitudes he finds in the play may differ from his own, whereas the approaches generated by these three assumptions are guaranteed to prove that the dramatist agrees with the critic, as we noted earlier. My hypothesis would make it much more difficult for us to reshape the play in our own image, because it requires us to respect the literal sequential structure in all its particularity. Some years ago Clifford Lyons pointed out that if this structure is ignored, then "the drama is as modelling clay in the hands of ingenious redesigners, who may . . . rearrange the play, as in the game of anagrams we rearrange given letters to find new meanings."[2] He was speaking of what he called the "popular critical sport" of "thematic anagrams," but his warning is if anything even more pertinent to the anagrammatists of the code-breaking and ironic schools.

Unlike these three schools, which we saw created a new meaning for the play that was increasingly distanced from its literal representation of particular human actions (and hence from the dramatic experience this produces), my proposal would have us start with that representation, which should be presumed to embody the play's primary meaning, until proven otherwise. It therefore places the burden of proof where it belongs—upon those who reject the most obvious and most reasonable initial working hypothesis in interpreting the play, and who ask us to substitute for it one of these three special assumptions which deny that the play can be what it appears to be. It would demand that a thematic reading begin by demonstrating that the play cannot be construed literally, and an idea-of-the-time or occasionalist reading by demonstrating that the play cannot be understood in terms of its own internal standard and structure, and an ironic reading by demonstrating that the play cannot be taken at face value.

This, I believe, is the most important consequence of my proposal. For it would mean that the critic could no longer justify a new reading merely by presenting selected evidence from the play which is (or appears to be) consonant with it. We saw that this can be done for *any* reading stemming from the approaches considered here, since they are all self-confirming. He would now have to confront the "old" reading of the play, fairly and squarely, and show us that it is less probable than his own. The burden of proof he must assume, then, is really a burden of disproof, whenever there is an established interpretation of the play he is dealing with. And even when there is none, he is still not relieved of the burden, for he must then test his interpretation by having it confront all other plausible interpretations which differ from it, and all the plausible objections which could be raised against it. Each proponent of a new reading, in other words, would have to become his own devil's advocate.

The methods used to determine whether one interpretation is more probable than another may be very complicated, and cannot be adequately treated here. But we can state the fundamental principle which should govern this determination, and which has already been invoked several times during the course of our investigation—namely, that the dramatist wanted to be understood. This principle is the real basis of my negative critique of the three approaches, as well as of my positive proposal, for if he wished to be understood (and possessed the necessary competence), we should begin with the assumption that his play probably means what it seems to mean, and what it has been taken to mean by most viewers and readers. And critics can employ this principle to adjudicate between two rival interpretations by hypothesizing, for each of them, what he would have been likely to do (or to avoid doing) if he had wanted to make it clear to his audience, and then comparing this with what he actually did. We can take, as a simple example, the argument advanced by two critics quoted in chapter 3 that during the treason scene in *Henry V* (II.ii) we are supposed to realize that the conspirators were really acting to support Mortimer's rightful claim to the throne, and so sympathize with them against Henry. Had these critics accepted the principle I am advocating, they would have first asked themselves what they could expect to find in the scene if Shakespeare had meant us to see the motivation of the conspirators in this light, and what they could expect to find if he had not. And had they asked those questions, they would surely have abandoned their interpretation, since it is obvious that Shakespeare did none of the things he could have done to make us aware of Mortimer's cause, and did everything he could do to make us believe the conspirators' sole motive was "the gilt of France." And this is confirmed, again, by the traditional response to the scene, for we have no reason to think that anyone viewing or reading it was affected by the unmentioned Mortimer before the advent of these new readings.

I certainly do not pretend that all problems in interpretation can be solved so easily by my proposal, or even that they all have a solution. There will always be some critical disagreement about some plays; but I believe that its range would be considerably decreased, and the chances of developing a fruitful dialogue about it considerably increased, if the parties holding the different opinions adopted the procedure I have suggested and the principle from which it derives. For when we agree that the dramatist wanted the audience to grasp his intention, we then have a ground for settling disputes (or at least clarifying them) in the concrete facts of the play and in the general response they have evoked in most viewers and readers over the years, which should constitute, if he has been successful, the dramatic experience that the play was designed to produce, and hence the ultimate test of any interpretation. We will not be impressed, therefore, when the enthusiastic reviewer of a book quoted from several times in chapter 3, which attempted to ironize almost all Shakespearean tragedy, praises it as "a triumphant vindication of a new approach to the plays that unfolds in them depths of meaning hitherto largely unsuspected," because those depths could have remained unsuspected for almost four centuries only if Shakespeare had not wished to communicate them or had not the skill to do so. This does not mean, of course, that an informed and sensitive critic will not see more in the play than a groundling, or that a painstaking analysis of it will not reveal more than one visit to the theater will; but we would still expect these further insights to represent a refinement or enrichment of the common experience of the play—not something quite different from that experience, and certainly not its opposite.[3] And thus we would also expect that the better interpretations will come from an approach which leads us back into this experience, to sharpen and deepen it, instead of leading us away from it like the three approaches surveyed here.

In the unlikely event that my proposal won universal acceptance, we might have a moratorium on the new readings resulting from these approaches, but that would not put us out of business. For this proposal points to many kinds of studies which can enhance our understanding of the specific structure or physiognomy of each play and of the way it works upon us, and our ability to make discriminations among plays (discriminations in terms of their relative seriousness, for instance, or their artistic merit, which we saw were obscured or even obliterated by the thematic and ironic approaches). And while the conclusions reached by such studies may not be as spectacular as those new readings, they should have a more permanent value, since, unlike the new readings, they do not simply cancel each other out. Many studies of this type, of course, have been and are now being conducted by able critics who share the working hypothesis I am advocating, which is obviously not my discovery; it is already, as I have argued, the basis of most of our best interpretations. And this hypothesis also allows us to investigate all of the elements focused upon in the other approaches—the ideas or motifs in the play, the topical allusions and contemporary concerns, the mythic reverberations, the social and psychic conflicts, and the ironies—by examining them, not as ends in themselves, but as functional components, sometimes very important ones, which contribute to the overall dramatic effect. Nor does it preclude other pursuits associated with these approaches, because there are many things one can do with a play besides interpreting it. One can use it as data for inquiries in philosophy or history or religion or anthropology or sociology or psychology, or as a springboard for all sorts of fascinating speculations about life and art. But the value of most of these undertakings depends upon a prior satisfactory interpretation of the play itself, and that interpretation, I maintain, should begin with our actual dramatic experience, in its unique and concrete particularity.

My second proposal involves actions we might take collectively, as a profession, to improve the situation in which we find ourselves. We could initiate some changes in the education of our students, the critics of the future, to make them more sophisticated and self-conscious about the various interpretative approaches and their pitfalls. We could reduce some of the pressure on our younger teachers to publish so early and so often, and encourage them to seek other forms of publication instead of grinding out more new readings. But one of the most valuable things we could do, it seems to me, is to try to supplement the suggestion made earlier concerning the proper testing of interpretations. I said that everyone proposing a new reading should become his own devil's advocate by confronting it with all that can be said against it and in favor of the old reading (or other alternatives). Yet, human nature being what it is, we can expect that some critics, overcome with excitement at their discovery of the true but hitherto unnoticed meaning of a play (and at the prospect of publishing it), will not be able to state the devil's case very forcefully, and when they cannot do this, then we, as their colleagues and well-wishers, should be willing to give them a helping hand, both before and after publication. Consultants for the scholarly journals and presses could be much more rigorous in pointing out the defects in the manuscripts submitted to them; their authors may not welcome such attention at first, but in the end they will be thankful, and so will the rest of us who have to read the resulting books and articles. And if the result is the abandonment of the discovery before it reaches print, that too should be cause for thanksgiving.

We could also do a better job with our book reviews, which are now all too often merely summaries, or vaguely impressionistic generalizations, or excuses for the reviewer to present his own opinions on the subject. The review of a book of "close readings," for instance, should itself be a close reading of those readings, a conscientious attempt to explain and to evaluate the nature of the author's argument in all of its significant aspects (including its assumptions, its methodology, and its use of evidence), rather than a simple pronouncement of agreement or disagreement with his conclusions. And could we not begin to provide some kind of meaningful reviews for articles as well? They now rarely receive any commentary, except by the author of the next reading, who usually disposes of them in his opening paragraphs or footnotes (as we saw in our investigation of the "my-theme-can-lick-your-theme" gambit). If they were worth publishing, then, presumably, they are worth criticizing, and should be subject to the same public accountability as books. This could be managed in surveys of the recent work on particular playwrights or plays or aspects of the drama. There are a few broad surveys of this type now, but most of them do not descend to articles,

and those which do have to cover so many that they can seldom devote
more than one or two sentences to each. Even a bad article deserves a
fuller discussion than that, if its author, and those who accepted it for
publication, and readers who may have been convinced by it are ever
going to learn why it is bad. If we also had other surveys more specialized in scope, they would be able to examine the articles as well as the
books in greater depth.

In any event, we could certainly use more surveys, since they can serve
a very important function—if they are done well—not only in criticizing
the individual studies coming under their purview, but also in helping us
to comprehend the current critical scene and the bewildering variety of
conflicting interpretations it presents. They can show us the evolution
and the contours of this scene, the major areas of controversy that have
developed within it, and their causes, and so give us the kind of knowledge we must have in order to identify our problems and begin to do
something about them. In any ongoing intellectual enterprise, some form
of stocktaking is necessary to digest the work that has been produced;
but in our field the need is now especially urgent, because the amount of
material we are being given to digest is so large and so confusing. If we
are to have any chance of making sense out of it, we must rely upon such
surveys to tell us just where we stand in each area, and how we got
there, and in what directions we can profitably proceed. But perhaps
their greatest contribution would be to help overcome the attitude of
cynical laissez-faire noted earlier, by demonstrating that the profession
as a whole really does care about what gets published.

It is of course a good deal easier to make these suggestions than to
implement them, for that would require some reordering of our scale of
values. We would have to recognize that an intelligent review of a book
of even moderate complexity (or of a group of articles) takes at least as
much time and effort as the concoction of another new reading, and is
likely to prove much more useful, and that a really effective survey of the
kind just described is a major scholarly achievement in its own right.
And we would have to reward them accordingly. If we began to do that,
we would then be able to persuade more of our senior colleagues to take
them on, and to take them seriously. The younger members of the
profession would also come, with some encouragement, to consider this as
an alternative and honored route to publication, one which offered an
escape from the dilemma between publishable novelty and unpublishable
credibility into which we now force them. And the editors of our journals
would be more willing to commission and to provide space for such
studies.

There are also other ways in which these editors might promote the testing of interpretations. They could add a "forum" to their journals, if they do not already have one, where readers would have a chance to criticize the articles, and authors a chance to reply to them. And they could devote special issues to an exchange between several critics on a single work or a single interpretative problem. We have special issues now, to be sure, but they are almost always a mere collection of independent papers on the same topic which do not directly engage each other, much like the panels at our scholarly meetings. But we could do something about those panels as well, by arranging it so that in at least a few of them the participants can enter into a genuine debate, instead of presenting us with the usual solo performances. And additional procedures for furthering this kind of critical discussion in person or in print would be developed, I am sure, once we were convinced that it had an important purpose.

That purpose, I hope it is clear, is not to enforce some sort of orthodoxy in interpretation, which would be neither possible nor desirable. Nor is it to provide the excitement of seeing or reading one critic attack another. As I stated in my opening chapter, the purpose would be to initiate something approaching a rational conversation in our field. This should, one hopes, help to locate and to clarify the problems of interpretation now facing us, and so lead us eventually, if not to greater agreement, then at least to a greater insight into the nature of our disagreements, their causes, and their consequences. And it should improve our own critical efforts. Criticism will never be a collective enterprise; it must always come down, in the final analysis, to the individual critic confronting the literary work in solitude. But each of us can learn a great deal from other critics, even—I would say especially—from those with whom we differ, as they can learn from us, if we are able to talk to each other about what we are doing and why we are doing it. It is to such a conversation that this book is dedicated.

Appendix

The Figures of Fluellen

The technique which I call Fluellenism was not invented by Shakespeare's Welsh captain, but it is beautifully epitomized in the mode of reasoning he employs when he is inspired at Agincourt to undertake a demonstration that King Henry is a second Alexander the Great. Having established that Henry was born in Monmouth and Alexander in Macedon, he proceeds to his proof:

> If you look in the maps of the 'orld, I warrant you sall find, in the comparisons between Macedon and Monmouth, that the situations, look you, is both alike. There is a river in Macedon, and there is also moreover a river at Monmouth. It is call'd Wye at Monmouth; but it is out of my prains what is the name of the other river. But 'tis all one; 'tis alike as my fingers is to my fingers, and there is salmons in both. If you mark Alexander's life well, Harry of Monmouth's life is come after it indifferent well; for there is figures in all things. . . . As Alexander kill'd his friend Cleitus, being in his ales and his cups, so also Harry Monmouth, being in his right wits and his good judgments, turn'd away the fat knight with the great-belly doublet.
>
> *Henry V*, IV.vii.22–46

And so also, Fluellen would be pleased to learn, another fine example of his technique has been produced in our own day by another British connoisseur of the "figures in all things," living near another river with

209

fish in it, who is moved by another momentous event beyond the seas to draw another comparison between another pair of national heroes:

> The similarities between the murder of President Lincoln and that of President Kennedy nearly a century later are astonishing. Both were shot on a Friday, in the back of the head, and with his wife seated at his side. Both never regained consciousness. Both were killed at a time when they were fighting on the civil rights issue more outspokenly than any other Presidents have done. . . . More obscure similarities have been noted—that Lincoln was elected in 1860 and Kennedy in 1960; that the names of both Presidents contain seven letters; that the wife of each President lost a son while she was First Lady; that the names of the assassins, John Wilkes Booth and Lee Harvey Oswald, each contain fifteen letters. . . .[1]

At first sight this may seem much more convincing than Fluellen's demonstration, as the author obviously intended; but a moment's reflection will reveal that it is based upon the same kind of logic parodied by Shakespeare. Our latter-day Fluellen has found a larger number of similarities between his two heroes, it is true, but each of them turns out to be merely another "salmon"—an isolated and insignificant coincidence. Indeed, the number itself is without significance, since Fluellen could easily have equaled it by adding more fish (Macedon and Monmouth begin both with a letter, Alexander and Henry both rode horses and brought armies across the water, and so on), and we could easily surpass it by compiling a very much longer list of dissimilarities that the second comparison has omitted: one president was shot in April and the other in November, one was inside and the other outside, one felled by a pistol at point-blank range and the other by a rifle at some distance, etc. And we could also show that some of the "salmons" have been described in such a way as to conceal further differences—the two presidents have the same number of letters in their surnames but not in their first or full names, and conversely the two assassins have the same number of letters in their full names but not in their first or last names; both presidents were elected in '60, but one was reelected in '64 and killed in his second term, which was not true of the other.

The Fluellenist, however, ignores all the differences between the two objects he is equating, which is one of the secrets of his success: even if a census of the Wye turns up cod, dace, hake, pike, and salmon, while the nameless Macedonian river yields only gudgeon, lamprey, spichcock, umbrina, and salmon, he can still claim they are alike because "there is salmons in both." A second secret is that he ignores all the other objects which may also exhibit the particular points of similarity he has seized upon: even if every river in Europe contains salmon, he can still claim his two rivers are alike because "there is salmons in both." His procedure is necessarily self-confirming; having decided to equate two objects (or persons or events), he sifts through as many facts about them as he can, and from these selects only the facts that establish parallels between them (or can be made to sound as if they establish parallels). He is therefore in complete control of the "evidence" and cannot possibly fail to prove his case. Any two objects in the universe, no matter how diverse they may seem, must have similarities; one could work up quite a respectable list comparing King Henry to an oyster. And the more specific the class to which both objects belong, the more similarities can be found; there will be many more if Henry is compared to another man (or dramatic character), and still more if he is compared to another king or general— any king or general. It is thus in the nature of things that the Fluellenist will never lack for material, which he can then manipulate by means of his trade secrets in order to demonstrate whatever equation he wants.

When Fluellenism is employed by literary scholars or critics, the cause of the similarities it discovers is not located in some mysterious "figures in all things" or providence (where it presumably resides in the examples just quoted and in other "folk" comparisons), but in the conscious or unconscious mind of an author. In the scholarship of earlier generations it was most commonly used to accumulate "parallels" between two works in order to prove that they were both written by the same person, or that one work influenced the other. These attribution and source studies are no longer in fashion, partly because their obvious abuses have been so thoroughly exposed,[2] but also, I believe, because their emphasis was historical rather than critical, since the alleged similarities did not enter directly into the interpretation of either work, and so did not yield a "new reading." To produce such a reading, the Fluellenist must claim that the similarities he has discovered were deliberately created by the author, who wanted them to be recognized by the audience and to affect their response to his work. This, then, is the typical form that Fluellenism has taken in recent studies of English Renaissance drama, where it has proved very useful to several modes of interpretation (which is why I call it a technique rather than an approach). In fact, we have already seen it operating in two of the approaches examined earlier—in the ironic readings to set up those "odious comparisons" between the critic's target and a baser character, and in the occasionalist readings of *Measure for Measure* to establish a connection between the play and the *Basilicon*

Doron.³ Its most popular use in our day, however, has been to equate or relate one of the characters in the play to some extraliterary personage.

Several examples of this kind of Fluellenist equation can be found in modern treatments of Duke Vincentio of *Measure for Measure*. One critic, for instance, demonstrates that in him "the actions of God are anthropomorphically represented":

> We know that he had long since ordained laws the breach of which he has never himself punished, because his personal intervention would seem "too dreadful" (I.iii.34); he has withdrawn himself into invisibility from the world of which he is the Lord, but remains as it were omnipresent and omniscient, in the guise of a priest, seeking to draw good out of evil; he reappears "like pow'r divine" (V.i.364) in righteousness, majesty and judgement in the last scene. It is not very difficult to see what is here suggested on the anagogical plane.

But another critic discerns in him another member of the Trinity:

> The Duke, like Jesus, is the prophet of a new order of ethics. . . .
> After rebuking Pompey the bawd very sternly but not unkindly, he concludes:
> > Go mend, go mend! (III.ii.24)
> His attitude is that of Jesus to the woman taken in adultery:
> > Neither do I condemn thee: go, and sin no more.
> > (John 8:11)
> Both are more kindly disposed towards honest impurity than light and frivolous scandal-mongers, such as Lucio, or Pharisaic self-righteousness such as Angelo's. The Duke's ethical attitude is exactly correspondent with Jesus': the play must be read in the light of the Gospel teaching, if its full significance is to be apparent.

A third critic, however, argues that the Duke is being related, much less favorably, to St. Paul, primarily in terms of his arbitrary judgments which are characterized in Claudio's speech on "the demigod, Authority" (I.ii.107–10):

> Why critics who draw upon Christian teaching to support the illusion of a sympathetically conceived Duke should pass over the play's most easily identifiable Biblical excerpt is easy to understand. Here indeed is the kind of power divine which Vincentio wields. . . . We are not listening to the Sermon on the Mount but to St. Paul's legalistic defense of God's inscrutable, apparently contradictory, ways with sinful men, specifically his letter to the Roman church.

A fourth critic, whom we met in chapter 4, rejects what he calls this "theological exegesis" and claims instead that the portrayal of the Duke contains a "radical historical dimension" because he was intended to exhibit a flattering resemblance to King James:

> It [is] impossible to believe that Shakespeare, just by odd luck, had created a Duke of Vienna who agreed with the new King not only in his dislike of the "Aves" of the crowd, but also in his concept of virtue-in-action, his irritation at the "unreverent speeches" of the common people, his insistence that a ruler should first subdue his own appetites before he attempted to subdue them in his subjects, and his wish to appear to the "envious," in his "own bringings-forth," both a scholar and a statesman.

But a fifth critic sees a very different historical dimension in a very unflattering parallel between the Duke's use of Angelo and Cesare Borgia's use of Remiro de Orco, as recorded in Innocent Gentillet's *Anti-Machiavel:*

> The underlying situations in *Measure for Measure* and the episode of "Messiere Remiro de Orco" are the same; in each, the ruler appoints a deputy to do an unpopular job. In the scene (I.iii) in which he explains the appointment, Shakespeare's Duke gives, in all, four reasons for making Angelo his deputy.... All four of these reasons appear in Gentillet's treatment of the story of Remiro de Orco.

And finally, a sixth critic, who denies both the theological and the historical-political dimensions of the Duke, finds in him yet another kind of parallel:

> It surely appears that the Duke's activity in presenting what I have called his Interlude of Justice bears some analogy with the activity of a writer of tragi-comedy, when he propounds a situation from which no happy issue seems possible, and then deploys a power strong enough to avert the expected ill.... I think it probable, therefore, that—whether by a train of thought or some swifter, intuitive process—Shakespeare acknowledged a correspondence between the Duke's undertaking and his own.

Although no evidence in these arguments is actually false, the reader with sensitive nostrils will detect some rather fishy salmon. The first critic conveniently omits the remainder of the passage in which the Duke explains why his intervention would seem "too dreadful," because it is so obviously inappropriate to God the Father:

> I do fear, too dreadful.
> Sith 'twas my fault to give the people scope,
> 'Twould be my tyranny to strike and gall them
> For what I bid them do.
>
> [I.iii.34–37]

Critic four just as conveniently forgets that the Duke wishes to appear, in his "own bringings-forth," not only a scholar and a statesman but also a soldier (III.ii.134), which clearly does not apply to King James, as we noted before. And when critic five reaches the Duke's last reason for appointing Angelo, he finds its parallel in "Gentillet's pious hope" rather than in one of Borgia's reasons for appointing Remiro.

Other instances of this kind of sleight of hand could be cited, but they are not really to the point, because even if all the evidence were above suspicion, one would still have to conclude that something is radically wrong with the Fluellenian technique itself when it is so readily adapted to equating the same character to six different persons. It will be easier to examine that basic methodological problem if we concentrate first upon the most frequently encountered equation of this type, which is represented by critic two—the assertion that a character is a "figure" of Christ. This will provide the greatest number of examples of the technique in its clearest and most influential form, and what we learn about it here will apply as well to its other manifestations, including its important role in the production of "James figures" for the historical approach, as seen in critic four. (Critic six shows how it can serve another current fashion, the "reflexive" branch of thematism discussed in chapter 2, which treats the play as a statement about itself or the nature of drama.)

Anyone familiar with recent Shakespearean criticism need not be told how popular the pursuit of Christ figures has become. It is because of this popularity that we are now confronted with an embarrassment of riches which is the converse of the embarrassment already noted and reflects the same methodological difficulty.[4] For just as the Fluellenian technique allows critics to equate many different extradramatic persons to any given character, so it allows them to equate many different characters to any given extradramatic personage. And this can easily occur within a single play; in *Measure for Measure*, for instance, the Duke is not the only character to be elevated to Christ figurehood. A seventh critic has proposed Isabella:

> The holy Isabella, like Christ in the wilderness, at once discerns
> that a laying down of her life in obedience to the will of this
> Devil is not the allowable answer to the problem posed by the

fact of human sin. . . . At this point the teaching of one whom
she recognizes as her spiritual Father . . . shows her how to go
beyond the rules of Old Testament law. In the spirit of faith, she
consents to play a part in a sort of Passion-play (in an ambiguous sense, being analogous on the one hand to Christ's
Passion, on the other to human passion) which culminates in the
overcoming and binding of the adversary, and the freeing of sinful man (represented in Claudio), whom the adversary, by a
kind of justice, was holding in prison.

And an eighth has proposed Mariana:

> The great action of Christ is duplicated, shadowed, or re-enacted
> on another plane . . . the substitution of Mariana for Isabella,
> an action which saves Angelo from sin and makes him eligible
> for redemption, may be regarded as a shadow of that great
> selfless and loving action. . . . Mariana's substitution for
> Isabella, which is made at the instigation of the Duke, reflects
> Christ's atonement for the sins of humanity because of God's
> love in doing good.

And a ninth, most recently, proposed Angelo, by virtue of his position as
the Duke's substitute:

> Christ, by taking our sins, was the supreme substitute. . . .
> Suppose we ask, who, in this play, most obviously corresponds
> to the figure of Christ? It is not surprising that this question has
> been avoided. The answer is both unthinkable and only too
> plain. . . . One element in the traditional doctrine which is obsti-
> nately unclear is the phrase "took upon his shoulders our sins."
> . . . Yet that is what is required of Angelo. In the atonement of
> *Measure for Measure* the implications of vicarious guilt are
> followed out to the very end. Angelo takes on his shoulders the
> necessary sins of human judgement.

The search for Christ figures in Shakespeare's other plays has also
been very fruitful. Although few of them have been as prolific as *Measure for Measure*, a great many have yielded at least one such figure by
now, and several have two. (Usually these are discovered in rival interpretations, but not always—one critic claims that in *Twelfth Night* Viola
and Sebastian embody "the dual manifestation of Christ's action in the
world. . . . Viola's role alludes to the human dimension, Christ's role as
patient servant, willing sufferer . . . Sebastian reflects the divine dimension . . . in the role of judge and punisher";[5] and another divides the
Christ figure of *The Merchant of Venice* between "Antonio representing

Christ's physical nature, which offered a physical body as sacrifice, and Portia representing Christ's divine nature, offering forgiveness.") The sheer quantity of these results might seem a remarkable achievement, considering that the operation has been under way for less than fifty years, and has been under attack for over a decade. But although that attack, which received its most comprehensive statement in Roland Frye's *Shakespeare and Christian Doctrine* of 1963 (and its wittiest in Frederick Crews's *Pooh Perplex* of 1965), has put the Christ-figure hunters on the defensive—of which more later—it certainly has not subdued them, perhaps because it has for the most part been directed to the high ground of aesthetic theory, dealing with such questions as the possibility of Christian tragedy, the relation of art to belief, and the nature of allegory and allegorical exegesis (the main concern of Frye's book), where arguments are rarely decisive, rather than to the level of critical practice—to the demonstrable weaknesses of the Fluellenian method used to produce these figures.

From the perspective already gained on this method it should now be clear that the number of Christ figures found in Shakespeare is not so remarkable after all. It is absurdly easy to discover one in a play because of the many aspects of Christ's earthly career that can be drawn upon to work up the necessary parallelism (unlike the much more abstract God the Father, who has proved to be much less popular with the Fluellenists). Any character who represents true authority or opposes false authority, who moves from a higher station or "world" to a lower one, who resists temptation or combats evil, who suffers or dies (or merely disappears for a time), who loves another or helps him or forgives him or substitutes for him or judges him or refuses to judge him, can qualify for this role; and since almost all of the major sympathetic characters in the plays (and even some of the minor and antipathetic ones, as we have seen) come under at least one and usually several of these heads, there will never be any shortage of candidates. And in addition to these more general parallels, the critic has available to him a great number and variety of specific incidents in the Gospel story and later commentaries that he can choose from to establish further connections with the candidate he is championing. Since specific connections of this type are made so much of in so many of these interpretations, it should be instructive to examine a few representative examples.

We can begin with the first such example in the preceding quotations, the equation set up by critic two between Duke Vincentio's interview with Pompey and Christ's with the woman taken in adultery, which has been singled out by Patrick Murray, in that survey of modern Shakespearean criticism described earlier, to justify his assertion that this critic is "able to cite numerous parallels to show how again and again [the Duke's] ethical attitude is exactly correspondent with that of Jesus."[6] The two attitudes will seem to correspond, however, only if we have forgotten our Bible or our Shakespeare. In the account of St. John, when the scribes and Pharisees asked Jesus whether the woman should be stoned, as "Moses in the law commanded,"

> he lifted up himself, and said unto them, He that is without sin
> among you, let him first cast a stone at her. And again he
> stooped down, and wrote on the ground. And they which heard
> it, being convicted by their own conscience, went out one by
> one, beginning at the eldest, even unto the last: and Jesus was
> left alone, and the woman standing in the midst. When Jesus
> had lifted up himself, and saw none but the woman, he said unto
> her, Woman, where are those thine accusers? Hath no man
> condemned thee? She said, No man, Lord. And Jesus said unto
> her, Neither do I condemn thee: go, and sin no more. [8:7–11][7]

And in *Measure for Measure* the following dialogue takes place when the Duke comes upon Pompey in the custody of the constable:

Duke.   Fie, sirrah! a bawd, a wicked bawd!
        The evil that thou causest to be done,
        That is thy means to live. Do thou but think
        What 'tis to cram a maw or clothe a back
        From such a filthy vice. Say to thyself,
        "From their abominable and beastly touches
        I drink, I eat, array myself, and live."
        Canst thou believe thy living is a life,
        So stinkingly depending? Go mend, go mend!
Pom.   Indeed, it does stink in some sort, sir. But yet, sir, I
        would prove—
Duke.   Nay, if the devil have given thee proofs for sin,
        Thou wilt prove his. Take him to prison, officer.
        Correction and instruction must both work
        Ere this rude beast will profit.

                                [III.ii.16–30]

Surely it would be more accurate to say that the ethical attitudes of Jesus and the Duke are diametrically opposed: each is confronted with a sexual offender, but whereas one explicitly refuses to condemn the offender and circumvents the punishment that "the law commanded," the other explicitly condemns the offender (whether in a manner "not unkindly," I leave the reader to judge) and insists upon his legal punishment—"Take

him to prison." Yet because both tell the offender to reform, our critic
seizes upon this one lonely salmon which these two wholly different
rivers have in common, and so can claim (and persuade Mr. Murray)
that they are "exactly correspondent."

This example was taken from one of the earliest Christ-figure interpretations, originally published in 1930, but the method remains unchanged
in one of the latest discoveries: "No one has noted that Hamlet's ranting
challenge of Laertes at Ophelia's grave, introduced by the interjection
''Swounds' for 'God's wounds,' equates him with Christ: 'Woo't drink up
esill?'" (V.i.261–63). It would be difficult to imagine situations more
dissimilar than that of Jesus on the cross, being given the sponge filled
with vinegar, and that of Hamlet in the graveyard, grappling with
Laertes and challenging him to contests in weeping, fighting, fasting,
self-tearing, vinegar-drinking, and crocodile-eating; but, again, the critic
hooks onto the single salmon (even though it is a real object in one case and
merely a verbal formula in the other) which, according to Fluellenian
logic, "equates" them. (We may more charitably pass over without
comment that minnow represented by "'Swounds.")

As might be expected, the Crucifixion and the events leading up to it
have become a favorite source of material for these studies, and have
been equated by this same mode of reasoning to the deaths of Julius
Caesar, Cordelia, Desdemona, Duncan, Hamlet, Hector, Hotspur,
Richard II, and Timon, among others, in order to establish their Christ
figurehood. Nor is it always necessary for the character to die. One critic
tells us that in *The Winter's Tale*, "Hermione, refusing to fear the death
that is offered her as a form of justice, proclaimed a strumpet on every
post, and hurried into a place in the open air before she has her strength
—all this should suggest readily enough, even to a modern reader, the
familiar career of Jesus from Gethsemane to Golgotha." (Of course, even
a modern reader, if he stops to think about it, should recognize readily
enough the obvious differences between these two ordeals in the nature
of the accusation, the conduct of the trial, the verdict, the sentence and
its execution, even in the reasons for the refusal to fear death and for the
loss of strength—in just about every element, that is, except the "open
air" where both occur.) Hero's feigned death in *Much Ado about
Nothing* is similarly elevated, according to a second critic, since it
"imaged forth . . . the concept of love as redemptive sacrifice," whose
"ultimate archetype [is] Christ's death and resurrection." And so is
Helena's in *All's Well That Ends Well*, according to a third, who adds,
for good measure, another kind of figurative "death" for the Christ
figure:

Like Christ, Helena dies in demonstrating her love, or at least
leads others to believe in her death. And finally like Christ she
is resurrected from apparent death to make a final demonstration
of her holy power. Perhaps one may say Helena also dies figu-
ratively in the sexual sense as a substitute sacrifice to Bertram's
lust.

But the character need not even feign death (or suffer coitus) in order
to qualify. A fourth critic has recently announced that Orlando in *As
You Like It* "assumes symbolic stature" because "his action of redeeming
Oliver by his own blood is clearly reminiscent of the Christian mystery
of man's redemption; like Christ, Orlando has conquered, by the gratuitous expression of love, the moral evil symbolized by the snake." We
may have some trouble reconciling this account of the action with the
one given in the play, for there the snake slithers off as soon as Orlando
happens upon the scene, before he has a chance to express his gratuitous
love or anything else (IV.iii.110–13); and when he does act he cannot be
"redeeming Oliver by his own blood" in the Christian sense, since his
blood is not offered as a sacrifice for Oliver but is lost quite unintentionally while battling the lioness (ll.146–48). And other alleged "figures"
of the Crucifixion seem to be directly contradicted by the dramatic facts.
One critic asserts, for instance, that Richard II "take[s] on the aspect of
Christ" because, "betrayed and scorned, he undergoes his ordeal pa-
tiently and is made to recall the supreme example of patience in suffering," but does not note that he later explicitly rejects this attitude:
"Patience is stale, and I am weary of it" (V.v.103). And another tells us
that Richard "face[s] his executioners with such a manifestation of regality in death that Exton, like the centurion at the foot of the cross, . . .
is compelled to acknowledge it," but fails to mention that his manifestation of regality, in which he kills two of these executioners and consigns them to a "room in hell" and the "never-quenching fire" (ll.107–8), is
just the opposite of Jesus' ("Father, forgive them; for they know not what
they do").[8]

There really was no need for such reticence on the part of these last
two critics, because they could easily have transformed this very contradiction into further evidence for their case by falling back upon the
convenient concept of "parody," as we see in the argument of another
critic relating Timon's death to Christ's:

After his rejection by men, he dwells for a time in a suggestive
cave, emerging to condemn all humanity. And the parodic
pattern is completed when, instead of rising from the cave to be

transfigured, he descends from it to be merely obliterated in the
sands of the seashore.

Although this use of the "parodic" parallel is relatively new to Shakespearean Christ-figure studies, it was anticipated (and parodied) in the
final point made by Shakespeare's own exemplar of their method: "As
Alexander kill'd his friend Cleitus, being in his ales and his cups, so also
Harry Monmouth, being in his right wits and his good judgments, turn'd
away the fat knight." It is, in fact, the third and ultimate secret of
Fluellenism, one that I call the "heads-I-win-tails-you-lose" gambit since
it guarantees the critic's success by enabling him to exploit with equal
effectiveness all differences as well as all similarities between the two
objects under comparison, and so to dispose of any possible objections.
(That final point of Fluellen's, of course, was answering the objection to
his equation raised by Gower: "Our King is not like him in that. He never
kill'd any of his friends.") Thus in the preceding example, Timon's cave is
supposed to be "suggestive," as is his rejection by men, because it is like
something in Christ's career, while his condemnation of humanity and
descent into oblivion are supposed to be just as suggestive because they
are unlike that career. And the same sort of two-way logic lies behind
another argument of this critic, presented in question form: "What is the
banquet [in I.ii], in other words, but a monstrous parody of the Communion of the Last Supper, with every guest playing Judas Iscariot to
Timon's Christ?" What indeed?

The Last Supper, incidentally, has by now become almost as popular
as the Crucifixion in these studies, which are turning up many versions
of it, both "straight" and "parodic," within the canon. It is not always
necessary for these meals to be seen on the stage:

> Other examples of Christ figures who partake of a Last Supper
> ... [include] Antonio, to whose supper Shylock goes "to feed
> upon / The prodigal Christian" (II.v.14–15), Shakespeare as-
> signing the same cannibalistic images to Shylock as he does to
> Timon's false friends and creditors.[9]

> Macbeth, welcoming Duncan to the banquet in his castle, plays
> the part of Judas at the Last Supper.[10]

Nor do they always have to be meals, so long as some ingestion occurs:

> Could not Caesar's offering of wine to the conspirators [II.ii.126]
> be taken as his "last supper"?

> Hailing Juliet's beauty as a feast of light, [Romeo] raises and
> drinks his cup of poison—a kind of blind *figura* of the Christian
> Mass. Since in the time scheme of the play it is now Thursday

night, we recognize here a celebration which travesties the
Thursday Last Supper of Christ.

And in one striking instance not even that is required:

> At a Last Supper during which Christ speaks of his body as a
> memorial unto the "forgiveness of sins," Judas arises from the
> table to go out into the night to keep his bargain of betrayal with
> a kiss. Likewise Othello, in a final scene of bedroom communion
> with Desdemona, has no mind for forgiveness but instead, in
> loyalty to his own blind sense of justice, mocks the reality of
> communion by celebrating it perversely with a deadly kiss.

The reader will recognize that the connective "likewise" here has the
same logical status as Fluellen's "so also."

Perhaps we have now seen enough of these Shakespearean Christ
figures and their Last Suppers. Further examples would simply confirm
what we have learned about the Fluellenian technique, which is really
nothing more than the accumulation of parallels of this kind, which are
themselves nothing more than pieces of special pleading, in that they
have always been subjected to a double screening in advance by the
Fluellenist: out of all the facts in the play he selects only those suiting his
purpose, and since each of these chosen facts has many aspects, he selects
again those of its aspects that he will consider relevant and ignores all the
others.[11] The result is therefore never in doubt, so that when one of the
critics quoted above announces that he has discovered an "astonishing
congruence" between *Measure for Measure* and the Gospel story, we will
manage to control our wonder. That is just what we would expect. If he
had been searching for such a congruence (or any other) by the use of this
method and had failed to discover it, that would indeed be astonishing.
But no such failure has ever been recorded.

We still have to consider the defense of this method offered by these
critics themselves in the face of the attacks mentioned earlier. Its principal lines can be seen clearly enough in the typical statements of two
studies published after 1960, one on *The Merchant of Venice* and the
other on *Timon of Athens*. The first explains that

> the overingenuity and the religious special pleading that has
> marred some "Christian" criticism of Shakespeare make manifest
> the need for rigorous standards of evidence and argument in such
> investigations. The present study does not claim that all of
> Shakespeare's plays approach as closely as *The Merchant of
> Venice* appears to do to the themes and methods of the morality

play. Nor does it imply anything about Shakespeare's personal religious convictions. . . . The study does, however, uncover in *The Merchant of Venice* patterns of Biblical allusion and imagery so precise and pervasive as to be patently deliberate; it finds, moreover, that such language clearly reveals an important theological dimension in the play and points toward consistent and unmistakable allegorical meanings.

And the second begins in similar fashion by acknowledging that previous comparisons of Timon to Christ

are flawed by an extravagance of claims and a lack of hard evidence that Roland Frye charges are typical of most efforts to make "Christ-figures" out of Shakespeare's protagonists. Much of Frye's very trenchant attack on such loose "theologizing" . . . is valid, but I think he is wrong in denying (presumably) that Shakespeare would ever invest a character's career with overtones and metaphors of the Christ-story, without actually forcing a one-to-one identification. . . . The verbal and plot correspondences that I discuss above as a pattern are certainly remarkable . . . I do not see how, in themselves, they can be denied or dismissed. Perhaps Frye as a theological historian is incensed by the careless use of "type" by writers in Knight's critical school. I am not prepared to argue that Timon is a *typos* of Christ in the strict exegetical sense.

There is no need to linger over the concessions on Shakespeare's other plays or his personal religious convictions or the strict exegetical sense of *typos*, which seem to be diversionary tactics designed to propitiate the enemy in advance. The essential strategy, in each case, is to assert that the earlier Christ-figure studies now under attack represent an *abuse* of the method which the critic will be using, so that they can be surrendered in order to secure his own position.[12] And that position depends upon the hardness and rigor of the "evidence," which is supposed to distinguish these two studies from their predecessors and therefore establish their claim to validity. But it is subject to immediate qualification, for the second critic admits there is no "one-to-one identification" of Timon's career with Christ's, and the first, after insisting upon "rigorous standards of evidence and argument," explains on the next page that the "dimensions of allegorical significance" are "not consistently maintained throughout the play and not susceptible of analysis with schematic rigor."

In this respect, then, these two studies are no different from those previous "abuses" or from other examples of theological Fluellenism, both ante- and post-Frye, which regularly acknowledge that the parallelism they have discovered is not exact, sometimes even claiming this as a positive virtue. Critic eight, for instance, says of the relation of Mariana's "sacrifice" to Christ's: "No point-by-point equivalence may be found; nor, indeed, is such a perfect correspondence necessary or desirable." And the critic who made a Christ figure of Hermione warns us that "the kind of absolute correspondence, traceable point by point through every line of a poem, that is sometimes used as a criterion by academic allegory hunters is not a characteristic of this play—or, for that matter, of any really respectable literary work." It is not at all difficult to understand the need for such statements, since we have seen that the parallels are highly (and doubly) selective; but it is then most difficult to understand why these later studies are superior to the earlier ones which they condemn as overingenious and extravagant. For this qualification means that there has been no significant change in the nature of the Fluellenian comparisons. Consequently, the precise and pervasive biblical patterns and the undeniable and undismissable correspondences of which they boast turn out to be nothing more than the same old "astonishing congruence" we have already encountered, and their hard, rigorous evidence, nothing more than another mess of soft and slippery salmon. And this would confirm that the examples we have been looking at cannot be regarded as abuses of the method; they *are* the method itself.

There is also a tactical variant of this defense which depends ultimately upon the same kind of evidence, but shifts the burden of proof to the enemy:

> The evidence must be drawn from the play itself, using whatever aid a knowledge of the contemporary climate of opinion and of the dramatic practice can give us. The opponent of a critical interpretation must in turn show how the critic has wrenched or disregarded the text. But this is what Frye does not seek to do. One cannot very well present a rebuttal to what is merely assertion rather than an attempt at refutation.

The tactic is perfectly safe, for it must now be evident from what we have learned of the method that a Fluellenian equation cannot be refuted. The critic defending such an equation should take little comfort in that, however, because it necessarily follows that all rival equations established by this method are also irrefutable. While there is no way to prove that Duke Vincentio is not a Christ figure, neither is there any way to prove that he is not a God the Father figure, or a Saint Paul figure, or a King James figure, or a Cesare Borgia figure, or a Shakespeare figure, or

even an Alexander the Great figure, or conversely, to prove that the
Christ figure of *Measure for Measure* is not Isabella or Mariana or
Angelo or some fifth character. Nor is it possible to show that any one of
these equations is supported by more evidence than any of the others,
since we saw at the outset that such quantitative judgments of Fluellenism were meaningless. The evidence (i.e., the parallels between the
dramatic character and his alleged extradramatic prototype) is not re-
ducible to definite units that can be added up, because every parallel
could be divided into smaller units or combined with others into a larger
one; and even if it were, one could always find more of these parallels for
any given equation with little additional effort. Therefore, we must
conclude (as we did with the central themes) that all the Fluellenian
equations are equally true and equally false, which should be a much
more serious objection to them than any merely theoretical "assertion"
because it demonstrates a basic defect in the very nature of the method
used to establish them. But the most telling objection of all, we may feel,
is in that speech of Fluellen's, for how can we believe that Shakespeare
would write such a devastating parody of the selfsame method of "figure" hunting that he expected, according to these critics, of his own
audience?

Since our investigation has been concerned solely with Fluellenism as a
technique for interpreting the "evidence ... drawn from the play itself,"
no attempt has been made to consider its relationship to the whole
problem of external evidence and that "contemporary climate of opinion" referred to by the critic just quoted. Yet this would obviously have
to enter into any complete discussion of Shakespearean Christ figures.
The critics who traffic in them regularly justify their practice by invoking
various traits of the Elizabethan mentality and "the ideas of the time"
which supposedly required both playwrights and audiences to view the
drama allegorically or analogically or anagogically or symbolically or
typologically, and hence produced these theatrical figures of Christ. But
when we ask for specific evidence to support this kind of generalization,
they always give us something else—the writings of the Church fathers,
or Dante's letter to Can Grande, or the marginal glosses on the Geneva
Bible, or Tillyard's *Elizabethan World Picture*, or the like—none of
which can tell us whether an Elizabethan would have been at all likely to
create or to discern a Christ figure on the stage.[13] For the plain truth is
that they have no evidence: after more than forty years of searching,
these critics have not found anything to suggest that any character in any
play written by Shakespeare, or by any of his contemporaries, was ever
regarded as a figure of Christ, or of any other biblical personage, by

anyone in his time (or, for that matter, in any succeeding time down to the present century). Yet this surely is the sort of thing one would expect to be recorded somewhere—for instance, in the spirited debate that was then being waged about the morality of the drama, where it would have been especially relevant. Therefore, the absence of such evidence is itself very impressive evidence against these critics. If the conception of Shakespearean Christ figures depended upon the "contemporary climate of opinion," as they allege, it is certainly strange that those figures have only been discovered in our own day. Indeed, it would seem much more probable that this conception (like the other impositions of "ideas of the time" upon the drama which we treated in chapter 4) is really a modern anachronism.

The lesson to be derived from our examination of Shakespeare's Christ figures, however, is not restricted to this one form of "figure" hunting or to the works of this one playwright. It extends with equal force to what is apparently the second most popular manifestation of Fluellenism in recent interpretations of English Renaissance drama—the attempt to find a "historical dimension" in that drama by equating some of its characters to important contemporary personalities and particularly to King James, as exemplified in the fourth passage on Duke Vincentio quoted at the outset. This operation may even claim a wider influence than the search for Christ figures, since it has been applied to many more playwrights and has been with us for many more years (we noted in chapter 4, for instance, that Duke Vincentio was connected to King James as far back as 1766, whereas there is no reason to believe that anyone ever saw the figure of Christ in him before 1930). Moreover, we do have one indisputable case of James figurehood—the White King in Middleton's *A Game at Chess*—and enough solid external evidence (in the censorship, the arrests of authors, etc.) of contemporary sensitivity to the possibility of political allusion in the drama to suggest that, at least in theory, this kind of "figure" should be more plausible than the theological variety.

Yet if we turn to the actual arguments which have been advanced to produce the recent proliferation of these James figures, we encounter again all of the difficulties already seen in theological Fluellenism. The royal persona has been discovered in characters as widely and wildly diverse as Shakespeare's Bottom and Cymbeline and Fortinbras and Hamlet and Leontes and Pericles and Prospero and Vincentio, along with Gonzago in Marston's *The Fawn*, Henri IV in Chapman's *Byron* plays, Overdo in Jonson's *Bartholomew Fair*, the Cardinal in Middleton's *More*

Dissemblers Besides Women, the King in Beaumont and Fletcher's *Philaster*, the titular characters in Greene's *James IV* and Middleton's *The Phoenix*, and several others.[14] Like the figure of Christ, the James figure can also turn up in different characters in the same play, sometimes in the same reading. According to one critic, in *Hengist, King of Kent* "two utterly opposed characters, Vortiger and Constantius, suggest two contradictory sides of [James's] nature"; and another assures us that "no objection would be raised" by the original audience of *Cymbeline* "to the apparently illogical position of James I's somehow participating in two rôles at once: Cymbeline and Augustus."

The tactics deployed to explain away the many striking differences between these characters and their supposed real-life prototype do not inspire any more confidence. The most common is the same one used for Christ figures—the standard, all-purpose Fluellenian disclaimer, in which we are told that the playwright was "not attempting an allegorical representation of James" or aiming at a "point-by-point correspondence" or a "literal accord with history," or providing "tourists' guides to Whitehall," and so on. And this is sometimes supplemented by the postulation of a special audience with special viewing habits, for this political branch of Fluellenism is obviously related to the occasionalist approach, just as the theological branch was to thematism. Thus the court is invoked by the critic just quoted to support his bifurcation of the James figurehood of *Cymbeline*, as it was by another critic quoted in chapter 4 to allow him to turn the James figurehood of *Measure for Measure* on and off at will ("A court audience . . . would not press for consistency," etc.). Another favorite tactic, also encountered in chapter 4, is to assert that the differences between the James figure and James himself were deliberately introduced by the playwright because he wanted to "mask" the connection to the King in order to "avoid giving offence." It is not easy to see why, if that figure was meant to flatter James (which is the usual claim), the playwright would want to mask the connection; or how, if he succeeded in masking it from the King and (presumably) his officials, it could still be deciphered by others in the contemporary audience—let alone by a critic some 350 years later. But it is all too easy to see why this argument should be favored by this type of critic, since it allows him to treat these very differences as if they were evidence confirming his thesis. Like the "parody" ploy of the Christ-figure hunters, it is another case of "heads-I-win-tails-you-lose."[15]

The primary evidence in these James-figure studies is the accumulation of the usual "salmon"—particular parallels which are supposed to equate the dramatic character with the King. Earlier critics tended to seek the parallels in the episodes of James's life, thereby transforming the plays into extended and sometimes quite intricate historical allegories, with the required additional "figures" of Elizabeth, Mary Stuart, Darnley, Raleigh, etc. The most notable achievement of this form of Fluellenism that I have come across is a book on *Hamlet*, published in 1921, which demonstrates that the play is simultaneously enacting two separate series of events—James's succession in Scotland, and the Essex conspiracy in England—so that many of its characters take on a double figurehood: Hamlet is James in the Scottish allegory and Essex in the English, Claudius is Bothwell (actually both Bothwells) and Robert Cecil, Polonius is Rizzio and Burleigh, and so on.[16] (The obvious advantage here, of course, is that the critic can shift from one set of equations to the other whenever it suits his purpose.)

This sort of elaborate historical parallelism (single or double) is no longer in fashion, although one critic recently created some stir with his announcement that *The Winter's Tale* is "a wholly explicit and consistent allegory" designed to celebrate James's unification of England and Scotland. As he explains it, in the first part of the play Leontes, King of Sicilia, is the legendary Brutus who ruled over a united Britain but divided the kingdom, this being symbolized by the divorce of his wife Hermione and loss of his daughter ("Great Britain, alias Perdita"); and in the second part he is James himself, the "second Brutus," who reunited the kingdom through his reunion with Hermione and Perdita. Sicilia is England and Bohemia is Scotland ("hence its sea-coast"), although it could not very well be Scotland in the first part, since Leontes-Brutus is supposed to rule all of Britain but does not rule Bohemia, this being the realm of Polixenes; presumably it becomes Scotland during the sixteen year interval between the two parts of the play, while Leontes-Brutus is becoming Leontes-James. And Polixenes's son Florizel is Prince Henry, James's heir, whose marriage to Perdita–Great Britain confirms the political union. (I was at first puzzled as to why Florizel-Henry is not the son of Leontes-James, as he was in real life, until I realized that then Perdita–Great Britain would be his sister, whom he could not marry without violating the powerful incest taboos of the time.) And the clinching point, we are told, is that King James's erection of statues of Queen Elizabeth and Mary, Queen of Scots, in a chapel of Westminster Abbey is "figured in the play" by Hermione's posing as a statue of herself in the chapel of Leontes-James. Of course, this means that Hermione can no longer be a portion of divided Britain, whose reunion with Leontes-James was going to symbolize the unification of the island, nor can she even be James's real-life wife, since she has apparently become his mother

(Mary) and/or his predecessor (Elizabeth) in the final stage of this wholly explicit and consistent allegory.

The same study also presents us with a much more generalized allegorical pattern which is supposed to confer James figurehood upon Pericles and Cymbeline and Prospero as well as Leontes, because each of them is, like King James, "a father figure wracked by adversity, brought near to death and disaster, but steadfast in his faith, constant in his purpose and protected by providence to bring his policies to a successful and joyous conclusion." Our critic does not add that this could just as truly be said of Aegeon in *The Comedy of Errors*, Theseus in *A Midsummer Night's Dream*, Antonio in *The Merchant of Venice*, Leonato in *Much Ado about Nothing*, Duke Senior in *As You Like It*, and several persons in the history plays, all of which were written during the reign of Queen Elizabeth; but then it could also be said of the Queen herself, and so these characters will qualify as Elizabeth figures.[17] Thus with this kind of evidence and this kind of logic we shall soon be able to prove that most of Shakespeare's Elizabethan plays are about Elizabeth and most of his Jacobean plays about James, which would have the added advantage of imparting a more precise significance to those two royal adjectives, now bandied about so loosely.

This study is something of a throwback, however, because today most attempts to create James figures resemble those examined in chapter 4, where the parallels between the dramatic character and the King are not sought in the specific events of James's career but in his personality and his beliefs, especially in the views on ethics and politics stated in the *Basilicon Doron*. But the resultant equations are no more convincing than the older historical allegories. The royal personality has proved sufficiently protean to accommodate itself to a number of very different dramatic characters, as was just noted, because the Fluellenist is free to seize upon any traits of the King and the character that will prove his point, and therefore is certain to find the likeness he is looking for. And the *Basilicon Doron* has turned out to be equally accommodating because, as we saw earlier, it is full of the platitudes of Renaissance moral and political doctrine which can be related to a great many characters in the plays of this period—again, if one is free to screen them in advance. In fact, the arguments surveyed in chapter 4 which were used to equate Duke Vincentio's actions and attitudes with the King's book are a perfect illustration of the Fluellenian method: they deal only with the similarities (the salmon) in the play and the treatise, while ignoring the presence of all the dissimilarities (there are many species of fish in the Wye that are not in the Macedonian river, and vice versa), and also ignoring the presence of those similarities in other plays and treatises (there are many rivers with salmon).

There is not much point, then, in extending our investigation to the other recent studies which seek to connect these James figures to the *Basilicon Doron*, because they are all subject to this same basic objection. Witness, for instance, one critic's demonstration that Chapman modeled Henri IV in his two *Byron* plays upon the King's book:

> King and dramatist appear to have agreed upon basic political maxims: a nation needs an absolute and just ruler who can save it from feudal chaos; subjects need and desire security; they owe their ruler, God's representative upon earth, absolute obedience; and although a king is above the "danger of the laws," he should recognize both his obligation to be a good example to his people and his responsibility to do all he can for their welfare.

We are supposed to believe, in the words of yet another James-figure producer who worked up a similar list of "ideas on kingcraft" shared by Middleton's *Phoenix* and the *Basilicon Doron* ("a king should rule wisely and well"; "virtue enables a king to stand more surely than birth or blood"; etc.), that "the correspondences between book and play are too extensive to be explained as mere coincidences." And he is not entirely wrong, for we have seen that such correspondences (or "astonishing congruence") can be explained not by coincidence but by the diligence of the Fluellenist and the special secrets of his trade.[18] We have also seen that, for this very reason, they have the same significance as the correspondence of salmon in the Wye and that river of Macedonia whose name was out of the Welshman's brains.

Notes

1. "Five Types of *Lycidas*," in *Milton's "Lycidas": The Tradition and the Poem*, ed. C. A. Patrides (New York: Holt, Rinehart and Winston, 1961), p. 214.

2. A. L. French makes this point in *Shakespeare and the Critics* (Cambridge: Cambridge University Press, 1972): "Critics habitually start from the assumption that there must be a way of 'explaining' everything that happens in a play: if there are things we can't explain that is the fault of our incompetent reading and not of Shakespeare" (p. 5).

3. There are exceptions; a recent book contains a chapter entitled "Some New Readings in Shakespeare," which treats the ironic reading of *Henry V* as rather old hat and concentrates instead upon genuinely new revelations, such as that Duncan in *Macbeth* "*must*, on the circumstantial evidence of these first scenes, not only have usurped the throne himself, but have done it in a particularly foul and gory manner."

4. This connection between newness and closeness is established at the outset of a recent article: "The contention of this essay is that the traditional interpretation of the scene is completely mistaken. A close reading of the text will indicate...."

5. "The Myth of Perfection," in *Conceptions of Shakespeare* (Cambridge: Harvard University Press, 1966), p. 37.

6. *Validity in Interpretation* (New Haven: Yale University Press, 1967), p. 3. See also Peter Conrad on "the critic's upstaging of the work he is nominally discussing": "Perversity of interpretation is a statement of possession, that the work has been made the critic's property.... In the same way people were able to chatter of 'the Brook *Dream*,' as if the director had appropriated the piece from Shakespeare" ("Grub Street and Dreaming Spires," *Times Literary Supplement*, 22 March 1974, p. 285).

7. *Complaint and Satire in Early English Literature* (Oxford: Clarendon Press, 1956), p. 256.

8. *"Love's Labor's Lost* and the Early Shakespeare," *Philological Quarterly*, 41 (1962): 19 (reprinted in *Shakespeare without Words and Other Essays* [Cambridge: Harvard University Press, 1972]).

Chapter 2

1. Probably the best known comparative study of this kind is Stith Thompson's *Motif-Index of Folk-Literature* (rev. ed.; Bloomington: Indiana University Press, 1955–58). See also the discussion of such studies by Harry Levin, "Thematics and Criticism" in *The Disciplines of Criticism: Essays in Literary Theory, Interpretation, and History*, ed. Peter Demetz et al. (New Haven: Yale University Press, 1968), and by Howard Lee Nostrand, "Theme Analysis in the Study of Literature" in *Yearbook of Comparative Criticism*, vol. 2, *Problems of Literary Evaluation*, ed. Joseph Strelka (University Park: Pennsylvania State University Press, 1969).

2. The critic who tells us of "Shakespeare's near obsession with the antithesis between appearance and reality" is concerned about this: "Recurrent themes are by now such a recognized feature of Shakespearian drama that we are perhaps in danger of underrating them. And when one begins to reconsider Shakespeare's use of the most recurrent theme of them all...this caveat seems especially apropos. For everyone knows that Shakespeare manipulates this theme in play after play throughout his career, and it all begins to seem tediously old hat."

3. This complaint appeared in 1961; it could hardly be made today—certainly not about *A Midsummer Night's Dream*, as we shall see later.

4. It is only fair to add that the author concludes this reading with a disclaimer: "I am not necessarily trying to contend that *Much Ado* is a neo-Platonic homily."

5. The special affinity of thematism to the Morality play will be discussed in the final section of this chapter.

6. The theme of time is also disposed of by the critic quoted on p. 39, who uses another version of this gambit, and by A. S. Knowland in a very different kind of argument: "Hector is not killed by 'time,' nor are the 'values' he 'represents' killed by time. Hector is killed by Achilles" (*"Troilus and Cressida,"* *Shakespeare Quarterly*, 10 [1959]: 355). This of course is not a thematic refutation (i.e., a demonstration that my theme can lick your theme), but a refutation of thematism.

7. Since these lines were written I have come upon a single exception, a reading of *A Midsummer Night's Dream* published in the early days of thematism (1951) which concludes that the Pyramus and Thisby playlet "appears to have no connection... with what I regard as the central theme of the play" (namely, 'love-madness"). No thematist today, I believe, would have any trouble discovering such a connection.

8. E. D. Hirsch discusses this problem in *Validity in Interpretation* (New Haven: Yale University Press, 1967), pp. 190–92.

9. The relationship is not as obvious as this critic seems to think, since it depends on prior philosophic commitments: a Platonist would agree that avarice is a type of folly; but they would be placed in separate categories by men of a different persuasion, including Jonson himself, who uses his double-plot structure here to distinguish English folly from Italian vice. Thus another arbitrary element may be added to this argument from "inclusiveness."

10. One critic has in fact recommended "appearance versus reality" as "the primary

theme" of *The Turn of the Screw* because it "has the virtue of extreme inclusiveness."

11. This is critic ten, who took folly "in its widest Renaissance sense of a false estimation of reality or the Nature of Things."

12. John Dryden on *Epicene*; Nicholas Rowe on *The Merry Wives of Windsor*; Samuel Johnson on *Henry IV*, *Troilus and Cressida*, and *The Merry Wives of Windsor*. This attitude persisted down to recent times, as Clifford Leech observed: "In the childhood of people yet living, Shakespeare's plays were valued firstly as portrait-galleries, marvelous for the variety of character they presented" ("The 'Capability' of Shakespeare," *Shakespeare Quarterly*, 11 [1960]: 124).

13. Dean Frye discusses this point in "The Question of Shakespearean 'Parody,'" *Essays in Criticism*, 15 (1965): 22–26.

14. "A complete whole in itself...with all the organic unity of a living creature" (*Poetics* xxiii.1459a19–21, Bywater trans.). Aristotle distinguishes between these two kinds of unity in *Metaphysics* V.xxvi.

15. See p. 35 for his version of my-theme-can-lick-your-theme, and p. 36 for the version which introduces the following reading of *Measure for Measure*.

16. This is critic fourteen, whose candidate was "the centrifugal personality."

17. One of these critics acknowledges this in his definition of "theme": "I use it in what I take to be its most commonly accepted meaning: a simple and generalized statement about the world which may be abstracted from a literary work, to which the larger part of the work contributes, and with which the rest is generally consistent."

18. The trend developed so rapidly that in the second edition the author could say, "In the four years since my book was published critical attitudes to the earlier comedies have changed significantly: my attempt to analyse the judgements informing them could now be presented without a reasoned apology and I could quote further responsible opinion on its behalf."

19. *Shakespeare Studies*, 3 (1967): 258; *Studies in English Literature*, 7 (1967): 375.

20. One of these critics complains that "when it is acted...this divine insight is reduced to nothing but an occasion for roars of laughter."

21. From a manuscript poem reproduced in C. H. Herford and Percy Simpson, *Ben Jonson*, vol. 1 (Oxford: Clarendon Press, 1925), p. 113 (attribution corrected in 11:398). All of the quoted terms in this sentence are taken from recent readings of these two plays.

22. This is the critic quoted on p. 15 who claimed that each of Shakespeare's plays is a "variation on one grand theme" of "order."

23. "The Myth of Perfection," *Conceptions of Shakespeare* (Cambridge: Harvard University Press, 1966), p. 35.

24. "Five Types of *Lycidas*," in *Milton's "Lycidas": The Tradition and the Poem*, ed. C. A. Patrides (New York: Holt, Rinehart and Winston, 1961), p. 215.

25. *Essays in Criticism*, 9 (1959): 83.

26. Copyright by Apollo Books, a division of Coshad, Inc. "Casyndekan" is "an acronym formed from *CA*talyst, *SYN*thesis, *DE*finition, Knowledge and *AN*alysis," these being "the major elements of sophisticated information handling." I take all this from the "Instructor's Introduction to the E-Z Learner Study Text Literature Series" and a pamphlet entitled "Effective Concept Acquisition and Recall (or Why Casyndekan?)," furnished by the publisher.

27. It is true that on p. 39 we saw some critics rejecting a theme proposed by their predecessors because it was the "ground" or "datum" or underlying "recognition" of the play; but they did this only to subsume it under their own candidate.

28. "The 'New Criticism' and *King Lear*," in *Critics and Criticism Ancient and*

Modern, ed. R. S. Crane (Chicago: University of Chicago Press, 1952), pp. 129–30.

29. *Shakespeare and Christian Doctrine* (Princeton: Princeton University Press, 1963), p. 20.

30. "*Measure for Measure*: A Question of Approach," *Shakespeare Studies,* 2 (1966): 150.

31. "Shakespeare's Romances: 1900–1957," *Shakespeare Survey,* 11 (1958): 11.

32. "The Myth of Perfection," p. 37. This seems an appropriate place to add to our honor roll some of the other voices, not yet cited in this chapter, which have been crying out in the thematic wilderness: William Hastings, "The New Critics of Shakespeare," *Shakespeare Quarterly,* 1 (1950): 165–76; R. S. Crane, *The Languages of Criticism and the Structure of Poetry* (Toronto: University of Toronto Press, 1953), especially pp. 117–28; Barbara Everett, "The Figure in Professor Knights' Carpet," *Critical Quarterly,* 2 (1960): 171–76; Sheldon Sacks, *Fiction and the Shape of Belief* (Berkeley: University of California Press, 1964), chaps. 1 and 6; Bernard Beckerman, "A Shakespearean Experiment: The Dramaturgy of *Measure for Measure,*" in *The Elizabethan Theatre II,* ed. David Galloway (Toronto: Macmillan, 1970), pp. 87–107; Marvin Rosenberg, *The Masks of King Lear* (Berkeley: University of California Press, 1972).

It is also the place for the key to the test on p. 59: A. *Measure for Measure;* B. *The Tempest;* C. *All's Well That Ends Well;* D. *Sejanus* and *Volpone;* E. *Antony and Cleopatra;* F. *Julius Caesar;* G. *Antony and Cleopatra;* H. *Julius Caesar;* I. *The Devil Is an Ass;* J. *Twelfth Night;* K. *All's Well That Ends Well;* L. *The Comedy of Errors;* M. *Richard II;* N. *The Winter's Tale;* O. *All's Well That Ends Well.* Item E is taken from "Cosmic Card Game," Alfred Harbage's parody of thematics, which was originally published in *The American Scholar,* 20 (1951), and reprinted in *Shakespeare without Words and Other Essays* (Cambridge: Harvard University Press, 1972). As can be seen from the other items, all published since 1960, this parody was leading its target.

Chapter 3

1. It is implicit in Aristotle's conception of the "complex plot" (*Poetics* x–xi).

2. I am not suggesting that these exhaust the meanings which "irony" has acquired. One critic has recently argued that our second sense is a "loose usage" of the term, and that its use in our first and third senses (which he combines) is "corrupt," since if someone says A while indicating that he really means B (the opposite), then "he has in effect simply said B, though in a roundabout manner . . . . Clearly, irony in the strict sense is not present unless we have discovered that our hypothetical speaker means *both* A and B, despite their being opposites." (On this position see Wayne Booth, *A Rhetoric of Irony* [Chicago: University of Chicago Press, 1974], p. 140 and the references there.) But the three senses distinguished above should be adequate to isolate and define the interpretative approach we are concerned with.

3. The only significant exception I can recall is that "unbelievably close reading" of *Henry IV* cited in chap. 1, which ironizes Falstaff up to "a covert St. John"; but this requires the ironizing down of most of the other characters, especially of Prince Hal (since "Falstaff is inevitably downgraded as compared to Hal by critics insensitive" to

the subtleties this author has discovered). He becomes "treacherous" and "unchristian"; his reformation and his honor are both "counterfeit"; etc.

4. In reviewing the study of Marlowe cited earlier, which ironized most of his tragedies, Robert Ornstein observes that its author "writes less as a critic than as a prosecuting attorney who will seize upon any scrap of evidence to build a case" (*Renaissance Quarterly*, 28 [1975]: 276).

5. The technique is even clearer in a later reading, which finds fault with Troilus for refusing to arm in act 1 and then for arming in act 5, with Hector and Ajax for engaging in their duel and then for breaking it off, with Achilles for not keeping his vow about fighting and with Hector for keeping his, with those who accept the chivalric code and those who reject it. All the major characters, whatever they do or fail to do, are always wrong.

6. It is only fair to add that this critic does suggest alternative courses for Hamlet: "At least three other choices are conceivable for a man in Hamlet's shoes. He might . . . offer himself for training in a Christian friars' Order. . . . Or, alternatively, Hamlet might have chosen a political role . . . by fleeing suspected tyranny and then in exile awaiting such evidence of misgovernment as might justify a military invasion to take away the tyrant's power. Or, thirdly, he might have charged Claudius publicly with treachery and challenged him to trial by combat." But none of these "conceivable" choices is conceived in the world of the play.

7. The second critic claims that his interpretation is "in accordance with one of the traditional functions of the Chorus," presumably in Greek tragedy. But there the chorus was identified as a group of people in the world of the play (Theban elders, women of Mycenae, etc.), and they responded directly to the action, sometimes even changing their attitudes. None of this is true of the Shakespearean chorus or prologue.

8. We are apparently asked to believe, however, that the comparison of Hamlet to a priest in a Black Mass was intended by Shakespeare; and other claims have been made that the dramatist set up such equations with reprehensible characters or actions outside the play which he expected his audience to recognize. One of the early ironic readings of *Henry V* says that the Battle of Agincourt was to be viewed as "the royal equivalent of the Gadshill robbery" in *Henry IV, Part I* (although the connection is "more or less under cover"), and one of the latest says that Henry's actions were presented as "indubitably updated echoes" of Marlowe's Tamburlaine. A reading of *The Tempest* asserts that Prospero is "paralleled with Medea" as well as with Circe, and another, that he "can be seen as a type of Satan."

9. Julia is also employed elsewhere to establish contrasts which enhance our sympathy for the Duchess and Antonio and our antipathy toward their persecutors: the Cardinal is indignant that the Duchess has feigned a pilgrimage to save herself and her family from him (III.iii.72–73), but praises Julia for using a similar excuse to carry on their liaison (II.iv.1–8); and in V.i he arranges to give to Julia, "as salary for his lust," the land which he had unjustly "ravish'd" from Antonio.

10. This reading, which was reprinted on the program, apparently inspired the disastrous 1974 production at Stratford, directed by Keith Hack.

11. We found there six different umbrellas used for this purpose (in addition to "the mistaken conception of honor"): "prideful will and appetite," the "effect of time," "the corruptive spirit," the idea of "evasion," "the overpowering of Right Judgment by Passion," and "the universal flaw in all human exchange."

12. After using this hypothetical example in an article, I came upon a refutation of the ending of *Hamlet* which claimed that Fortinbras's "accession means the defeat of

humanity and the perpetuation of genocide," and showed that it is now impossible to imagine an ironic interpretation so self-evidently absurd that it could not be proposed.

13. This interpretation was incorporated into John Barton's 1970 production, which has been enthusiastically endorsed by one critic: "There was a splendid production of this play at Stratford-upon-Avon in 1970, in which Isabella turned away from the Duke at the end and he had to make the best of it: that was, I think, a fully justified reading of the text, although Shakespeare has given us only Isabella's silence to go upon." Barton said he "actually intended...that Isabella's response should be open-ended," and that she was "puzzling about what she should do" ("Directing Problem Plays: John Barton Talks to Gareth Lloyd Evans," *Shakespeare Studies*, 25 [1972]: 66), but I understand that in the earlier productions of the season her actions implied a rejection of the Duke.

14. See, for example, *Richard III*, III.vii.144–45, and *Cymbeline*, II.iii.94. Shakespeare's comic resolutions include a number of other "silent women" whose consent we must assume: Luciana in *The Comedy of Errors*, Silvia in *The Two Gentlemen of Verona*, Helena and Hermia in *A Midsummer Night's Dream*, Diana in *All's Well That Ends Well*, and Miranda in *The Tempest*; and at the end of *The Winter's Tale* neither Paulina nor Camillo agrees to the match proposed by Leontes.

15. The use of this logic is not limited to the ending. One critic recently applied it to refute the scene in *Henry V* (II.ii) where Cambridge, Scroop, and Grey are sentenced for plotting to kill Henry. According to Holinshed, they were trying to secure the throne for Edmund Mortimer (who had a better claim to it than Henry), but this is not mentioned in the play; the only explanation given there, first in the Chorus and then in Henry's denunciation, is that they were bribed by French gold. Old-fashioned commentators had asked why Shakespeare altered his source, and arrived at the obvious answer—to make Henry more sympathetic and the plotters less. But not our critic. He insists that the reason given in Holinshed must be their "real motive," and that it would have been known to the audience, or at least to the "politically more sophisticated" among them. Therefore he does not ask why Shakespeare is silent about that motive but why the plotters are, and he finds the answer in their desire to protect their families. He never explains, however, why this explanation is not revealed to us, either through their own asides or through the Chorus, which has no reason to lie about them (unless we are also to imagine that Henry suborned it between the acts). But putting aside these details, we can see here the beginnings of an entirely new kind of source study. In *Henry IV, Part I*, to cite just one possibility, where conventional wisdom has it that Shakespeare made Hotspur much younger than he is in Holinshed in order to set him up as a rival to Hal, we can now recognize that his "real" age must be that given in Holinshed, and then go on to consider why he and the other characters conspire to pretend that he is youthful.

16. The critic to whom we owe that "grim path" has found a novel way around this difficulty. He argues that, since *Henry VI* was written before *Henry V*, "the portrait of the conqueror of France" could not have been "drawn without recollection of, and reflection upon, the bitter fruit of his conquest," which led Shakespeare to adopt "that peculiar, retrospective view through which the victory at Agincourt is, in *Henry V*, really defeat, both moral and spiritual." But even in *Henry VI* no one suggests that the Wars of the Roses were the fruit of Henry V's French conquest; in fact we are told there that "England ne'er lost a king of so much worth" and "ne'er had a king until his time," that "his deeds exceed all speech" and "he was a king bless'd of the King of Kings," etc. (*Henry VI, Part I*, I.i.1–30).

17. In John Barton's production of *Richard II* a mask was used at the end to equate Bolingbroke with Richard (see also note 13 on his treatment of Isabella at the end of *Measure for Measure*), and in the Jonathan Miller production of *The Merchant of Venice* Jessica was left alone on the stage to suggest her unhappy isolation, while some other recent productions close with Antonio in a similar situation. An account of Heiner Muller's German version of *Macbeth* says, "Perhaps Muller's best touch is the final line, in which it is not the loyal nobles but the witches hailing Malcolm as King of Scotland. Thus he begins as Macbeth had, and, rather than solving anything, the pessimistic conclusion of the play implies the recurrence of the same cycle" (*Shakespeare Newsletter*, 23 [1973]: 46; this version was first presented in Basel in 1972). The Polanski film also brings back the witches at the end, but here they hail Donalbain and so set him up as a future Macbeth. Charles Marowitz has published a revealing explanation of why he and Peter Brook felt the need to make a similar improvement on Shakespeare's ending of *King Lear* in their 1962 production: "One of the problems with *Lear* is that like all great tragedies, it produces a catharsis. The audience leaves the play shaken but reassured.... At the end of the play, the threat of a reassuring catharsis is even greater. I suggested that, instead of the silence and repose which follows the last couplet, it might be disturbing to suggest that another storm—a greater storm—was on the way. Once the final lines had been spoken, the thunder could clamor greater than ever before, implying that the worst was yet to come. Brook seconded the idea, but instead of an overpowering storm, preferred a faint, dull rumbling which would suggest something more ominous and less explicit" ("Lear Log," *Tulane Drama Review*, 8 [1963]: 113–14). The ironic director, like the ironic critic, sees the terminality of the ending as a "problem" or "threat" to be overcome by extending the play beyond it; he can do it with an offstage sound, while the critic must rely on the refutative techniques.

18. According to Clive Barnes's review, Lucio was given this role in the 1975 production at Stratford, Ontario: "Mr. Phillips [the director] makes him, rather than the Duke, the conscience of the play, the ironic Brechtian commentator, who stands in the center of the action, all-knowing, all-seeing" (*New York Times*, 13 June 1975, p. 22).

19. Many of Shakespeare's tragic heroes do attain a limited kind of success at the very end when, within the narrow range of action still open to them, they are at least able to win an honorable death. I would include here Hamlet's killing of Claudius and Othello's suicide, so that the attempts noted earlier to condemn these acts in terms of the ideas of the time really amount to a refutation of an important aspect of the play's final favorable judgment of the hero.

20. Sometimes his failure to admit to these charges is itself presented as another charge against him: the initial quotation on *The Changeling* made Alsemero inferior to Deflores, "whose animality...has at least the merit of being undisguised," and a reading of *Henry V* finds that Henry is worse than Richard III, who "was still conscious of his evil." Here again we see the ironic critic placing the character who is his target in an impossible dilemma—if he confessed, he would be guilty; since he does not, he is more guilty.

21. In a prologue or chorus, which, we have seen, the ironic critics reject. Some even reject the play's exposition or reports of offstage action: one critic asserts that we need not believe Ulysses' account of Aeneas's praise of Troilus (IV.v.96–112) because "it depends on mere hearsay" which "makes the praise dubious," although he does not explain what motive Ulysses could possibly have for misrepresenting Aeneas (who is

present), or how we could possibly know that he was; and another, one of the most relentless refuters of Shakespeare, has discovered that Hamlet's letter to Ophelia (II.ii.109–24) was forged by Polonius. But in narrative literature this distrust can go even further; one critic dealing with James's *The Turn of the Screw*, not content with the usual ironic reading which has the governess imagining the ghosts, argues that she really imagined the entire story: "We may still maintain that her manuscript is not a true story at all, that it is a work of fiction she had already committed to paper before relating orally to Douglas. Or she may have made it up as she went along and then written it down." He assures us, however, that other interpretations "are not necessarily invalidated" by this breakthough.

22. *Shakespearian Comedy* (London: Methuen, 1938), p. 43.

23. Alfred Harbage has some shrewd remarks on this in "The Myth of Perfection," *Conceptions of Shakespeare* (Cambridge: Harvard University Press, 1966).

24. The last critic quoted also asserts, as further evidence of the "spoofing," that "Letitia-Frank-Letitia, a boy actor playing a girl playing a boy playing a girl, can only be Jonson's scornful bid for a record in this event." But Letitia cannot set any record because the same thing happens to Martia in *The Widow*, a comedy of about 1616 in which Jonson may have had a hand. It also happens in *As You Like It* to Rosalind, who plays the role of Ganymede who plays the role of Rosalind for Orlando's mock courtship, although this final twist involves no disguise. Actually the point of Letitia's transformations is not their number—record or not—but the reversal they make possible when it is revealed that her pretended identity is her real one, which is what Jonson emphasizes in his "short characterism of the chief actors": "the boy, the Host's son, set up for Letitia, the younger sister, which she proves to be indeed." The same situation obtains in *As You Like It* and also in *The Carthaginian* of Plautus, who is a most unlikely target for Jonsonian scorn.

25. *The Moral Vision of Jacobean Tragedy* (Madison: University of Wisconsin Press, 1960), p. 155.

26. This view of the boy actors has been challenged by Ejner Jensen, "The Style of the Boy Actors," *Comparative Drama*, 2 (1968): 100–114; J. A. Lavin, "The Elizabethan Theatre and the Inductive Method," in *The Elizabethan Theatre II*, ed. David Galloway (Toronto: Macmillan, 1970), pp. 78–80; and Michael Shapiro, *Children of the Revels: The Boy Companies of Shakespeare's Time and Their Plays* (New York: Columbia University Press, 1977).

27. Earlier statements of this view are summarized and criticized by Frank Hook in the introduction to his edition (*The Life and Works of George Peele*, vol. 3 [New Haven: Yale University Press, 1970]).

28. For an exchange of arguments on whether the Induction to *Antonio and Mellida* contains such a suggestion, see "The Critical Forum" in the July 1972 and July 1974 issues of *Essays in Criticism*.

29. See A. L. French's discussion of this point in "Purposive Imitation: A Skirmish with Literary Theory," *Essays in Criticism*, 22 (1972): 109–30, especially p. 124: "Even if they *were* meant parodically, [they] remain obstinately at the level of what they are allegedly criticising; and you cannot criticise bad poetry *merely* by being equally bad."

30. " 'It appears so by the story': Notes on Narrative-Thematic Emphasis in Shakespeare," *Shakespeare Quarterly*, 9 (1958): 293.

31. Yet this critic tells us, apparently without any awareness of the contradiction, that there were "precedents for a forgiving husband" in other works of the time, and

that "in no Elizabethan or Jacobean tragedy does a character blamelessly decline forgiveness to a penitent."

32. This is another example of the misuse of sources, discussed in the section on refuting the ending. See note 15 there for a different ironic reading of this scene which claims that even the theater audience was supposed to be aware of Mortimer.

33. *A Rhetoric of Irony*, p. 172.

Chapter 4

---

1. See especially Edward Hubler, "The Damnation of Othello: Some Limitations on the Christian View of the Play," *Shakespeare Quarterly*, 9 (1958): 295–300; Robert Ornstein, "Historical Criticism and the Interpretation of Shakespeare," *Shakespeare Quarterly*, 10 (1959): 3–9; William Empson, "Mine Eyes Dazzle," *Essays in Criticism*, 14 (1964): 80–86; Herbert Howarth, "Put Away the World-Picture," *The Tiger's Heart: Eight Essays on Shakespeare* (New York: Oxford University Press, 1970); Harriett Hawkins, "What Kind of Pre-Contract had Angelo? A Note on Some Non-problems in Elizabethan Drama," *College English*, 36 (1974): 173–79; and Arthur H. Scouten, "An Historical Approach to *Measure for Measure*," *Philological Quarterly*, 54 (1975): 68–84. See also the historical survey of this approach by J. W. Lever, "Shakespeare and the Ideas of his Time," *Shakespeare Survey*, 29 (1976): 79–91, and the theoretical analysis (which does not deal directly with Elizabethan drama) by Ronald Crane, "On Hypotheses in 'Historical Criticism': Apropos of Certain Con-temporary Medievalists," *The Idea of the Humanities and Other Essays Critical and Historical* (Chicago: University of Chicago Press, 1967).

2. *The Shakespearian Scene: Some Twentieth Century Perspectives* (London: Longmans, Green, 1969), pp. 145–49.

3. *A Remonstrance of the Most Gracious King James I . . . for the Right of Kings and the Independence of Their Crowns, Against an Oration of the Most Illustrious Cardinal of Perron* (Cambridge, 1616), p. 270. In this passage James denies the Cardinal the right to cite William Barclay in support of the Pope's power to depose kings: "Barclaius, alleged by the Cardinal, meddles not with deposing of kings, but deals with disavowing them for kings, when they shall renounce the right of royalty, and of their own accord give over the kingdom. Now he that leaves it in the King's choice, either to hold or to give over his crown, leaves it not in the Pope's power to take away the kingdom." (Spelling and punctuation have been modernized.)

4. "Put Away the World-Picture," p. 170. Marvin Rosenberg, in *The Masks of King Lear* (Berkeley: University of California Press, 1972), p. 41, also cites Charles's abdication in this connection, and notes that it was praised by Montaigne in his *Essays*, 2:8.

5. 1 Kings 1:48 (King James Version).

6. See for example entries L499, L531, and L532 in Morris Tilley, *A Dictionary of the Proverbs in England in the Sixteenth and Seventeenth Centuries* (Ann Arbor: University of Michigan Press, 1950).

7. See also *Hamlet*, III.ii.370–71: " 'Tis now the very witching time of night, / When churchyards yawn"; and *The Tempest*, V.i.48–49: "graves at my command / Have wak'd their sleepers, op'd, and let 'em forth."

8. Robert Ornstein, in *A Kingdom for a Stage: The Achievement of Shakespeare's History Plays* (Cambridge: Harvard University Press, 1972), points out "the inherent bias of the historical method toward what is conventional and orthodox in Elizabethan culture, because any search for the 'norms' of Elizabethan thought must lead to a consensus of truisms and pieties" (p. 4).

9. This critic begins, as usual, with "the context of ideas in which [the play] must be approached," which is the "orthodox pneumatological theory" of the time. This theory held, according to him, that "any kind of magic" was "a damnable, unlawful art," for "no general acceptance of a beneficent magic as lawful is evident during the period. Both church and state condemned it." Therefore, "a Jacobean audience familiar with the orthodox attitudes toward magic black or white" would have seen Prospero's "identification with the evil sorcerer of orthodox tradition." But David Woodman has shown, in *White Magic and English Renaissance Drama* (Rutherford, N.J.: Fairleigh Dickinson University Press, 1973), that a tradition of beneficent magic did exist then; and this would suggest another valuable contribution of studies in the ideas of the time—they can serve to correct the impressionistic vagaries of the ideas-of-the-time approach.

10. Some of them appeared in chap. 2, since an idea of the time can also be treated as the thematic idea which the play is about. It is thus possible for a reading to use all three approaches.

11. So far as I know, no ideas-of-the-time critic of English Renaissance literature has yet gone that far; but some members of the medievalist branch of this school have, arguing that every poem written in their period, from *Piers Plowman* down to the simplest lyric, must embody the same theological doctrine. (These are the critics Ronald Crane deals with in the essay cited in note 1.)

12. Or, as Edward Hubler puts it, such literature "gives us a picture of humanity as it was taught to be, not as it was" ("The Damnation of Othello," p. 299). There are of course other kinds of evidence which could provide better insights into the actual attitudes of the people of this time—their letters and journals, their litigation and legislation, and, above all, their recorded behavior. (A noted historian of the period once told me that if he wanted to know how the Elizabethans really felt about premarital intercourse, he would not go to the moral treatises, which would obviously condemn it, but to the parish registers, to see how many marriages produced a child in less than nine months.) But the ideas-of-the-time critics do not seem to consult such evidence, perhaps because it is much more difficult to survey than the homiletic literature, and gives us a much less simplistic and pietistic picture of the ideas of the time.

13. Unless we are to suppose that these attitudes underwent a drastic change in the relatively short period between the production of the play and the first recorded response, and thereafter remained constant down to our own day. This seems to be the assumption behind the advertisement for a book quoted earlier that used the ideas of the time to condemn Juliet: "A strikingly new interpretation which contravenes virtually all that has been written about the play since 1660 by taking the view of Elizabethan rationalistic moral-psychology."

14. "*Love's Labor's Lost* and the Early Shakespeare," *Philological Quarterly*, 41 (1962): 19–20 (reprinted in *Shakespeare without Words and Other Essays* [Cambridge: Harvard University Press, 1972]); see his statement on "ghostly precedents" cited in chap. 1, and *Shakespeare and the Rival Traditions* (New York: Macmillan,

1952), p. 116. See also David Bevington, *Tudor Drama and Politics: A Critical Approach to Topical Meaning* (Cambridge: Harvard University Press, 1968), p. 10.

15. Bernard Beckerman, in his survey of 144 plays presented at court from 1590 to 1642, could find only one prior to 1620 which apparently had its premiere there, and even that was uncertain (*Shakespeare at the Globe* [New York: Macmillan, 1962], pp. 20, 219, 235).

16. *Shakespeare's Occasional Plays: Their Origin and Transmission* (London: Edward Arnold, 1965), p. 3. The wedding took place on 14 February 1613, and the list of plays in the Chambers Accounts is reprinted by E. K. Chambers, *William Shakespeare: A Study of Facts and Problems* (Oxford: Clarendon Press, 1930), 2:343.

17. The fragment of the Revels Accounts which notes this performance has been challenged as a forgery, but most scholars now accept E. K. Chambers's defense of it—see *The Elizabethan Stage* (Oxford: Clarendon Press, 1923), 4:136–41, and *William Shakespeare*, 2:330–31.

18. A noted Shakespearean, in his review of two of the occasionalist studies of *Measure for Measure*, concludes that this play treats "the King's own views and interests...more explicitly" than *Macbeth*.

19. Thomas Tyrwhitt, *Observations and Conjectures upon Some Passages of Shakespeare* (Oxford, 1766), pp. 36–37; George Chalmers, *A Supplemental Apology for the Believers in the Shakespeare-Papers* (London, 1799), pp. 404–8; Charles Knight, *Studies of Shakespeare* (London, 1849), p. 319; Louis Albrecht, *Neue Untersuchungen zu Shakespeares Mass für Mass* (Berlin, 1914), pp. 129–244.

20. The author is quoting one of these studies.

21. In the section of *The Shakespearian Scene* cited at the outset, Patrick Murray treats the discovery of this relationship as another major contribution of "the historical approach": "In *Measure for Measure* there are obscurities both of speech and action which can be satisfactorily dealt with only in historical terms. The Duke's enigmatic behaviour and his various idiosyncrasies...have long puzzled critics.... Historical critics explain such puzzling features of the Duke's role by suggesting that *Measure for Measure* was written as a compliment to King James and that the Duke is an idealized image of Shakespeare's new sovereign, endowed by him with several of those qualities for which James expressed the greatest admiration in works such as *Basilikon Doron*.... All the Duke's more eccentric preoccupations and actions can be closely paralleled either in the writings of the King or in contemporary accounts of his behaviour" (p. 149).

22. I use James Craigie's edition of the 1603 Waldegrave octavo (Scottish Text Society; Edinburgh: W. Blackwood, 1944–50) for all quotations and citations. (Spelling and punctuation have been modernized.)

23. The conventional sources of James's ideas are discussed by Craigie in his edition, 2:63–87, and of Shakespeare's by Elizabeth Pope, "The Renaissance Background of *Measure for Measure*," *Shakespeare Survey*, 2 (1949): 66–82.

24. See E. H. C. Oliphant, "How Not to Play the Game of Parallels," *Journal of English and Germanic Philology*, 28 (1929): 1–15.

25. See Matt. 5:15; Mark 4:21; Luke 8:16, 11:33; and Morris Tilley, *A Dictionary of the Proverbs in England*, C39.

26. Some critics try to relate this action to the King's advice to "haunt your session, and spy carefully their proceedings" (p. 147); but that is to distort his meaning, which is made explicit in his next sentence: "Spare not to go there...." The Duke never does

go to Angelo's court, and his sort of "spying" is clearly not what James had in mind.

27. We will see in the appendix that a parallel has been noted to an action of Cesare Borgia's recorded in Innocent Gentillet's *Anti-Machiavel*.

28. Another critic, who is not one of the group examined here, also finds a central theme in the play that fits the occasionalist thesis, although he is not trying to prove this thesis but accepts it as an established truth: "In *Measure for Measure*, Shakespeare is dramatizing for James I at court on December 26, 1604, the fact that in order for law to benefit mankind and lead men to virtue, it must be administered with equity."

29. Another critic says that the Duke's final words to Lucio ("Slandering a prince deserves it" [V.i.519]) are "addressed more to King James than to the fictions of the play."

30. His personal motto was *"Beati Pacifici."* One critic simply drops the "soldier" in summarizing this point, and another tries to explain it away: "The last, King James certainly was not, yet as a monarch he must be versed in warfare, as he advises his son."

31. See also *Hamlet*, I.v.141: "As you are friends, scholars, and soldiers"; *The Merchant of Venice*, I.ii.105: "a scholar and a soldier"; and T. M. Pearce, "The Ideal of the Soldier-Scholar in the Renaissance," *Western Humanities Review*, 7 (1953): 43–52; and compare our own use of "a gentleman and a scholar" and "an officer and a gentleman."

32. See Mary Lascelles, "Sir Thomas Elyot and the Legend of Alexander Severus," *Review of English Studies*, 2 (1951): 305–18, and J. W. Lever's introduction to the Arden edition (Cambridge: Harvard University Press, 1965), pp. xliv–xlvii. The "disguised ruler" role in the drama is discussed at length by Rosalind Miles, *The Problem of "Measure for Measure": A Historical Investigation* (London: Vision Press, 1976), pp. 135–60.

33. Two of these plays written after his ascension have fallen prey to the occasionalists. Four separate studies have argued that *The Phoenix* was intended for King James (one is entitled "Middleton's *The Phoenix* as a Royal Play"), despite the fact that it contains jokes about his sale of knighthoods (I.vi.150, II.iii.4). One critic says that "surely these trifling jokes would have passed almost unnoticed in the mass of material calculated to please"; but neither he nor any of the others ever explains why they are there, if the play was composed to please the King. And another critic has claimed that *Bartholomew Fair* was "designed (partly at least) for a royal occasion," citing *Measure for Measure* as a precedent, although Jonson's disguised ruler, Justice Adam Overdo, is a comic butt.

34. One critic tries to get around this: "The second reference to a distaste for crowds comes from Angelo, the other ruler in the play, and so emphasizes the universality of the experience." Another, however, claims that Angelo steps out of his role "in order to rationalize, momentarily to be sure, the point of view of James himself.... His speech, therefore, may be considered as direct, bold flattery of James." But the point of view is not that of the crowd's victim, and the flattery, if it exists, is anything but direct.

35. In the note to his edition (Cambridge: Cambridge University Press, 1922), John Dover Wilson says, "It seems probable that both passages were *additions*, written expressly for the Court performance of 1604." The second he feels is "almost certainly so," since it makes Angelo's speech too long for the interval between the servant's announcement of Isabella and her entrance.

36. The one quoted at the outset, for example, which in one stroke occasionalized *Cymbeline, The Winter's Tale,* and *The Tempest,* tells us that the theatrical companies' "salaried status in the royal households could only increase the likelihood that commissioned work would be required of them in return for their privileged status," and that this would be especially true of Shakespeare because of his "personal position as a Groom of the Chamber in the service of King James himself."

37. See Chambers, *William Shakespeare,* 2:270. There was also a legend that King James issued playwriting directives to Jonson—see C. H. Herford and Percy Simpson, *Ben Jonson,* vol. 1 (Oxford: Clarendon Press, 1925), p. 180.

38. I can testify from my own experience to the connection between these ideas. An ironical defense of Shakespearean occasionalism which I once wrote was read "straight" and reprinted in two anti-Stratfordian journals, presumably because the editors saw the claim that these plays were designed for the aristocracy as evidence that their author was an aristocrat himself.

Chapter 5

---

1. One of the thematists treated in chap. 2 acknowledges that "the present generation of critics" is "deeply indebted to the movement we call the New Criticism. Our chief debt is what we have learned about the means of discovering the theme, the principle of coherence, in a literary work: the techniques of the New Critics have made possible a kind of rational investigation into the ways in which poetry conveys meaning that earlier generations simply could not formulate." Note again the assumption that the "principle of coherence" in each work must be a theme.

2. "'It appears so by the story': Notes on Narrative-Thematic Emphasis in Shakespeare," *Shakespeare Quarterly,* 9 (1958): 288.

3. Harriett Hawkins has stated this position very well in *Likenesses of Truth in Elizabethan and Restoration Drama* (Oxford: Clarendon Press, 1972): "Drama is by its nature a public medium, and though there may be a great many things in a play which do not reveal themselves at a first hearing or even a second, there are certain primary effects which do so reveal themselves. And the accumulated experience of intelligent audiences and readers really represents the best judgment of what these primary effects are. In spite of the fact that they may very well fail to take into account subtleties later discovered by individual critics, the recorded responses of audiences and readers over the years provide us with the best evidence of a given play's overt emotional and intellectual impact" (p. 24).

Appendix

---

1. John Cottrell, *Anatomy of an Assassination* (London: Frederick Muller, 1966), pp. 13–14; see also Homer Bigart, *New York Times,* 14 April 1965, p. 28.

2. See, for instance, Ephim Fogel, "Salmons in Both, or Some Caveats for Canonical Scholars," *Bulletin of the New York Public Library,* 63 (1959): 223–36, 292–308; and E. H. C. Oliphant, "How Not to Play the Game of Parallels," cited in chap. 4.

3. These readings differed from the traditional source study, we found, in their claim that Shakespeare expected his audience to recognize and respond to the borrowing, which therefore becomes a crucial aspect of the play's meaning.

4. We also encountered this double embarrassment of riches in the thematic scene, where many different central themes were found in the same play, and many different plays were found to have the same central theme, which would suggest that the alleged connection between a character and the extradramatic personage he is supposed to "figure" is just as arbitrary as that between a play and the theme it is supposed to be "about."

5. This critic also collects a Fluellenian list of parallels within the play to prove that "there is a remarkable identity" in the careers of Viola and Sebastian: "both endure a sea tempest, both are saved and aided by good sea captains, both are wooed by and in a manner of speaking woo Olivia, both are forced to a duel with Andrew Aguecheek, both give money to Feste, both are in the end betrothed to their proper lovers." "In a manner of speaking" is a particularly fine touch.

6. *The Shakespearian Scene: Some Twentieth Century Perspectives* (London: Longmans, Green, 1969), p. 137.

7. I quote from the King James Version, which this critic used.

8. Richard II is a favorite of some of these critics because he is the only character in Shakespeare who is explicitly compared to Christ (in III.ii.132; IV.i.170–71, 239–41). All three comparisons, however, are made by Richard, so while they certainly prove that he thinks of himself as a Christ figure at these times, we cannot assume that Shakespeare shares this view, for he has shown in Richard a marked tendency toward self-glorification and self-pity. We surely are meant to realize that in the first comparison he is completely wrong, since the men he calls "Judases" were killed because of their loyalty to him, and that he is at least partly wrong in the other two, since by the analogy he is denying his own guilt, which Shakespeare took considerable pains to demonstrate earlier. Therefore I cannot see how these speeches make him a Christ figure, any more than his comparisons of himself to a lion (I.i.174) and to the sun (III.ii.36–53) make him a lion or sun figure.

9. The final clause shows that this trend has now reached the stage of a self-sustaining chain reaction, where a character's credentials for Christ figurehood need no longer go back to biblical parallels but can be established by comparing him to other alleged Christ figures. The same critic finds it "significant" that three lines in Flavius's account of Timon (IV.ii.42–44) "are similar to France's words about the rejected Cordelia, another Christ figure."

10. Actually Macbeth does not welcome Duncan on this occasion (I.vi); but then Judas does not welcome Christ to the Last Supper. The next sentence of this study adds that Macbeth's "dismay when Duncan proclaims Malcolm the Prince of Cumberland [I.iv] is like Lucifer's dismay when God announces the begetting of His Son," which makes Malcolm a second Christ figure. A third is produced by another critic's comparison of the Porter scene (II.iii) to the "Harrowing of Hell" in the mystery cycles: "Christ comes to hell in these plays and awakens hell and its porter with his thunderous command, *Attollite portas*, etc. Macduff is the Christ-figure who hammers at the door of Macbeth's hell." Another critic finds a fourth such figure in Fleance, because the play makes a "direct comparison" of his escape in III.iii "to Christ's escape from Herod's massacre of the innocents of Bethlehem." And we would have a fifth if some director followed the suggestion of another critic that the play be staged with "an image of the 'naked new-born babe' [I.vii.21], the Christ child, that becomes increas-

ingly visible as the tragedy proceeds." I believe this sets a record for the number of Christ figures in a single play.

11. The most amusing example of this second screening that I have seen comes from the Old Testament branch of theological Fluellenism: "What story then, familiar to Shakespeare and to his audience, does this *Tempest* story of a man and woman exiled from their natural inheritance for the acquisition of a forbidden knowledge resemble? An answer leaps readily to mind; it resembles the story of Adam and Eve." Of course, if this critic had identified Prospero and Miranda by any of their other aspects— father and daughter, adult and infant, etc.—nothing would have leaped readily to mind to connect these biblical and Shakespearean rivers.

12. The same line of defense is taken by two other critics who published rejoinders to an earlier version of this appendix, which appeared as an article. The first says he "must admit that among those moderns who engage in [figure hunting] are a fair number of misguided enthusiasts who sometimes give the appearance of playing at an irresponsible parlor game," but claims this is "the abuse of the practice, not...the practice itself." And the second acknowledges that many attempts to relate a Shakespearean character to Christ "impose such a comparison where it is not justified, but this...[is] an abuse of critical method, not the use of an inherently invalid one." Neither one tells us, however, which of these alleged Christ figures are legitimate and which represent an "abuse," or how we are to distinguish between them.

13. One of the critics quoted earlier even gives us Shakespeare's parody as evidence: "[The] Renaissance audience...would have been responsive to such a use of symbolic techniques, for it had not yet outgrown the medieval habit of analogical thought.... The world in which it lived was still...a microcosm with which all other levels of being corresponded and in which, as Fluellen noted, 'there is figures in all things.'"

14. This proliferation also seems to have reached the self-sustaining stage, as can be seen, for instance, in a study of *Believe as You List* which finds that Prusias is a James figure because his traits "bear some resemblance to the traits Massinger attributes to Roberto in *The Maid of Honour*, who is undoubtedly intended as a portrait of the English king."

15. One critic has gone a step further by arguing that the differences between a character and the King can themselves create a kind of James figurehead: "If James seemed to unite Britain...Lear sought to divide it. In this important respect, Lear is James's 'anti-type,' his figural antithesis."

16. In the English part of the allegory Fortinbras also is King James, which may explain why he and Hamlet (who is James in the Scottish part) have such nice things to say about each other. One of the high points of the book is its attempt to connect Hamlet's remark on Alexander the Great (V.i.184–98) to the Earl of Essex by means of a comparison that brings us right back to Fluellen: "like Alexander, Essex had travelled widely, and met his enemies in distant lands and, like him, he too perished in his youth." (These early examples of figure hunting were parodied by Baldwin Maxwell in "The Original of Sir John Falstaff—Believe It or Not," *Studies in Philology*, 27 [1930]: 230–32, where he proved that Falstaff was really Robert Greene.)

17. They will, that is, for Fluellenists who approve of Elizabeth and believe that Shakespeare did (which always amounts to the same thing). A recent book by one who clearly disapproves of her, however, tells us that "Shakespeare associated her in his dramatic imagination with such characters as King John and Bolingbroke, Richard III and Edmund, Macbeth and his 'fiend-like queen.'"

18. I do not mean to imply that these critics are trying to deceive us, for I am sure that they (like Fluellen himself) are completely convinced by their logic, if I can judge from my own experience. My first publication was a Fluellenian exercise (it was even titled "A New Reading") demonstrating that Joyce's *Dubliners* was based on the *Odyssey*, and I can still remember, after these many years, the excitement I felt in working up the equation, and my impatience with any recalcitrant facts that did not seem to fit it, and with any skeptics who doubted its validity. There is a bit of Fluellen, I suspect, in most of us, which is all the more reason why we need some stern devil's advocate who would, like his counterpart in Rome, present the strongest possible case against these elevations to figurehood before we commit ourselves to them.

List of New Readings

All of the unidentified studies quoted from or referred to in each chapter to illustrate the approaches are listed here, by author, in alphabetical order.

Chapter 1. Readings and Approaches

Battenhouse, Roy. "Falstaff as Parodist and Perhaps Holy Fool." *PMLA* 90 (1975): 32–52.

Berry, Ralph. *Shakespeare's Comedies: Explorations in Form.* Princeton: Princeton University Press, 1972.

Chatterji, Ruby. "Theme, Imagery, and Unity in *A Chaste Maid in Cheapside.*" *Renaissance Drama* 8 (1965): 105–26.

Gould, Gerald. "A New Reading of *Henry V.*" *English Review* 29 (1919): 42–55.

Michel, Laurence. *The Thing Contained: Theory of the Tragic.* Bloomington: Indiana University Press, 1970.

Tromly, Frederic. "Macbeth and His Porter." *Shakespeare Quarterly* 26 (1975): 151–56.

Chapter 2. Thematic Readings

Adams, John. "*All's Well That Ends Well*: The Paradox of Procreation." *Shakespeare Quarterly* 12 (1961): 261–70.

Allen, Don Cameron. Book review. *Shakespeare Studies* 2 (1966): 370–71.

Arnold, Judd. "Lovewit's Triumph and Jonsonian Morality: A Reading of *The Alchemist*." *Criticism* 11 (1969): 151–66.

Bacon, Wallace. "The Magnetic Field: The Structure of Jonson's Comedies." *Huntington Library Quarterly* 19 (1956): 121–53.

Barish, Jonas. "The Double Plot in *Volpone*." *Modern Philology* 51 (1953): 83–92.

Barnet, Sylvan, ed. *Twentieth Century Interpretations of "The Merchant of Venice*." Englewood Cliffs, N.J.: Prentice-Hall, 1970. Introduction.

Bennett, Josephine Waters. "The Storm Within: The Madness of Lear." *Shakespeare Quarterly* 13 (1962): 137–55.

Berkeley, David, and Eidson, Donald. "The Theme of *Henry IV, Part 1*." *Shakespeare Quarterly* 19 (1968): 25–31.

Berry, Ralph. "Pattern in *Othello*." *Shakespeare Quarterly* 23 (1972): 3–19.

_____. *Shakespeare's Comedies: Explorations in Form*. Princeton: Princeton University Press, 1972.

Black, James. "The Unfolding of *Measure for Measure*." *Shakespeare Survey* 26 (1973): 119–28.

Bowling, Lawrence. "Antony's Internal Disunity." *Studies in English Literature* 4 (1964): 239–46.

Bradbrook, Muriel C. *Themes and Conventions of Elizabethan Tragedy*. Cambridge: Cambridge University Press, 1935.

Brown, John Russell. *Shakespeare and his Comedies*. London: Methuen, 1957; 2d ed. rev., 1962.

Bryant, Jerry H. "*The Winter's Tale* and the Pastoral Tradition." *Shakespeare Quarterly* 14 (1963): 387–98.

Bryant, Joseph A., Jr. *The Compassionate Satirist: Ben Jonson and His Imperfect World*. Athens, Ga.: University of Georgia Press, 1973.

_____. *Hippolyta's View: Some Christian Aspects of Shakespeare's Plays*. Lexington: University of Kentucky Press, 1961.

Burge, Barbara. "*Hamlet*: The Search for Identity." *Review of English Literature* 5 (1964): 58–71.

Calhoun, Jean. "*Hamlet* and the Circumference of Action." *Renaissance News* 15 (1962): 281–98.

Canuteson, John. "The Theme of Forgiveness in the Plot and Subplot of *A Woman Killed with Kindness*." *Renaissance Drama* n. s. 2 (1969): 123–41.

Carpenter, Nan Cooke. "Infinite Riches: A Note on Marlovian Unity." *Notes and Queries* 196 (1951): 50–52.

Chang, Joseph. "The Language of Paradox in *Romeo and Juliet*." *Shakespeare Studies* 3 (1967): 22–42.

Coghill, Nevill. "The Basis of Shakespearian Comedy." In *Shakespeare Criticism 1935–1960*, edited by Anne Ridler. London: Oxford University Press, 1963.

Cook, David. "*Timon of Athens*." *Shakespeare Survey* 16 (1963): 83–94.

Cope, Jackson. "*Bartholomew Fair* as Blasphemy." *Renaissance Drama* 8 (1965): 127–52.

Coursen, Herbert R., Jr. "Prospero and the Drama of the Soul." *Shakespeare Studies* 4 (1968): 316–33.

Danby, John. *Elizabethan and Jacobean Poets: Studies in Sidney, Shakespeare, Beaumont and Fletcher*. London: Faber and Faber, 1965 (first published as *Poets on Fortune's Hill*, 1952).

Davidson, Clifford. "*Coriolanus*: A Study in Political Dislocation." *Shakespeare Studies* 4 (1968): 263–74.

Davis, Walter, ed. *Twentieth Century Interpretations of "Much Ado about Nothing."* Englewood Cliffs, N.J.: Prentice-Hall, 1969. Introduction.

Dennis, Carl. "The Vision of *Twelfth Night*." *Tennessee Studies in Literature* 18 (1973): 63–74.

_____. "Wit and Wisdom in *Much Ado about Nothing*." *Studies in English Literature* 13 (1973): 223–37.

Dessen, Alan. *Jonson's Moral Comedy*. Evanston, Ill.: Northwestern University Press, 1971.

Donaldson, Ian. "*Volpone*: Quick and Dead." *Essays in Criticism* 21 (1971): 121–34.

Doran, Madeleine. "'Yet Am I Inland Bred.'" *Shakespeare Quarterly* 15 (1964): 99–114.

Enck, John. *Jonson and the Comic Truth*. Madison: University of Wisconsin Press, 1957.

Evans, Oliver. "James's Air of Evil: *The Turn of the Screw*." *Partisan Review* 16 (1949): 175–87.

Faber, M. D., and Skinner, Colin. "*The Spanish Tragedy*: Act IV." *Philological Quarterly* 49 (1970): 444–59.

Fiskin, A. M. I. *"The Alchemist"* Notes. Lincoln, Nebr.: Cliff's Notes, 1967.

Fly, Richard. "'I Cannot Come to Cressid but by Pandar': Mediation in the Theme and Structure of *Troilus and Cressida*." *English Literary Renaissance* 3 (1973): 145–65.

Frye, Northrop. *Anatomy of Criticism: Four Essays*. Princeton: Princeton University Press, 1957.

Goddard, Harold. *The Meaning of Shakespeare*. Chicago: University of Chicago Press, 1951.

Godshalk, W. L. *"Measure for Measure*: Freedom and Restraint." *Shakespeare Studies* 6 (1970): 137–50.

Goldberg, S. L. "Folly into Crime: The Catastrophe of *Volpone*." *Modern Language Quarterly* 20 (1959): 233–42.

Goldstein, Melvin. "Identity Crises in a Midsummer Nightmare: Comedy as Terror in Disguise." *Psychoanalytic Review* 60 (1973): 169–204.

Greene, Thomas. "Ben Jonson and the Centered Self." *Studies in English Literature* 10 (1970): 325–48.

Halio, Jay. *"All's Well That Ends Well."* *Shakespeare Quarterly* 15 (1964): 33–43.

Hall, Lawrence Sargent. "Isabella's Angry Ape." *Shakespeare Quarterly* 15 (1964): 157–65.

Hallett, Charles. *Middleton's Cynics: A Study of Middleton's Insight into the Moral Psychology of the Mediocre Mind*. Jacobean Drama Studies, no. 47. Salzburg: Universität Salzburg, 1975.

————. "The Satanic Nature of Volpone." *Philological Quarterly* 49 (1970): 41–55.

Hallstead, R. N. "Idolatrous Love: A New Approach to *Othello*." *Shakespeare Quarterly* 19 (1968): 107–24.

Hawkes, Terence. "The Word against the Word: The Role of Language in *Richard II*." *Language and Style* 2 (1969): 296–322.

Hays, H. R. "Satire and Identification: An Introduction to Ben Jonson." *Kenyon Review* 19 (1957): 267–83.

Heilman, Robert B. *Magic in the Web: Action and Language in "Othello."* Lexington: University of Kentucky Press, 1956.

————. "More Fair than Black: Light and Dark in *Othello*." *Essays in Criticism* 1 (1951): 315–35.

————. *This Great Stage: Image and Structure in "King Lear."* Baton Rouge: Louisiana State University Press, 1948.

————. "The Unity of *King Lear*." *Sewanee Review* 56 (1948): 58–68.

Heninger, S. K., Jr. "The Pattern of *Love's Labour's Lost*." *Shakespeare Studies* 7 (1974): 25–53.

Henn, T. R. Book review. *Shakespeare Quarterly* 10 (1959): 231–34.

Henze, Richard. "*The Comedy of Errors*: A Freely Binding Chain." *Shakespeare Quarterly* 22 (1971): 35–41.

———. "*The Tempest*: Rejection of a Vanity." *Shakespeare Quarterly* 23 (1972): 420–34.

Hethmon, Robert. "The Case for *All's Well*: What is Wrong with the King?" *Drama Critique* 7 (1964): 26–31.

Holaday, Allan. "Antonio and the Allegory of Salvation." *Shakespeare Studies* 4 (1968): 109–18.

Huston, J. Dennis. "'Some Stain of Soldier': The Functions of Parolles in *All's Well That Ends Well*." *Shakespeare Quarterly* 21 (1970): 431–38.

Jackson, Gabriele Bernhard. *Vision and Judgment in Ben Jonson's Drama*. Yale Studies in English, no. 166. New Haven: Yale University Press, 1968.

Jayne, Sears. "Charity in *King Lear*." *Shakespeare Quarterly* 15 (1964): 277–88.

Jensen, Ejner. "The Changing Faces of Love in English Renaissance Comedy." *Comparative Drama* 6 (1972–73): 294–309.

———. "Kyd's *Spanish Tragedy*: The Play Explains Itself." *Journal of English and Germanic Philology* 64 (1965): 7–16.

Jones, Myrddin. "Sir Epicure Mammon: A Study in 'Spiritual Fornication.'" *Renaissance Quarterly* 22 (1969): 233–42.

Kaufmann, R. J. "Bond Slaves and Counterfeits: Shakespeare's *Measure for Measure*." *Shakespeare Studies* 3 (1967): 85–97.

———. "Ford's 'Waste Land': *The Broken Heart*." *Renaissance Drama* n. s. 3 (1970): 167–87.

Kelly, Michael. "The Values of Action and Chronicle in *The Broken Heart*." *Papers on Language and Literature* 7 (1971): 150–58.

Kermode, Frank. "*Macbeth*." In *The Riverside Shakespeare*, edited by G. Blakemore Evans et al. Boston: Houghton Mifflin, 1974.

———. "The Mature Comedies." *Early Shakespeare*. Stratford-upon-Avon Studies, vol. 3, edited by John Russell Brown and Bernard Harris. London: Edward Arnold, 1961.

Kernan, Alvin, ed. *Volpone*. The Yale Ben Jonson. New Haven: Yale University Press, 1962. Introduction.

King, Walter. "Much Ado about *Something*." *Shakespeare Quarterly* 15 (1964): 143–55.

———. "Shakespeare and Parmenides: The Metaphysics of *Twelfth Night*." *Studies in English Literature* 8 (1968): 283–306.

Klevar, Harvey. "*King Lear*: The Unnatural Nuptial Breach." *Shakespeare Quarterly* 23 (1972): 117–21.

Knight, G. Wilson. *Byron and Shakespeare.* New York: Barnes and Noble, 1966.

————. *The Christian Renaissance.* New York: W. W. Norton, 1962.

————. *The Crown of Life: Essays in Interpretation of Shakespeare's Final Plays.* London: Methuen, 1948.

————. *The Imperial Theme: Further Interpretations of Shakespeare's Tragedies, Including the Roman Plays.* 3d ed. London, Methuen, 1951.

Knights, L. C. *Drama and Society in the Age of Jonson.* London: Chatto and Windus, 1937.

————. *Further Explorations.* London: Chatto and Windus, 1965.

————. *Some Shakespearean Themes.* London: Chatto and Windus, 1959.

Knoll, Robert. *Ben Jonson's Plays: An Introduction.* Lincoln, Nebr.: University of Nebraska Press, 1964.

Levin, Harry. "Jonson's Metempsychosis." *Philological Quarterly* 22 (1943): 231–39.

Lewalski, Barbara. "Biblical Allusion and Allegory in *The Merchant of Venice.*" *Shakespeare Quarterly* 13 (1962): 327–43.

Lewis, Allan. "*A Midsummer Night's Dream*—Fairy Fantasy or Erotic Nightmare?" *Educational Theatre Journal* 21 (1969): 251–58.

McCollom, William. "The Role of Wit in *Much Ado about Nothing.*" *Shakespeare Quarterly* 19 (1968): 165–74.

McKenzie, D. F. "Shakespeare's Dream of Knowledge." *Landfall* 18 (1964): 40–48.

Nandy, Dipak. "The Realism of *Antony and Cleopatra.*" In *Shakespeare in a Changing World,* edited by Arnold Kettle. London: Lawrence and Wishart, 1964.

Nowottny, Winifred. "Lear's Questions." *Shakespeare Survey* 10 (1957): 90–97.

Ormerod, David. "Faith and Fashion in *Much Ado about Nothing.*" *Shakespeare Survey* 25 (1972): 93–105.

Partridge, Edward. *The Broken Compass: A Study of the Major Comedies of Ben Jonson.* New York: Columbia University Press, 1958.

Pearce, Howard. "*Virtù* and *Poesis* in *The Revenger's Tragedy.*" *ELH* 43 (1976): 19–37.

Peck, Russell. "Edgar's Pilgrimage: High Comedy in *King Lear.*" *Studies in English Literature* 7 (1967): 219–37.

Pope, Elizabeth. "The Renaissance Background of *Measure for Measure.*" *Shakespeare Survey* 2 (1949): 66–82.

Presson, Robert. "The Structural Use of a Traditional Theme in *Troilus and Cressida.*" *Philological Quarterly* 31 (1952): 180–88.

Price, Hereward. *Construction in Shakespeare.* University of Michigan Contributions in Modern Philology, no. 17. Ann Arbor: University of Michigan Press, 1951.

————. "The Function of Imagery in Webster." *PMLA* 70 (1955): 717–39.

Prosser, Eleanor. *Hamlet and Revenge.* Stanford, Cal.: Stanford University Press, 1967; 2d ed. rev., 1971.

Rabkin, Norman. *Shakespeare and the Common Understanding.* New York: Free Press, 1967.

Ramsey, Jarold. "The Perversion of Manliness in *Macbeth.*" *Studies in English Literature* 13 (1973): 285–300.

Reno, Raymond. "Hotspur: The Integration of Character and Theme." In *Renaissance Papers 1962*, edited by George Walton Williams and Peter Phialas. Durham, N.C.: Southeastern Renaissance Conference, 1963.

Reynolds, Robert. "Ironic Epithet in *Julius Caesar.*" *Shakespeare Quarterly* 24 (1973): 329–33.

Ribner, Irving. *Jacobean Tragedy: The Quest for Moral Order.* New York: Barnes and Noble, 1962.

————. *Patterns in Shakespearian Tragedy.* London: Methuen, 1960.

Rickey, Mary Ellen. " 'Twixt the Dangerous Shores: *Troilus and Cressida* Again." *Shakespeare Quarterly* 15 (1964): 3–13.

Robinson, James. "*Bartholomew Fair:* Comedy of Vapors." *Studies in English Literature* 1 (1961): 65–80.

Rossiter, A. P. *Angel with Horns, and Other Shakespeare Lectures.* Edited by Graham Storey. London: Longmans, 1961.

Sanders, Norman. "The Shift of Power in *Julius Caesar.*" *Review of English Literature* 5 (1964): 24–35.

————. "The Year's Contributions to Shakespearian Study. 1. Critical Studies." *Shakespeare Survey* 26 (1973): 151–68.

Schanzer, Ernest. "The Central Theme of *A Midsummer Night's Dream.*" *University of Toronto Quarterly* 22 (1951): 233–38.

Schlösser, Anselm. "Das Motiv der Entfremdung in der *Komödie der Irrungen.*" *Shakespeare-Jahrbuch* 100–101 (1964–65): 57–71.

Scott, William. "Proteus in Spenser and Shakespeare: The Lover's Identity." *Shakespeare Studies* 1 (1965): 283–93.

Shalvi, Alice. " 'Honor' in *Troilus and Cressida.*" *Studies in English Literature* 5 (1965): 283–302.

Sicherman, Carol. "*Coriolanus:* The Failure of Words." *ELH* 39 (1972): 189–207.

Slater, Ann Pasternak. "Variations within a Source: From Isaiah xxix to *The Tempest.*" *Shakespeare Survey* 25 (1972): 125–35.

Snyder, Susan. "*Othello* and the Conventions of Romantic Comedy." *Renaissance Drama* n. s. 5 (1972): 123–41.

Southall, Raymond. "*Troilus and Cressida* and the Spirit of Capitalism." In *Shakespeare in a Changing World*, edited by Arnold Kettle. London: Lawrence and Wishart, 1964.

Storey, Graham. "The Success of *Much Ado about Nothing.*" In *More Talking of Shakespeare*, edited by John Garrett. London: Longmans, 1959.

Taylor, Michael. "*As You Like It:* The Penalty of Adam." *Critical Quarterly* 15 (1973): 76–80.

————. "The Darker Purpose of *A Midsummer Night's Dream.*" *Studies in English Literature* 9 (1969): 259–73.

Taylor, Myron. "Shakespeare's *Julius Caesar* and the Irony of History." *Shakespeare Quarterly* 24 (1973): 301–8.

Thayer, C. G. *Ben Jonson: Studies in the Plays.* Norman: University of Oklahoma Press, 1963.

Tomlinson, Maggie. "*Henry IV.*" *Melbourne Critical Review* 6 (1963): 3–15.

Townsend, Freda. *Apologie for "Bartholmew Fayre": The Art of Jonson's Comedies.* New York: Modern Language Association of America, 1947.

Traversi, D. A. *An Approach to Shakespeare.* 3d ed. Garden City, N.Y.: Doubleday, 1969.

Uphaus, Robert. "Virtue in Vengeance: Prospero's Rarer Action." *Bucknell Review* 18 (1970): 34–51.

Van Niel, Pieter Jan. "*The Relapse*—Into Death and Damnation." *Educational Theatre Journal* 21 (1969): 318–32.

Vawter, Marvin. "'Division 'tween Our Souls': Shakespeare's Stoic Brutus." *Shakespeare Studies* 7 (1974): 173–95.

Wain, John. "Guides to Shakespeare." *Encounter* 22 (1964): 53–62.

Walton, J. K. Book review. *Review of English Studies* 23 (1972): 338–41.

Weld, John. "Christian Comedy: *Volpone.*" *Studies in Philology* 51 (1954): 172–93.

Westlund, Joseph. "Fancy and Achievement in *Love's Labour's Lost.*" *Shakespeare Quarterly* 18 (1967): 37–46.

Whitaker, Virgil. *The Mirror up to Nature: The Technique of Shakespeare's Tragedies.* San Marino, Cal.: Huntington Library, 1965.

Williams, Gwyn. "*The Comedy of Errors* Rescued from Tragedy." *Review of English Literature* 5 (1964): 63–71.

Wilson, Harold S. *On the Design of Shakespearian Tragedy.* Toronto: University of Toronto Press, 1957.

Yoder, R. A. "'Sons and Daughters of the Game': An Essay on Shakespeare's *Troilus and Cressida.*" *Shakespeare Survey* 25 (1972): 11–25.

Chapter 3. Ironic Readings

Andrews, Michael. "*Jack Drum's Entertainment* as Burlesque." *Renaissance Quarterly* 24 (1971): 226–31.

Anson, John. "*Julius Caesar:* The Politics of the Hardened Heart." *Shakespeare Studies* 2 (1966): 11–33.

Auden, W. H. *The Dyer's Hand.* London: Faber and Faber, 1963.

Ayres, Philip. "Marston's *Antonio's Revenge:* The Morality of the Revenging Hero." *Studies in English Literature* 12 (1972): 359–74.

Battenhouse, Roy. "Falstaff as Parodist and Perhaps Holy Fool." *PMLA* 90 (1975): 32–52.

———. "Recent Studies in Elizabethan and Jacobean Drama." *Studies in English Literature* 12 (1972): 391–428.

———. "The Relation of Henry V to Tamburlaine." *Shakespeare Survey* 27 (1974): 71–79.

———. *Shakespearean Tragedy: Its Art and Its Christian Premises.* Bloomington: Indiana University Press, 1969.

Berland, Ellen. "The Function of Irony in Marston's *Antonio and Mellida.*" *Studies in Philology* 66 (1969): 739–55.

Berry, Ralph. "Shakespearean Comedy and Northrop Frye." *Essays in Criticism* 22 (1972): 33–40.

———. *Shakespeare's Comedies: Explorations in Form.* Princeton: Princeton University Press, 1972.

Bond, Edward. "The Duke in *Measure for Measure.*" *Gambit* 5 (1970): 43–45.

Bradbrook, Muriel C. "*The Comedy of Timon:* A Reveling Play of the Inner Temple." *Renaissance Drama* 9 (1966): 83–103.

Bromley, John. *The Shakespearean Kings.* Boulder: Colorado Associated University Press, 1971.

Canuteson, John. "The Theme of Forgiveness in the Plot and Subplot of *A Woman Killed with Kindness.*" *Renaissance Drama* n. s. 2 (1969): 123–41.

Champion, Larry. *Ben Jonson's "Dotages": A Reconsideration of the Late Plays.* Lexington: University of Kentucky Press, 1967.

Cutts, John. *The Left Hand of God: A Critical Interpretation of the Plays of Christopher Marlowe*. Haddonfield, N.J.: Haddonfield House, 1973.

————. *Rich and Strange: A Study of Shakespeare's Last Plays*. Pullman: Washington State University Press, 1968.

Danson, Lawrence. *Tragic Alphabet: Shakespeare's Drama of Language*. New Haven: Yale University Press, 1974.

Davidson, Clifford. "Middleton and the Family of Love." *English Miscellany* 20 (1969): 81–92.

Dessen, Alan. *Jonson's Moral Comedy*. Evanston, Ill.: Northwestern University Press, 1971.

Doebler, John. "The Tone of George Peele's *The Old Wives' Tale*." *English Studies* 53 (1972): 412–21.

Duncan, Douglas. "Ben Jonson's Lucianic Irony." *Ariel* 1 (1970): 42–53.

————. "A Guide to *The New Inn*." *Essays in Criticism* 20 (1970): 311–26.

Evans, Gareth Lloyd. "Directing Problem Plays: John Barton Talks to Gareth Lloyd Evans." *Shakespeare Survey* 25 (1972): 63–71.

Finkelpearl, Philip. "Beaumont, Fletcher, and 'Beaumont & Fletcher': Some Distinctions." *English Literary Renaissance* 1 (1971): 144–64.

Foakes, R. A. "John Marston's Fantastical Plays: *Antonio and Mellida* and *Antonio's Revenge*." *Philological Quarterly* 41 (1962): 229–39.

————. *Shakespeare: The Dark Comedies to the Last Plays: From Satire to Celebration*. London: Routledge and Kegan Paul, 1971.

————. "Tragedy at the Children's Theatres after 1600: A Challenge to the Adult Stage." In *The Elizabethan Theatre II*, edited by David Galloway. Toronto: Macmillan, 1970.

French, A. L. *Shakespeare and the Critics*. Cambridge: Cambridge University Press, 1972.

————. "The World of *Richard III*." *Shakespeare Studies* 4 (1968): 25–39.

Frost, David. "*Antony and Cleopatra*—All for Love; or the World Ill-Lost?" *Topic* 7 (1964): 33–44.

Gelb, Hal. "Duke Vincentio and the Illusion of Comedy or All's Not Well that Ends Well." *Shakespeare Quarterly* 22 (1971): 25–34.

Goddard, Harold. *Alphabet of the Imagination*. Edited by Eleanor Worthen. Atlantic Highlands, N.J.: Humanities Press, 1974.

————. *The Meaning of Shakespeare*. Chicago: University of Chicago Press, 1951.

Godshalk, W. L. "*Measure for Measure*: Freedom and Restraint." *Shakespeare Studies* 6 (1970): 137–50.

Gould, Gerald. "A New Reading of *Henry V*." *English Review* 29 (1919): 42–55.

Harrison, G. B., ed. *Shakespeare: The Complete Works.* New York: Harcourt, Brace and World, 1952. Introductions.

Hassel, R. Chris. "Antonio and the Ironic Festivity of *The Merchant of Venice.*" *Shakespeare Studies* 6 (1970): 67–74.

Hobday, C. H. "Imagery and Irony in *Henry V.*" *Shakespeare Survey* 21 (1968): 107–13.

Holleran, James. "Character Transmutation in *The Alchemist.*" *College Language Association Journal* 11 (1968): 221–27.

Holmes, David. *The Art of Thomas Middleton: A Critical Study.* Oxford: Clarendon Press, 1970.

Houser, David. "Armor and Motive in *Troilus and Cressida.*" *Renaissance Drama* n. s. 4 (1971): 121–34.

Huston, J. Dennis. "'When I Came to Man's Estate': *Twelfth Night* and the Problems of Identity." *Modern Language Quarterly* 33 (1972): 274–88.

Jackson, Gabriele Bernhard. *Vision and Judgment in Ben Jonson's Drama.* Yale Studies in English, no. 166. New Haven: Yale University Press, 1968.

Jeffrey, David, and Grant, Patrick. "Reputation in *Othello.*" *Shakespeare Studies* 6 (1970): 197–208.

King, Walter. "Much Ado about *Something.*" *Shakespeare Quarterly* 15 (1964): 143–55.

Knoll, Robert. *Ben Jonson's Plays: An Introduction.* Lincoln, Nebr.: University of Nebraska Press, 1964.

Kott, Jan. *Shakespeare Our Contemporary.* Translated by Boleslaw Taborski. Garden City, N.Y.: Doubleday, 1964.

Leech, Clifford. Book review. *Modern Language Quarterly* 34 (1973): 100–102.

_____. "The Incredibility of Jonsonian Comedy." In *A Celebration of Ben Jonson,* edited by William Blissett et al. Toronto: University of Toronto Press, 1973.

_____. *John Webster: A Critical Study.* London: Hogarth Press, 1951.

_____, ed. *The Two Gentlemen of Verona.* Arden Shakespeare. London: Methuen, 1969. Introduction.

Levitsky, Ruth. "All-In-All Sufficiency in *Othello.*" *Shakespeare Studies* 6 (1970): 209–21.

McAlindon, T. "Language, Style and Meaning in *Troilus and Cressida.*" *PMLA* 84 (1969): 29–43.

McElroy, John. *Parody and Burlesque in the Tragicomedies of Thomas Middleton.* Jacobean Drama Studies, no. 19. Salzburg: Universität Salzburg, 1972.

Mansell, Darrel. "'Seemers' in *Measure for Measure*." *Modern Language Quarterly* 27 (1966): 270–84.

Marsh, D. R. C. "The Mood of *Measure for Measure*." *Shakespeare Quarterly* 14 (1963): 31–38.

Michel, Laurence. *The Thing Contained: Theory of the Tragic*. Bloomington: Indiana University Press, 1970.

Moody, A. D. *Shakespeare: "The Merchant of Venice."* Studies in English Literature, no. 21. London: Edward Arnold, 1964.

Murray, Peter. *A Study of John Webster*. Studies in English Literature, no. 50. The Hague: Mouton, 1969.

Ormerod, David. "Faith and Fashion in *Much Ado about Nothing*." *Shakespeare Survey* 25 (1972): 93–105.

Palmer, D. J. "Tragic Error in *Julius Caesar*." *Shakespeare Quarterly* 21 (1970): 399–409.

Partridge, Edward. *The Broken Compass: A Study of the Major Comedies of Ben Jonson*. New York: Columbia University Press, 1958.

Pearson, D'Orsay W. "'Unkinde' Theseus: A Study in Renaissance Mythography." *English Literary Renaissance* 4 (1974): 276–98.

———. "'Unless I Be Reliev'd by Prayer': *The Tempest* in Perspective." *Shakespeare Studies* 7 (1974): 253–82.

Price, Hereward. "Shakespeare as a Critic." *Philological Quarterly* 20 (1941): 390–99.

Prior, Moody. "The Search for a Hero in *Julius Caesar*." *Renaissance Drama* n. s. 2 (1969): 81–101.

Reibetanz, John. "Hieronimo in Decimosexto: A Private-Theater Burlesque." *Renaissance Drama* n. s. 5 (1972): 89–121.

Rice, Julian. "Desdemona Unpinned: Universal Guilt in *Othello*." *Shakespeare Studies* 7 (1974): 209–26.

———. "*Julius Caesar* and the Judgment of the Senses." *Studies in English Literature* 13 (1973): 238–56.

Richmond, Hugh. "The Dead Albatross: 'New Criticism' as a Humanist Fallacy." *College English* 33 (1972): 515–31.

———. *Shakespeare's Sexual Comedy: A Mirror for Lovers*. Indianapolis: Bobbs-Merrill, 1971.

Rockey, Laurilyn. "*The Old Wives Tale* as Dramatic Satire." *Educational Theatre Journal* 22 (1970): 268–75.

Ryder, Frank, and Bennett, Benjamin. "The Irony of Goethe's *Hermann und Dorothea*: Its Form and Function." *PMLA* 90 (1975): 433–46.

Seward, James. *Tragic Vision in "Romeo and Juliet."* Washington: Consortium Press, 1973.

Shalvi, Alice. "'Honor' in *Troilus and Cressida.*" *Studies in English Literature* 5 (1965): 283–302.

Slights, William. "The Trickster-Hero and Middleton's *A Mad World, My Masters.*" *Comparative Drama* 3 (1969): 87–98.

Stabler, A. P. "The Source of the German Hamlet." *Shakespeare Studies* 5 (1969): 97–105.

Vawter, Marvin. "'Division 'tween Our Souls': Shakespeare's Stoic Brutus." *Shakespeare Studies* 7 (1974): 173–95.

Vyvyan, John. *The Shakespearean Ethic.* London: Chatto and Windus, 1959.

Weil, Herbert. "Comic Structure and Tonal Manipulation in Shakespeare and Some Modern Plays." *Shakespeare Survey* 22 (1969): 27–33.

_____. "The Options of the Audience: Theory and Practice in Peter Brook's *Measure for Measure.*" *Shakespeare Survey* 25 (1972): 27–35.

Wentersdorf, Karl. "The Conspiracy of Silence in *Henry V.*" *Shakespeare Quarterly* 27 (1976): 264–87.

Wickham, Glynne. *Shakespeare's Dramatic Heritage: Collected Studies in Mediaeval, Tudor, and Shakespearean Drama.* New York: Barnes and Noble, 1969.

Willen, Gerald, ed. *A Casebook on Henry James's "The Turn of the Screw."* New York: Thomas Y. Crowell, 1960. Introduction.

Wilson, John Dover, ed. *Titus Andronicus.* Cambridge: Cambridge University Press, 1948. Introduction.

Yoder, R. A. " 'Sons and Daughters of the Game': An Essay on Shakespeare's *Troilus and Cressida.*" *Shakespeare Survey* 25 (1972): 11–25.

Chapter 4. Historical Readings

Alexander, Peter. Book review. *Modern Language Quarterly* 28 (1967): 478–88.

_____. *Shakespeare.* London: Oxford University Press, 1964.

Battenhouse, Roy. *Shakespearean Tragedy: Its Art and Its Christian Premises.* Bloomington: Indiana University Press, 1969.

Bawcutt, N. W. "Middleton's *The Phoenix* as a Royal Play." *Notes and Queries* n. s. 3 (1956): 287–88.

Bennett, Josephine Waters. *"Measure for Measure" as Royal Entertainment.* New York: Columbia University Press, 1966.

Bradbrook, Muriel C. "Shakespeare and His Collaborators." In *Shake-

speare 1971: Proceedings of the World Shakespeare Congress, Vancouver, August 1971, edited by Clifford Leech and J. M. R. Margeson. Toronto: University of Toronto Press, 1972.

Camden, Carroll. "The Elizabethan Imogen." *Rice Institute Pamphlet* 38 (1951): 1–17.

Campbell, Lily B. *Shakespeare's Tragic Heroes: Slaves of Passion.* Cambridge: Cambridge University Press, 1930.

Canuteson, John. "The Theme of Forgiveness in the Plot and Subplot of *A Woman Killed with Kindness.*" *Renaissance Drama* n. s. 2 (1969): 123–41.

Davidson, Clifford. "Middleton and the Family of Love." *English Miscellany* 20 (1969): 81–92.

Dodson, Daniel. "King James and *The Phoenix*—Again." *Notes and Queries* n. s. 5 (1958): 434–37.

Donaldson, Ian. *The World Upside-Down: Comedy from Jonson to Fielding.* London: Oxford University Press, 1970.

Draper, John. "Shakespeare and King James I." *Rivista di Letterature Moderne e Comparate* 22 (1969): 5–9.

Fergusson, Francis. *Shakespeare: The Pattern in His Carpet.* New York: Dell, 1971.

Foakes, R. A., ed. *King Henry VIII.* Arden Shakespeare. Cambridge: Harvard University Press, 1957. Introduction.

Frost, David. "*Antony and Cleopatra*—All for Love; or the World Ill-Lost?" *Topic* 7 (1964): 33–44.

Harris, Bernard. "'What's Past is Prologue': *Cymbeline* and *Henry VIII.*" *Later Shakespeare.* Stratford-upon-Avon Studies, vol. 8, edited by John Russell Brown and Bernard Harris. London: Edward Arnold, 1966.

Harrison, G. B., ed. *Shakespeare: The Complete Works.* New York: Harcourt, Brace and World, 1952. Introductions.

Hassel, R. Chris. "Antonio and the Ironic Festivity of *The Merchant of Venice.*" *Shakespeare Studies* 6 (1970): 67–74.

Howarth, Herbert. "Shakespeare's Flattery in *Measure for Measure.*" *Shakespeare Quarterly* 16 (1965): 29–37.

Jeffrey, David, and Grant, Patrick. "Reputation in *Othello.*" *Shakespeare Studies* 6 (1970): 197–208.

Jones, Emrys. "*Othello,* 'Lepanto' and the Cyprus Wars." *Shakespeare Survey* 21 (1968): 47–52.

Kaula, David. "*Measure for Measure* and John Mush's Dialogue." *Shakespeare Studies* 6 (1970): 185–95.

Klevar, Harvey. "*King Lear:* The Unnatural Nuptial Breach." *Shakespeare Quarterly* 23 (1972): 117–21.

Knight, W. Nicholas. "Equity and Mercy in English Law and Drama (1405–1641)." *Comparative Drama* 6 (1972): 51–67.

Knoll, Robert. *Ben Jonson's Plays: An Introduction.* Lincoln, Nebr.: University of Nebraska Press, 1964.

Lawrence, William W. "*Measure for Measure* and Lucio." *Shakespeare Quarterly* 9 (1958): 443–53.

Leech, Clifford. *John Webster: A Critical Study.* London: Hogarth Press, 1951.

Lever, J. W., ed. *Measure for Measure.* Arden Shakespeare. Cambridge: Harvard University Press, 1965. Introduction.

Levitsky, Ruth. "All-In-All Sufficiency in *Othello.*" *Shakespeare Studies* 6 (1970): 209–21.

McKenzie, D. F. "Shakespeare's Dream of Knowledge." *Landfall* 18 (1964): 40–48.

McManaway, James G. Address at the Modern Language Association convention, Chicago, 1967. Quoted in Ralph Berry. *Shakespeare's Comedies: Explorations in Form.* Princeton: Princeton University Press, 1972.

Mason, H. A. *Shakespeare's Tragedies of Love.* New York: Barnes and Noble, 1970.

Mendilow, A. A., and Shalvi, Alice. *The World and Art of Shakespeare.* Jerusalem: Israel Universities Press, 1967.

Nathan, Norman. "The Marriage of Duke Vincentio and Isabella." *Shakespeare Quarterly* 7 (1956): 43–45.

Paul, H. N. *The Royal Play of "Macbeth."* New York: Macmillan, 1950.

Pearson, D'Orsay W. "'Unless I Be Reliev'd by Prayer': *The Tempest* in Perspective." *Shakespeare Studies* 7 (1974): 253–82.

Power, William. "*The Phoenix*, Raleigh, and King James." *Notes and Queries* n. s. 5 (1958): 57–61.

Presson, Robert. "The Structural Use of a Traditional Theme in *Troilus and Cressida.*" *Philological Quarterly* 31 (1952): 180–88.

Prosser, Eleanor. *Hamlet and Revenge.* Stanford, Cal.: Stanford University Press, 1967; 2d ed. rev., 1971.

Ranald, Margaret Loftus. "The Indiscretions of Desdemona." *Shakespeare Quarterly* 14 (1963): 127–39.

Ribner, Irving. *Patterns in Shakespearian Tragedy.* London: Methuen, 1960.

Rice, Julian. "Desdemona Unpinned: Universal Guilt in *Othello.*" *Shakespeare Studies* 7 (1974): 209–26.

Richmond, Hugh. *Shakespeare's Sexual Comedy: A Mirror for Lovers.* Indianapolis: Bobbs-Merrill, 1971.

Rose, Brian. "Friar-Duke and Scholar-King." *English Studies in Africa* 9 (1966): 72–82.

Rose, Steven. "Love and Self-Love in *Much Ado about Nothing.*" *Essays in Criticism* 20 (1970): 143–50.

Schanzer, Ernest. *The Problem Plays of Shakespeare.* London: Routledge and Kegan Paul, 1963.

Seward, James H. *Tragic Vision in "Romeo and Juliet."* Washington: Consortium Press, 1973.

Stevenson, David. "The Role of James I in Shakespeare's *Measure for Measure.*" *ELH* 26 (1959): 188–208. Reprinted in *The Achievement of Shakespeare's "Measure for Measure."* Ithaca, N.Y.: Cornell University Press, 1966.

Taylor, Myron. "Tragic Justice and the House of Polonius." *Studies in English Literature* 8 (1968): 273–81.

Velz, Sarah. "Man's Need and God's Plan in *Measure for Measure* and Mark iv." *Shakespeare Survey* 25 (1972): 37–44.

Wasson, John. "*Measure for Measure*: A Text for Court Performance?" *Shakespeare Quarterly* 21 (1970): 17–24.

Whitaker, Virgil. *Shakespeare's Use of Learning: An Inquiry into the Growth of His Mind and Art.* San Marino, Cal.: Huntington Library, 1953.

Wickham, Glynne. "From Tragedy to Tragi-Comedy: *King Lear* as Prologue." *Shakespeare Survey* 26 (1973): 33–48.

———. "Shakespeare's Investiture Play: The Occasion and Subject of *The Winter's Tale.*" *Times Literary Supplement*, 18 December 1969, p. 1456.

Williamson, Marilyn. "*The Phoenix*: Middleton's Comedy *de Regimine Principum.*" *Renaissance News* 10 (1957): 183–87.

Chapter 5. Some Modest Proposals

Brooks, Cleanth. *The Well Wrought Urn: Studies in the Structure of Poetry.* New York: Reynal and Hitchcock, 1947.

Goddard, Harold. *The Meaning of Shakespeare.* Chicago: University of Chicago Press, 1951.

Knoll, Robert. *Ben Jonson's Plays: An Introduction.* Lincoln, Nebr.: University of Nebraska Press, 1964.

Milward, Peter. "Theology in Shakespeare." *Shakespeare Studies* (Tokyo) 9 (1970–71): 56–69.

Rabkin, Norman. *Shakespeare and the Common Understanding.* New York: Free Press, 1967.

Wentersdorf, Karl. "The Conspiracy of Silence in *Henry V.*" *Shakespeare Quarterly* 27 (1976): 264–87.

Appendix. The Figures of Fluellen

Battenhouse, Roy. "*Measure for Measure* and the Christian Doctrine of Atonement." *PMLA* 61 (1946): 1029–59.

———. *Shakespearean Tragedy: Its Art and Its Christian Premises.* Bloomington: Indiana University Press, 1969.

Bryant, Joseph A., Jr. "Figure Hunting." *PMLA* 90 (1975): 117–18.

———. *Hippolyta's View: Some Christian Aspects of Shakespeare's Plays.* Lexington: University of Kentucky Press, 1961.

Coghill, Nevill. "The Basis of Shakespearian Comedy." In *Shakespeare Criticism 1935–1960,* edited by Anne Ridler. London: Oxford University Press, 1963.

———. "Comic Form in *Measure for Measure.*" *Shakespeare Survey* 8 (1955): 14–26.

Cole, Howard. "The 'Christian' Context of *Measure for Measure.*" *Journal of English and Germanic Philology* 64 (1965): 425–51.

Davison, Peter. "The Serious Concerns of *Philaster.*" *ELH* 30 (1963): 1–15.

Dennis, Carl. "*All's Well That Ends Well* and the Meaning of *Agape.*" *Philological Quarterly* 50 (1971): 75–84.

Finkelpearl, Philip. *John Marston of the Middle Temple: An Elizabethan Dramatist in His Social Setting.* Cambridge: Harvard University Press, 1969.

Fortin, René. "'Tongues in Trees': Symbolic Patterns in *As You Like It.*" *Texas Studies in Literature and Language* 14 (1973): 569–82.

Gill, Roma. "'Necessitie of State': Massinger's *Believe As You List.*" *English Studies* 46 (1965): 407–16.

Holland, Norman. "*Measure for Measure:* The Duke and the Prince." *Comparative Literature* 11 (1959): 16–20.

———. *Psychoanalysis and Shakespeare.* New York: McGraw-Hill, 1966.

Hunter, G. K. "*Macbeth* in the Twentieth Century." *Shakespeare Survey* 19 (1966): 1–11.

Jones, Emrys. "Correspondence on *King Lear.*" *Critical Quarterly* 3 (1961): 72–75.

_____. "Stuart Cymbeline." *Essays in Criticism* 11 (1961): 84–99.

Kennedy, Edward. "James I and Chapman's Byron Plays." *Journal of English and Germanic Philology* 64 (1965): 677–90.

Knight, G. Wilson. *The Wheel of Fire: Interpretations of Shakespearian Tragedy with Three New Essays.* 4th ed. rev. London: Methuen, 1949.

Lascelles, Mary. *Shakespeare's "Measure for Measure."* London: Athlone, 1953.

Levin, Richard, and Shattuck, Charles. "First Flight to Ithaca: A New Reading of Joyce's *Dubliners.*" *Accent* 4 (1944): 75–99.

Lewalski, Barbara. "Biblical Allusion and Allegory in *The Merchant of Venice.*" *Shakespeare Quarterly* 13 (1962): 327–43.

_____. "Love, Appearance and Reality: Much Ado about Something." *Studies in English Literature* 8 (1968): 235–51.

_____. "Thematic Patterns in *Twelfth Night.*" *Shakespeare Studies* 1 (1965): 168–81.

Milward, Peter. *Shakespeare's Religious Background.* Bloomington: Indiana University Press, 1973.

Nuttall, A. D. "*Measure for Measure:* Quid Pro Quo?" *Shakespeare Studies* 4 (1968): 231–51.

Pollin, Burton. "Hamlet, A Successful Suicide." *Shakespeare Studies* 1 (1965): 240–60.

Power, William. "*The Phoenix*, Raleigh, and King James." *Notes and Queries* n. s. 5 (1958): 57–61.

_____. "Thomas Middleton vs. King James." *Notes and Queries* n. s. 4 (1957): 526–34.

Ramsey, Jarold. "Timon's Imitation of Christ." *Shakespeare Studies* 2 (1966): 162–73.

Siegel, Paul. "Figure Hunting." *PMLA* 90 (1975): 119–20.

_____. *Shakespearean Tragedy and the Elizabethan Compromise.* New York: New York University Press, 1957.

_____. *Shakespeare in His Time and Ours.* Notre Dame, Ind.: University of Notre Dame Press, 1968.

Spakowski, R. E. "Deification and Myth-Making in the Play *Julius Caesar.*" *University Review* 36 (1969): 135–40.

Stevenson, David. *The Achievement of Shakespeare's "Measure for Measure."* Ithaca, N.Y.: Cornell University Press, 1966.

Toole, William. *Shakespeare's Problem Plays: Studies in Form and Meaning.* New York: Humanities Press, 1966.

Wickham, Glynne. "From Tragedy to Tragi-Comedy: *King Lear* as Prologue." *Shakespeare Survey* 26 (1973): 33–48.

_____. *Shakespeare's Dramatic Heritage: Collected Studies in Medi-*

aeval, Tudor, and Shakespearean Drama. New York: Barnes and Noble, 1969.
Winstanley, Lilian. *Hamlet and the Scottish Succession.* Cambridge: Cambridge University Press, 1921.

List of Plays

This list includes every English play mentioned in the text, with its author, followed by the page numbers of all references to it. If passages from the play are quoted or cited, the edition used is also given here. For all of Shakespeare's plays the edition of Irving Ribner and George Lyman Kittredge (Waltham, Mass.: Xerox College Publishing, 1971) has been used, and for all of Jonson's, that of Charles Herford and Percy and Evelyn Simpson (11 vols., Oxford: Clarendon Press, 1925–52). Old-spelling texts have been modernized.

Index

This index does not include material in the List of New Readings and the List of Plays. Works appear under the author's name.